The Investor's Dilemma

How Mutual Funds Are Betraying Your Trust and What to Do about It

Louis Lowenstein

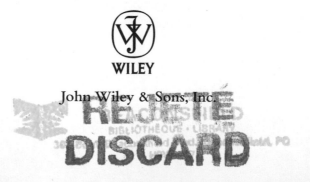

WILEY

John Wiley & Sons, Inc.

Published by John Wiley & Sons, Inc., Hoboken, New Jersey.
Published simultaneously in Canada.

For general information on our other products and services or for technical support, please
contact our Customer Care Department within the United States at (800) 762-2974,
outside the United States at (317) 572-3993 or fax (317) 572-4002.

Wiley also publishes its books in a variety of electronic formats. Some content that appears
in print may not be available in electronic books. For more information about Wiley
products, visit our web site at www.wiley.com.

Library of Congress Cataloging-in-Publication Data:

Lowenstein, Louis.
    The investor's dilemma : how mutual funds are betraying your trust and
what to do about it / Louis Lowenstein.
        p. cm.
    Includes bibliographical references and index.
    ISBN 978-0-470-11765-1 (cloth)
        1. Mutual funds—United States.   2. Investments.   I. Title
    HG4930.L689 2008
    332.63'27—dc22

                                                                    2007043553

Printed in the United States of America.

10 9 8 7 6 5 4 3 2 1

To Helen,
For all that you've created, shared, inspired

Contents

Foreword

My mother is an independent woman in her mid-seventies, with graduate degrees in social work and psychotherapy. Having built a successful therapeutic practice, she is financially comfortable. To the best of my knowledge, she has never missed a mortgage payment, defaulted on a loan, nor ever been in any financial stress. Yet she cannot legally invest in her son's hedge fund, since she does not meet the minimum net worth requirements as stipulated by the Securities and Exchange Commission. Hedge funds are deemed too risky for Mom. As any reader of the financial press is aware, hedge funds are "unregulated" pools of capital permitted to invest in a plethora of financial products and to lever up. Sounds scary, no? So the SEC, in its wisdom, does not permit hedge funds to advertise or market so as to protect the average investor, and does not allow individuals with less than a $5 million net worth to invest in most hedge funds.

Fortunately for my mom and millions like her, there are mutual funds. They are deemed safe. They file prospectuses with the SEC. They have theoretical oversight by an independent board of directors. They are regulated in the fees they can charge and the strategies they may employ. They have soothing names such as Fidelity or Alliance or Evergreen, and invest

for the "long-term." For the unsophisticated investor, mutual funds remain
the most popular vehicle for individual participation in the stock market.
The image of the mutual fund industry, in other words, is safe, sound, and
sober.

Unlike hedge funds, mutual funds are permitted to dig deep into
Madison Avenue's bag of tricks. They are permitted to employ armies of
stockbrokers and pay them handsomely—actually it's the investor who
ultimately pays—to market their product. They can take out four-color
ads in the Sunday paper. Pick up any financial publication, and it will be
filled with banner headlines selling mutual funds, as Professor Louis
Lowenstein puts it, "like soap." A recent full-page color ad in the
New York Times for Ameriprise Financial features a sexy blond in a trans-
lucent wet suit. The page positively purrs, "It's not just about where your
dreams will take you, it's where you take your dreams." An ad for Van
Kampen investments in *Barron's* features a picture of a lighthouse, painted
against dark clouds. "Not every kind of storm shows up on weather
radar," it says. "Look for the right Lighthouse. Van Kampen." A reasonable
person might ask, what does any of this have to do with stock market
investing?

*The Investor's Dilemma: How Mutual Funds Are Betraying Your Trust and
What to Do about It* combines dispassionate scholarship with the keen eye
of a professional marksman to report on what has gone wrong with the
institutions that invest so much of America's money. Professor Lowenstein
describes the evolution of a business that was launched in this country in
the 1920s. Then, as now, there were firms that viewed themselves as
trusted guardians of their clients' capital, and firms that took advantage of
public greed to embezzle and dissemble. Then as now, in the words of one
executive, the purpose of mutual funds (known as trust funds at the time),
was to bring "professional investment management" to those who had
"neither the means nor the experience, nor the necessary time at their
disposal."

What has changed in the interim? For one thing, costs increased, as
companies devised clever ways to saddle investors with marketing fees,
sales commissions, and other ingenuous methods to separate investors
from their money. Along with that, the number of offerings has changed.
Whereas most companies were launched with a single investment vehicle

that management could stand behind, the industry has morphed into a financial supermarket offering investors a range of choices, or, flavors of the month. Mostly, however, what has changed is the sheer number of investors and amount of capital given professional managers to invest in the stock market. Mutual funds rule.

Thanks to the adoption of 401(k) plans combined with the late twentieth century bull market, the mutual fund industry hit pay-dirt during the past several decades. Roughly 90 million Americans today are invested in mutual funds. In the United States, total assets under management have grown from $135 billion in 1980 to over $10 trillion today. That's roughly seven times the size of the hedge fund industry. Globally, the numbers are even more lopsided—$22 trillion in mutual funds versus nearly $2 trillion invested in hedge funds. In other words, most people's personal savings are far more likely to be invested in a mutual fund than a hedge fund.

Reading the financial press, the power and scope of the mutual fund industry is only hinted at. Based on the headlines, one might reasonably assume that hedge funds ruled the financial waters. In 2006, hedge funds were three times more likely to be the subject of *New York Times* headlines than mutual funds were. At the *Wall Street Journal*, the relationship was almost as skewed.[1] Let's face it, hedge funds are sexy; they breed billionaires. Hedge funds are scary; they are known to have fabulous collapses. They are short-term trading machines and huge generators of trading commissions. Plus, they are "secretive," barred from advertising or marketing, lest unsuspecting investors be lured into their trap.

Professor Lowenstein does not choose sides between hedge funds and mutual funds. Nor is all bleak in *The Investor's Dilemma*. The book sprang from research Professor Lowenstein did following the collapse of the stock market in the period between 2000 and 2002. Repeating a similar examination Warren Buffett performed of value managers in the 1980s, Professor Lowenstein reviewed the management of 10 value-oriented mutual funds that outperformed expectations during the years 1999–2003. What did they have in common?

In his chapter "Searching for Rational Investors in a Perfect Storm," Professor Lowenstein shows that there were several common attributes shared by these managers. First, during the "irrational exuberance" that characterized the Internet era, virtually all of these managers faced pressure from investors for underperforming the overall market during such heady times. "I would rather lose half my shareholders than lose half my shareholders' money," said one manager. And what other attributes did these managers share? They owned a limited number of stocks; they had relatively low portfolio turnover; they "ate their own cooking"—meaning they personally invested in their own funds; and they all shared an allegiance to Graham and Dodd–style value investing.

On the flip side of the coin, Professor Lowenstein discusses a *Fortune* magazine article from August 2000 with the ignominious title, "10 Stocks to Last the Decade," that inadvertently pointed readers to the road to ruin. The list included a who's who and a what's what of stocks that were hot at the time. The names included Enron, Broadcom, Nortel, and Nokia. This portfolio, *Fortune* intoned, was a "buy and forget" portfolio readers could one day retire on. By year-end 2002, the 10 stocks had declined on average 80 percent.

In a capitalist society, it is all well and good that companies are run for the benefit of shareholders and not necessarily for customers. In theory, so long as disclosure is adequate, consumers will make up their own minds as to who offers the best products, and there will be a cozy consistency between those who offer the best products and those who make the most money. Certainly over the past decade Apple, Research in Motion, Google, and others have seen the popularity of their products and their stocks soar in tandem. Similarly, our economy is littered with companies that lost their way, such as the U.S. auto industry, or companies that were overtaken by changes in technology, such as Blockbuster video.

Then what is one to make of an industry that seems to consistently take advantage of its own customers, yet sees its bottom line thrive? In my favorite chapter, "Greed Is Good," Professor Lowenstein examines how investors fared who gave mutual funds their money, versus investors in mutual fund management. Not surprisingly, an investor would have been better off investing in a mutual fund management company than in the typical mutual fund. Professor Lowenstein scrutinizes the business of T. Rowe Price Group, a respected Baltimore-based mutual fund behemoth.

In many ways, T. Rowe is an exemplary industry leader. It avoided the recent mutual fund timing scandals, and its funds are all "no-load," meaning investors can buy into one of the funds without paying the typical sales charge to a broker. Finally, T. Rowe makes very limited use of 12b-1 marketing fees and the company has kept its management fees relatively low. So what's wrong? Nothing, if you happen to be a T. Rowe shareholder. Between 2001 and 2005, assets under management grew by over 70 percent and net income almost doubled. In 2005, the company achieved a staggering 80 percent return on net tangible operating assets. Given these financial metrics, between 2003 and 2006 T. Rowe's stock rose 240 percent. T. Rowe's management did similarly spectacularly. The firm's chief investment officer owned or controlled about 1.7 million shares, at $75 per share, for a total stake of over $100 million. The sum total of his investment in T. Rowe's funds, however, appeared to be a relatively paltry $1 million.

So how did T. Rowe's investors fare during this period? Professor Lowenstein cites the results for five of the largest Price funds, and the results do not impress. Over a 10-year period, three of the funds did slightly better or worse than the S&P 500 index, while two fell short of the index by a significant margin. Professor Lowenstein quotes an analyst at the mutual fund watchdog group, Morningstar: "You would feel good about your granny investing" in the Price funds, the analyst says. The professor adds: "Maybe his grandma, but not mine."

Given the dominance of mutual funds in our financial life, one would think that journalistic inquiries are commonplace. In reality, there is a shortage of critical reporting of the industry in the financial press, and there have been a paltry few hard-hitting books about it. Just why this is the case is a matter of some reasoned speculation. Could it be that mutual fund companies, unlike hedge funds, remain influential advertisers in the financial press? I don't think so, but the fact bears noting. Perhaps it is the perception that traditional money managers are boring, again a notion that will be debunked by anyone leafing through this book.

Part of the reason the industry is so poorly covered, I suspect, is that mutual fund companies took a decided shift in the way they market to investors several years ago. Until then, mutual fund companies routinely touted their superstar managers, putting their pictures in advertisements, allowing them to sit for interviews in *Barron's*, or appear on CNBC. Then the mutual fund companies, never fools when it came to marketing, got even smarter. Why create stars when the value was in the corporation? Why make managers famous and indispensable when they could use their fame to negotiate higher salaries, be lured to other mutual fund companies, or start their own hedge funds? Why not promote the corporate brand, and instead allow mutual fund managers to become faceless drones, not truly critical to the firm's overall success?

This shift in marketing strategy was a brilliant way to suppress the careers of the mutual fund industry's rising stars. Today, the big-name money managers tend to run hedge funds. We forget that only a short time ago it was Mario Gabelli, Bill Miller, and Peter Lynch, among other well-known mutual fund managers, who were lionized by the media. By toning down the star system, mutual fund companies could concentrate on building their corporate brand, and today fund companies are either public or are traded like playing cards to banks and insurance companies. Hedge funds, with their star managers and their outsized compensation, are still largely unsellable, given that so much of the value of the enterprise is tied to the identity of the hedge fund manager.

Who today can name their mutual fund manager?

While the subject of *The Investor's Dilemma* is mutual funds, I would be remiss if I did not use this opportunity to compare the stodgy mutual fund industry with the hedge fund world I inhabit daily. In particular, I think it worth commenting on the different ways managers are paid in the two industries. Mutual fund managers are paid largely based on asset growth. The greater the assets managed by the fund, the higher the fees, the greater the profits. While hedge funds manage to charge relatively high management fees as well, the overwhelming bulk of manager compensation is based on performance; typically they receive 20 percent of gains. This structure would appear to create an asymmetry of rewards—managers clean up in the positive years, and investors eat the losses in down years. But because hedge funds pay managers based on performance, and because managers typically can't get paid until they recapture the losses from previous years, it is difficult for a fund to recover from a double-digit percentage loss. While mistakes occur all the time, this arrangement provides the hedge fund manager with a powerful incentive not to lose his or her investors' capital. But what of the mutual fund industry? As Professor Lowenstein demonstrates, there were countless funds at major mutual fund companies that squandered more than 70 percent of their investors' capital during the bear market earlier this decade, only to later trot out new funds with new strategies and new names. As Professor Lowenstein points out, thanks to the consultants, mutual fund managers are typically judged not on how they perform in absolute terms, but on how they do against their asset class, such as small-cap growth or large-cap value.

Put another way, if any hedge fund had a single year like the three the mutual fund industry had in 2000, 2001, and 2002, it would be out of business.

Nowadays, when critics examine business books, it is fashionable to look for axes to grind. Books on mutual funds or hedge funds are almost invariably penned by writers with an economic interest in one industry or the other, and the analysis is attendantly skewed. Not so with *The Investor's Dilemma*. Professor Lowenstein has no affiliation to protect, and no sacred cows to guard. His only bias is to a set of values nurtured over a long career in business and academia. The original principles of mutual fund investing that Professor Lowenstein espouses mirror principles of virtuous living—people matter; the business of investing should be based on trust, conservation of capital, a long-term focus, and quality of returns versus quantity of capital. It is these values that Professor Lowenstein believes have largely been lost in the gigantic mutual fund industry—to the long-term detriment of the industry's investors.

In closing, a personal note. In his distinguished career as attorney, businessman, and teacher, Professor Lowenstein has made several unwitting contributions to my own career. His 1992 book, *Sense and Nonsense in Corporate Finance,* helped shape my views on securities analysis and today remains one of the clearest critiques of what's right and wrong about corporate finance. His son, the author Roger Lowenstein, has been a close friend and colleague of mine for two decades. Finally, where I work, there resides a talented young partner by the name of Peter Carlin. In his job interview with me in 2002, I asked Peter what made him interested in investing. Not knowing of my acquaintance with Professor Lowenstein, Peter's reply was straightforward. "When I took Louis Lowenstein's class on investing, I knew that the law was not for me, and that inspired my passion." So that's three thank-yous I owe Professor Lowenstein. This book, even as it shines a harsh light on much of what is wrong with the mutual fund industry, also helps illuminate the brighter corners of the investment landscape for investors. At its best, *The Investor's Dilemma* will prove to be an inspiration for future students of investing. At the very least, it will serve as a stern warning that something has gone very wrong at the institutions that manage America's money.

NEIL BARSKY
Managing Partner
Alson Capital Partners, LLC

Preface

I have a varied background, as a lawyer, business executive, and Columbia professor. But I have always been a devotee of Graham and Dodd value investing. After the dot-com bubble burst, I wondered whether the value funds, ones that invest along the lines of a Warren Buffett, had bitten on the tech and media stocks that had been all the rage in the late 1990s. Remember, it was the New Economy, and no one needed an excuse to buy Broadcom, Enron, Oracle, and the like. An excuse? You needed one *not* to be there.

Given the names of 10 true-blue value mutual funds by a manager who himself is deeply committed to investing on fundamentals, I decided to see, first, if the group had steered clear of a *Fortune* list of high-flying stocks, ones selling at prices that bore little relationship to earnings, if indeed they had earnings. And then, the acid test, to see how the group performed over a five-year period that encompassed both the bubble and the collapse. As it turned out, they passed both tests with A+ grades. They had stuck to their principles, uniformly avoiding the Enrons of the day. And over the five-year test period, they far outperformed the market, each and every one of them.

The study attracted more attention than I had expected, as money managers picked it up, in *Barron's* or on the Web. (It was also the object of the inevitable brickbats from conventional economists, for whom no study inconsistent with their model is ever sufficient.) But I thought I was done with the subject. Then, in 2005, I spoke at a New York Society of Security Analysts dinner celebrating the 100th birthday of a distinguished value investor, Irving Kahn. Value managers may not be very numerous, but they are a tightly knit group. I decided to update the original 10 funds' results, and fatefully for me, to compare those results with a mainstream group of large-capitalization growth funds, the 15 survivors of the 20 largest such funds at year-end 1997.

Again, the results were remarkable; the value funds far outperformed the 15 large-cap growth funds. But it was not just the performance that was striking. The two groups manage their monies in very different styles, measured, for example, by the number of stocks in their portfolios, and the pace at which they traded in and out of stocks. The value funds were very picky, investing in just a few carefully researched choices, and then holding them for years. The more mainstream funds held huge portfolios, which they turned over at a frenetic pace, trying to catch the next new thing.

Now I was off in a universe radically different from that of the value managers where I had begun. Others have written about the excessive fee structures of mutual funds, but what captured my attention was the management of funds, or rather the *mismanagement* of them. Why were the major fund complexes proliferating new funds so rapidly that, even as I wrote, hundreds of new stock funds came onstream? To answer this and other questions, I dug into shareholder reports and talked with managers, to get a better sense of what they were trying to achieve.

There is a profound conflict of interest built into the industry's structure, one that grows out of the fact that the management companies are independently owned, separate from the funds themselves, and fund managers profit by maximizing the assets under management because their fees are based on assets, not performance. As a result, a fund family may have 100, even 300 different funds, to reach every niche in the market. And that's how the preponderance of funds are marketed and how they measure themselves—not by whether they made or lost money for their investors, but how well they did compared to a narrow benchmark of similar funds, whether it be a small-cap blend, mid-cap value, or whatever. Given the intense focus on marketing, at the expense of patient, careful stewardship, a fund group's distribution and promotional expenses can rival or exceed all the costs of managing the funds. And it works; several major fund complexes have $1 trillion or more under their wings.

Mutual funds matter to us. There are $6 trillion in stock funds alone. That puts a huge responsibility on those who manage the funds, particularly because Americans typically have modest financial skills and assets. After Eliot Spitzer, then the New York Attorney General, and the SEC had finished dealing with the market-timing abuses, many of us hoped we had seen an end to the corruption. A bubble inevitably breeds excesses, but with that behind us, we expected better. What I found instead was a story of incompetence and indifference, aggravated by greed and dishonesty. Even as I wrote, more scandals emerged.

As the reader will see, investors have been used and misused by outright thievery, but more importantly and lastingly by the fact that so many fund sponsors, and the brokers and other financial advisers through whom they market, are far too ready to manage monies—to steer their clients—in ways that violate the trust placed in them. That's the betrayal this book addresses.

I did not want to leave the reader adrift with a carload of bad news, and no sense of what to do about it. It is true that value funds, such as those 10 with which my journey began, are few and far between. Happily, however, they are visible above the crowd. The reader willing to invest some time and effort—not all that much, considering the rewards—will find the few he or she needs, using the handful of criteria discussed in the closing chapter. Yes, those funds do hold concentrated portfolios, on average for years at a time. And they are also known to close the funds to new investors for a while, so as to protect those already there. Most significantly, the managers almost invariably "eat their own cooking," investing significant personal bucks in the fund, not just in the management company. Finding two or three such funds that are currently open to new investors is not, therefore, just a matter of luck or hindsight.

LOUIS LOWENSTEIN

Larchmont, New York
January 2008

Acknowledgments

No one can do a book of this scope and detail without serious assistance, and I was privileged to have a group of people who were unstinting in their efforts. A number of highly knowledgeable fund managers helped me to grasp the realities of the marketplace, notably Jean-Marie Eveillard, Bill Nygren, Bob Rodriguez, and Marty Whitman. Michael Price had invaluable comments. Don Phillips of Morningstar and Kevin Laughlin of Vanguard had a world of data at their fingertips. The Columbia Law School library staff, too numerous to name, were generous in their support, even on weekends. Ken Berman and Mike Eisenberg provided sturdy advice into the often arcane legal structure of the industry.

Pamela van Giessen, my editor, has been just great. She knows finance and she knows how to translate what might otherwise be financial jargon into something accessible to a broad audience.

That leaves Roger, my son. When I would say that some revision he proposed was right on point, he would reply, "Okay, but it's yours now, Dad." He was simply understating and, for me, underscoring, the insights, the challenging queries, and the suggestions that made the give-and-take so glorious. A special thanks.

It's customary at this point to say the mistakes are all mine. In a book as factually intensive as this, there have surely been some; and yes, they're mine, all mine.

Introduction

There is something rotten in the mutual fund industry. One in every two households has entrusted their life savings to these funds, and the industry has betrayed their trust. You, the investor, are expecting a prudent protector and guardian. You go to the funds because you realize you are not personally equipped to manage money and you're counting on the funds for their expertise and care. Instead, the industry has treated you like a walk-in to a discount supermarket to whom they are peddling the latest brand of soap. They peddle all manner of poorly managed, ill-conceived, and unnecessary products, all the better to capture market share for themselves. It is not good for you, but it works wonders for the companies that manage the funds; they are raking in gigantic profits.

Rich or poor, directly or indirectly through retirement plans, over 90 million individuals, in 55 million households, own shares of mutual funds. It's easy to see why stock funds, in particular, are the way to go. Interest rates on bonds barely match inflation, and investors saw during the 1980s and 1990s that stocks will do better over time than bonds.

Twenty years ago there was less than $1 trillion invested in mutual funds of all kinds, and most of that was in bond or money market funds. Today, stock funds alone have $6 trillion in assets.[1] Toss in money market and other mutual funds, and the total is over $10 trillion.

Mutual funds conceal a deep, abiding conflict of interest between the shareholders of a fund and its managers. The companies that provide the fund management services are paid a fee based on the assets under management (AUM), whether investors in their funds are having a bad year or not. There are huge economies of scale in this business, meaning that the cost to manage $100 million of assets is nowhere near 10 times the cost to manage $10 million. And for a $10 billion fund, proportionately even less . . . and so on. But what's good for the managers is bad for investors, who inevitably suffer when funds become obese and inflexible. For a fund with $1 billion there is a far greater range of choices—many more opportunities to buy a sizable stake in a company without disrupting the market price—than for a fund 10 or 20 times that size.

This book examines how, as the dollars poured in, the mutual fund industry responded to the challenge. They had a choice. They could remain patient, prudent guardians of other people's money, creating the handful of funds for which they had managers in whom they had confidence. Or they could go a very different route and launch major marketing programs while spewing out a range of products, all in an effort to build really great businesses for themselves.

The industry succumbed to the temptations; it betrayed our trust. Today there are several fund sponsors, the American, Black Rock, Fidelity, and Vanguard groups, with $1 trillion or more under management—each of them with as much as all the mutual funds combined in 1990. And numerous others, including Franklin Templeton, Legg Mason, and T. Rowe Price, have hundreds of billions of dollars in assets. The funds' unrelenting focus is always the same: to gather more assets, sometimes within existing funds, sometimes by creating new ones—600 new funds just in 2005–2006—sometimes by acquiring the funds previously managed by others. Legg Mason now manages the funds previously run by Citigroup; Black Rock acquired the Merrill Lynch funds and is looking for more such deals overseas.

We harbor the conceit that while the fund sponsors are in it for the money, the people who are personally managing our money will do the best they can for us. Sorry, that's not what is happening. Most of us lack the experience, the time, and the patience needed to manage our investments. Being at a loss for how to proceed, we have turned to the 600,000 brokers, planners, and other financial advisers for guidance. To grasp how that betrayal played out, we need to see what the fund sponsors soon saw—that they could not gather hundreds of billions of dollars without major support from that army of brokers and other advisers. The major brokerage firms, such as Merrill Lynch and Edward Jones, have well-developed, geographically dispersed sales offices providing hands-on access to clients. The funds need those brokers; they have become the funds' true customers.

A fund manager mindful of his investors' success would turn over only about 20 percent of his stocks each year, meaning he would keep some well-researched choices on average for five years. He knows that trading is costly to the fund and its shareholders, who bear the ultimate tax burden. Not so for the run of managers, who are indifferent to these costs and may lack even the skill to select stocks one at a time. The Massachusetts Investors Growth Stock Fund, which we will examine close up, flipped its stocks an average of 250 percent per year for the five years through 2003, meaning that the stocks came and went every five months or so. They had said to investors they were picking stocks prudently, but in fact it was rank speculation. That fund was unusual perhaps, but hardly unique. The average fund turns over its 160-stock portfolio more than 100 percent a year.

The funds expend huge efforts and dollars to capture what they, like a Procter & Gamble or Nabisco, call "shelf space" at the retailers. The American Funds group, for example, sells only through intermediaries; sorry, they won't deal directly with the likes of you. Go to the web site of Edward Jones, and you can see the seven fund families that got on the "preferred" shelf, meaning the ones that offered the most dollars, plus marketing and support services for the Jones brokers—plus a golf trip or two. These so-called pay-to-play dollars are not trivial. In 2005 Edward Jones banked $172 million from the seven preferred families. It was money well spent for those seven, which for years were capturing almost the totality of the Edward Jones fund sales. Too bad, but Edward Jones clients were not told about the thousands of other funds, some of which might have been a better match for them.

The fund families have proliferated hundreds of superfluous "products"—as they call their funds—solely for the purpose filling every conceivable nook and cranny. The number of stock funds has exploded from less than 300 in 1980 to the roughly 4,800 today.[2] And those 4,800 funds contain over 11,000 different classes of stock, with expense structures designed to capture every segment of the market. Fidelity alone has over 300 different funds, with 24 different flavors just in the category of large-capitalization (cap) growth funds. The public does not need all these funds. There are obviously not enough topflight managers to cover them all. Where once Fidelity could boast of a Peter Lynch, now the managers are moved about from one fund to another, as if managers were fungible. Fidelity is a marketing construct, not something fashioned to enhance the welfare of investors. Consider, for example, that one board of directors oversees the performance and management of those 300+ funds.

The brokers have made it clear to the fund sponsors that each fund must adhere to its specific niche, such as large-cap growth, health care, or high tech, and then closely track a benchmark for that sector. A fund manager might think at some point that high tech is no longer a good place for investors' money. In the late 1990s, for example, the T. Rowe Price Science and Technology fund had soared, doubling just in the one year 1999. Still the fund stayed fully invested in its narrow sector, holding only a trivial amount of cash. The fund families know that it is up to the broker or adviser to rebalance your portfolio. For the fund manager to have taken money off the high tech table would have been to commit the tracking error that is a no-no. Sorry if you thought that the manager was pursuing your best interests, not some broker's.

The insidious aspect of the high fees and expenses the funds are harvesting is that the money is being used to manipulate the advice you receive and the management of your investments. The Franklin Templeton group, for example, spends more on marketing expenses, in one form or another, than *all the other costs of managing your money*. That group and several others that specialize in mutual funds are publicly owned companies, and we will pull back the curtain and see how profitable specific fund sponsors and the industry have become. If you had any doubts on this score, you will see how little, if any, the managers of your fund are likely to invest alongside you in the fund, and how they stack their personal dollars where the serious profits are: in the management company. You should have been told up front where the managers' money goes, but we will dig for it together.

Once the mutual fund industry came to focus on accumulating assets, rather than the prudent stewardship of your money, candor and full disclosure inevitably suffered. There are some hard facts you need to know *before* you decide to buy a fund, not afterward, which is when you get that densely written prospectus. Funds should tell us up front how rapidly they are spinning their stocks and what that will cost you, as well as how the fund has performed over a substantial period, 10 years, compared not just to some narrow benchmark that will make them look good, but relative to the market as a whole. And if the managers are splitting their time among several funds, tell us that, too. Efficient, yes; good stewardship and disclosure, no.

One way or another, all the profits are coming out of investors' pockets, and they are huge. We'll see in Chapter 8 an obscure little item, called a 12b-1 fee, which no longer has any reason to exist. Sorry, but it's costing investors $11 billion a year. This book, however, is not primarily about costs, important as they are. Others have written about the industry's failure to let investors share the economies of scale that accompanied the explosion of assets under management. No, the more serious problem is the fact that while those in the industry treat one another with respect, investors in the funds are simply sheep to be sheared. As Casey Stengel said, you can look it up. The industry's obsession with market timing and asset gathering has obscured the essential object of the enterprise—to guard our savings with skill and a long-term perspective. Who cares that a fund's expenses are 1 percent too high if the fund is hemorrhaging 10 to 20 percent a year?

Increasingly we are on our own. The good news is that we are living longer now. The not-so-good news is that two-thirds of all the corporate pension plans have been terminated or cut back, even at companies that remain profitable, such as DuPont. State and local government pension systems are also in dire straits. All told, they are delinquent on their funding by hundreds of billions of dollars. Fortunately, Social Security is still in place, but Washington has threatened to cut the benefits. In any event, unless something is done, the Social Security fund will dry up.

The picture is not totally bleak. There is a right way to run a fund, and that, in fact, is how mutual funds began, back in 1924. The first such fund, Massachusetts Investors Trust, was a *trust fund* in principle as well as in name. As time passed, however, the managers saw that they were missing the opportunity to get rich. Switching to an external management company, MFS, they soon sold it to a foreign insurance company, which adopted an array of tricks, some legal, some not, to increase the AUM. Too bad, but that buyer didn't have a clue about how to manage money.

Not all managers are sharks. We will take a direct, hands-on look at a representative group of tried-and-true value funds that have demonstrated a commitment to their investors' welfare. They select a handful of stocks with painstaking care, hold them for years at a time, and, having confidence in their own judgment, invest substantial personal dollars in their funds. Instead of proliferating new funds every few months, they will at times close a fund or two to new investors, rather than dilute the results for those already there. Remarkable as it may seem, no one had bothered to do a close-up of such a group, at least not since Warren Buffett did it in 1984. As we will see, their performance is outstanding.

Finally, we will set out a few important factors to look for when picking a stock fund. Once you know what to do, it's not that difficult. To illustrate the process, we will analyze two representative funds that are still open to new investors and not too large. It takes a little time, but remember it pays to be patient.

Chapter 1

Mutual Funds: A Painful Birth

In the Beginning

I nvestment companies, including what we now call mutual funds, gained a foothold in the United States in the 1920s. As the stock market was rising, and rising again, people who had previously relied on banks as a place for their savings turned toward the new investment companies as a convenient way to get into stocks. Riding with them, however, were some well-dressed—and quite respectable by the standards of the day—bankers and promoters who eagerly sponsored these investment funds not just for the management fees they could earn but also as easy targets for self-dealing and even outright theft. For readers who are aware of the recent market-timing and other mutual fund abuses, it is useful to see the veritable cesspool of abuses into which the industry was born.

But first, let's go back a bit. In the nineteenth century, the British had created investment companies or trusts to pool and manage money for smaller investors. The Foreign and Colonial Government Trust, founded in London in 1868, was the first such fund, and the purpose was to invest in the debt of various governments. (Stocks were thought to be too speculative for the general public back then.) By 1875, there were 18 similar trusts, including one, the Scottish American Trust Company, designed specifically to invest in the United States.[1]

Almost a century before, the Dutch had created similar trusts, also with the aim of permitting investors with limited means the opportunity to diversify and to achieve a greater degree of liquidity than the underlying investments could provide.[2] One of those early Dutch funds noted that it hoped to buy some "solid securities [at prices] *below their intrinsic value*" (italics added), suggesting it may have been the true forerunner of Benjamin Graham and then Warren Buffett.[3]

Is there nothing new under the sun? Within the past year the financial pages have carried lots of stories about a potential collapse of the so-called carry trade, wherein huge sums were being borrowed at extremely low interest rates in Japan, and to a lesser degree in Switzerland, and then flipped into high-yielding bonds in Europe, the United States, or New Zealand. It's a neat trick: borrow low, lend high. The difference in the two interest rates is the profit. Sounds too good to be true, right? The risk, and it's real, is that the Japanese yen will quickly increase in value, so that when the U.S. bonds, for example, are cashed in, they may not suffice to repay the yen due on the loan from the Japanese bank. (Indeed, as the book goes to press, the yen has risen precipitously to an 18-month high against the dollar.) But back in the 1880s, those ingenious Scots were already playing the same game, using their investment trusts to borrow in England at 3 percent and then lending to American railroad companies at rates up to 8 percent.[4] It sounded so good that by 1890, a trust mania was under way, and the Scots found that the supply of quality railroad mortgages was drying up, and only junk bonds remained. Too many railroads, too many shaky bonds, too many failures. Nothing new.

The bull market of the 1920s gave many Americans familiarity with stocks, and as the excitement rose, investment banks and brokers created hundreds of investment companies of one sort or another to meet the demand of the small investor looking for a convenient way to enjoy a diversified portfolio. Until 1926, there were still relatively few funds, and their assets totaled less than $1 billion in all. But over the next three years, hundreds more were formed. The individual accounts were small, mostly under $500, but the total invested grew to a more impressive $7 billion. To put that sum in context, the electric lighting industry, as it was called, was rapidly expanding during the 1920s, and it raised in all $14 billion to finance its growth.[5] Back then, the $7 billion in investment companies represented big bucks.

John Kenneth Galbraith liked to say that in prosperous times no one bothers to question how the money is being made; it's only after the tide runs out that we get to see the "bezzle," the inventory of undiscovered embezzlement.[6] By the late 1930s, the two million investors in these funds had lost $3 billion; only half the original 1,300 funds survived. Much of that money had been lost in the collapse of the market, of course. But beyond that, the promoters of the funds had committed just about every piece of skullduggery imaginable, and even some "duggery" that most skulls could *not* grasp. At 22 failed funds studied by the Securities and Exchange Commission (SEC), the security holders had lost, in all, 90 percent of their capital contributions of $560 million. Charles Kettering, a vice president and research director of General Motors, said that he did not understand investments but that he saw his $260,000 stake in a fund as somewhat akin to being deposited in a bank. In fact, the sales promotions had created the general impression that the funds were not unlike savings banks and insurance companies. Ultimately, Kettering lost all but $20,000 of his "deposit."

The promoters of the funds had largely used them as vehicles for self-dealing. Cash and negotiable securities are very flexible, mobile assets. Without the benefit of any real disclosure requirements, it was all too easy for the bankers to trade securities in and out of the funds to their own advantage. Sometimes they just stole the stocks. And complex capital structures, far beyond the ken of the small investor, allowed the management to dilute the holdings of the public and to monopolize the voting rights. Fund promoters issued securities to themselves at unfairly low prices.[7] Remember, these were the 1920s, when market manipulation, insider trading, and almost anything except outright theft were still considered legitimate. The public was just hoping to be part of the game, and to piggyback the insiders.

The public had assumed that in dealing with, say, Dillon, Read, they would enjoy the benefits of that estimable firm's expertise and the skills of Clarence Dillon. Dillon didn't see it that way. When the firm floated the United States and Foreign Securities Corporation in 1924, the public purchased a "*first* preferred" stock for $25 million, while the bankers bought an ostensibly junior "*second* preferred" for $5 million (of which $1 million was immediately recouped in underwriting fees). That may sound reasonable, but in fact "second" was better than "first." And then, by investing the trivial additional sum of $100,000 to buy the lion's share of the common stock, the bankers wound up with the voting rights plus 75 percent of the potential profits. Later, acting as the fund's banker, the firm proceeded, 16 times over, to unload into the fund large blocks of slumping railroad securities.[8]

Much as the public had been champing at the bit to sit alongside Dillon 80 years before, it was happening again in 2007, when investors stood in line to buy shares of Fortress Investment Group, the first U.S. hedge fund to go public. The offer was subscribed 25 times over by people hoping to sup at Fortress' table.[9] Here, too, the insiders kept all the so-called Class B shares, which, like Dillon's second preferred, owned the voting rights.[10] To be sure, the now enhanced disclosure requirements should have enabled investors to get a grasp on what was being offered, but with so many investors impatient to buy into Fortress, no one had time to read the small print. Nothing new?

Some examples of the looting back in the 1920s make gruesome reading even now. One fund, Utility and Industrial (U&I), had been organized by an investment bank, Byllesby & Co., which raised $30 million for the fund. Acting for its own account, Byllesby then sold to U&I the stock of Federal Public Service, a misleadingly named company that was about to go broke. It also sold to U&I a waterworks firm in Mexico, which was soon confiscated by the government. It sold U&I a block of Deep Rock Oil, which had been broke from its inception. In the end, the fund had lost all but $2 million.[11] The Senate hearings held in 1940 were filled with over 1,000 pages of tales of similar abuses.

The SEC had spent six years uncovering and cataloging where the "bezzle" went. The 5,000-page report ultimately issued in 1939 and 1940 was excellent, but the SEC had allowed far too much time to pass; it was truly a case where less would have been more. By 1940, with the clouds of World War II growing darker daily, and a less than sympathetic, anti–New Deal 76th Congress, the prospects for anything other than a compromise bill had dried up. Fortunately, the industry was eager for *some* bill to pass, so as to remove the taint and regain some credibility. There followed five weeks of intense closed-door negotiations between representatives of the fund industry and the SEC. A consensus bill emerged, representing what the SEC would call the minimum workable set of regulations. Self-dealing was outlawed, at least the more egregious forms; board approval of the management contracts would henceforth be required, and boards would need to include at least a minority of independent directors; independent audits and better disclosure became mandatory; and those complex, leveraged capital structures were outlawed. The bill was quickly adopted by both houses of Congress. As we will see in Chapter 9, the Investment Company Act of 1940, with some modifications over the years, has stood the test of time remarkably well.

A Good Idea

Was there no one back in the 1920s with a more constructive vision of what an investment company could provide for the small investor? With minor exceptions, all the funds were like those in Britain, the traditional closed-end companies, meaning that once the stock had been floated to the public, an investor who wanted to cash out his or her shares would have to find a buyer on Wall Street, with no assurance of receiving their fair value. The quality of disclosure by the funds was poor, allowing the fund sponsors to manipulate prices to their own advantage. Moreover, they had almost invariably injected debt and preferred stock into their funds' capital structures, which worked well enough when the market was rising but led to horrific results for the common stock when it crashed.

Lo and behold, Massachusetts Investors Trust (MIT), created in 1924, became the first *open-end* fund in the United States, or indeed anywhere, and it was conceived by some proper Bostonians as a new and useful vehicle for providing low-cost, professional management to those same small savers who were likely to be exploited elsewhere. In an open-end fund, investors who want to liquidate some or all of their investments could at any time sell them back to the *issuer*, MIT, at a price equal to the then value of the securities in the portfolio, divided by the number of shares of MIT outstanding at the time—the net asset value (NAV). (Subject to a front-end sales commission for a broker, they could also buy additional shares at the net asset value.) The fund was thus free from the speculative frenzy and skullduggery that had beset most closed-end funds, many of which refused to disclose what securities they were holding, indulged in insider trading, and often traded at prices that bore little relation to their intrinsic value. Think about it: Why would anyone pay more—or less—than the net asset value for a share of MIT? Given a policy of redemption on demand, MIT made a point of providing full disclosure of the trust's portfolio, long before federal law required it. This transparency and flexibility, and the security and comfort thus offered to small investors, made MIT a uniquely American contribution to finance.

Being open-ended, MIT was also a so-called Boston-type fund, meaning that it issued only one class of shares, the common. It would, of course, have been difficult to sell senior securities in a fund where the common holders could liquidate their holdings at any time.

In July 1924, when MIT published its first report, its portfolio consisted of industry leaders—companies that paid steady dividends, including 10 railroads, a handful of utilities, and even a few shares of General Motors. Twenty-five years later, in 1949, *Fortune* magazine found that MIT was still buying the stocks of industry leaders, and with minor exceptions, the then $250 million portfolio was largely invested in companies that had continuously paid dividends for at least 10 years.[12] Given its broadly based portfolio, the fund had roughly matched the S&P 500, which suited the public just fine. So popular was MIT that by 1949 it had become the largest owner of common stocks in the country.

Massachusetts Investors Trust was conceived as a *trust* fund, not just in form but in substance. As the then chairman explained in 1954, its purpose was to bring "professional investment management" to those who had "neither the means nor the experience, nor the necessary time at their disposal."[13] The structure of the fund had been the brainchild of a relatively obscure Boston securities salesman, Edward Leffler, who designed MIT and became one of its three initial trustees. Recognizing that investors rarely succeed when they buy stocks on their own, he studied the British and Dutch trusts, but realized that something was missing, notably a truly full-time management, and, in his words, "a provision that investors could present their shares and receive liquidating values at any time."[14] By creating continuous liquidity and the transparency that inevitably followed, Leffler put investors' interests first.

Good ideas usually have simple beginnings; it's the very simplicity of the concept that makes them ultimately successful. This one was brilliant.

Today almost every mutual fund is managed by an external corporation, often a bank or insurance company operating through a subsidiary, which is thus responsible to its own, separate shareholders to maximize fees and therefore income. MIT had avoided that conflict of interest by having the fund managed internally by trustees responsible solely to the fund's investors, trustees whose total pay would be a minor portion of the *income* generated by the trust, which was how management fees were calculated in those days. No income one year? Okay, no fee. Initially 6 percent, their compensation was soon reduced to 5 percent of income.[15] Then, in the 1940s, seeing how the fund had grown and concerned lest they be making *too good* a living, the trustees asked the shareholders to approve a further cut, to about 3.25 percent.[16] In 1949, the total management and all operating expenses were a very modest 0.4 percent of *net assets,* the formula by which fees and expenses are measured today; and by the 1960s, that already low annual expense ratio had dropped to a truly remarkable 0.19 percent of net assets.[17] (Today the annual all-in expense ratio of a fund is likely to be 10 times that, and the managers take their cut regardless of whether the fund turns a profit.) Unlike today, when investors casually flip in and out of funds, the investors in MIT redeemed less than 3 percent of their shares in 1949, and the turnover rate within the portfolio was just 3.6 percent that year.[18] Given a portfolio of industry leaders, there was little incentive for either share owners or managers to churn their holdings.

Cracks in the Good Idea

Times change, markets evolve, and one size, even if cut from such excellent cloth as MIT, will not fit all. As the industry grew, the inherent conflicts of interest came to the fore, overwhelming the sense of trusteeship that had infused the early days. Several distinct pressures were at work, as fund managers, seeing the growth, went about creating really good businesses for themselves. *First,* substantially all the fund managers gravitated away from the trusteeship model of MIT, using instead a structure whereby the funds would be managed by a separate, external corporation, owned by the managers. These management companies would provide not just advisory services but also the ancillary distribution, administration, and marketing functions. These were, of course, seen as profit centers, not merely service centers. The managers had their eyes on an eventual sale of their companies at prices that would enable them to harvest a handsome capital gain based on a substantial multiple of their profits.

When, in 1969, MIT also switched to an external management structure, now called Massachusetts Financial Services (MFS), it was clear that making too good a living had ceased to be of concern. The 0.19 percent expense ratio of 1968 would double to 0.39 percent by 1976, and then triple to 1.2 percent by 2003.[19] In 1981 MFS was sold to Sun Life of Canada. Subsequently, in 2006, after MFS had suffered sorely from the disclosure of its market-timing abuses and from poor perform-ance in some major funds, Sun Life tried to sell MFS, but for whatever reason soon took it off the market.

In addition to higher fees, the fund complexes have steadily focused on gathering more assets, whether within existing funds, by adding new ones, or by managing accounts for corporate retirement plans and other sponsors. There are huge economies of scale in the investment manage-ment business. The cost to manage $100 million of assets is nowhere near 10 times the cost to manage $10 million. The back office and administrative systems don't grow as rapidly as revenues, and the team that manages one fund may often manage others. The number of U.S. stock funds alone grew from 288 in 1980 to 1,099 in 1990 and to 4,770 in 2006, all in an effort to attract investors as they wander about the investment universe. Put a higher rate of fees on a larger pool of assets, and the impact is geometric; while MIT's assets grew seven times from 1969 to 1999, the total fees grew 36 times.[20] Guess what? The investors' interests no longer came first.

In addition to MIT, there was a second Boston-type, open-end fund created in 1924, State Street Investment Corporation, and like MIT, its history tells us much about the evolution of an industry. When the founders, a Cabot, a Paine, and a Saltonstall, discussed their pro-posed new concept with some veteran financiers, such as the treasurer of Harvard and members of J. P. Morgan & Company, they were met with incredulity. "Insane," they were told, to start a company that the stockholders could liquidate anytime they chose! So much for conventional wisdom.[21] State Street was managed more aggressively than MIT, and for the first 15 years or so it showed better results.

Like MIT, the partners at State Street could see during the 1970s that Fidelity Investments and other funds had formed separate management companies, which, if the managers chose, could then be sold to insurance companies and the like at what Paul Cabot called "ridiculously high prices." Echoing the views of the SEC, Cabot still thought that a "fiduciary does not have the right to sell his job to somebody else at a profit."[22] In 1982, however, one year after MIT was sold, the State Street Research & Management Company, joining the trend, was sold to Metropolitan Life. Under Met Life ownership, 32 new funds were created, and assets under management rose 15-fold, to $7.5 billion at year-end 1999.[23] But the end was nigh; values fell sharply in the dot-com crash, and assets under management fell by 60 percent. In 2004, Met Life called it quits, and the management contracts were sold to BlackRock, which promptly merged the funds into others.

American essayist and *Masterpiece Theater* host Russell Baker once observed, in a different context, "The new calendar reward[s] incessant and swift activity and penalize[s] the reflective pause."[24] Investment translation: Today, the average mutual fund trades in and out of its stocks about 100 percent a year, meaning that instead of investing carefully and patiently, as MIT had done years ago, it is furiously trying to stay abreast of the market trends, whatever they be. Investment translation #2: There are, indeed, a few funds, but very few, that still show the same patient, long-term perspective as had MIT. For the discerning investor, they illustrate the opportunities available when managers are willing to put their investors' interests first, even demonstrating their commitment by investing the bulk of their personal savings alongside the public's. Someone who, having done some homework and found one of these so-called value funds, can turn off CNBC, relax, and allow the manager to fret over whether the price of oil will help or hurt the portfolio. Investment translation #3: These managers, with their distinctive investment philosophy and willingness to be out of step at times, hold a useful mirror to the painful habits of the industry as a whole.

Let's take a look now at some of these patient, strong-minded funds.

Chapter 2

Searching for Rational Investors in a Perfect Storm

A Perfect Storm

I n October 1991, there occurred off the coast of Massachusetts a "perfect storm," a tempest created by a rare combination of events, primarily an Arctic cold front colliding with a hurricane, that would create waves 30 meters high and of course wreak havoc and death among the fishermen caught in its path.[1] In the late 1990s, there was another perfect storm, a rare coincidence of forces that created such turbulence in our financial markets that stock prices were distorted out of all relationship to their normal patterns. Like that nor'easter, there were huge costs to the innocents caught in its grip.

The speculative excesses of the 1990s threw a harsh light on efficient market theory (EMT), which for decades has been a cornerstone of economic theory and scholarship.[2] No B-school student has escaped it; no economics professor has won tenure without paying EMT due respect. And EMT has also had significant impact on public policy and investment practices. It is, of course, an appealing concept: In order to make money in the stock market one must compete against the smart money, the so-called rational investors, who are constantly scouring the market for opportunities. Because of them, all relevant new information is quickly captured by the market. There is no point in doing research oneself. Trust prices; the rational investors will already have erased almost any discrepancy between price and value.[3]

Since you cannot beat the market, buy a broadly diversified portfolio, say a Standard & Poor's 500 index fund. Trust prices! And indeed, for reasons both good and bad, huge numbers of us have done just that; in all, our investment in plain-vanilla, S&P 500 index funds rose from a modest $4 billion in 1990 to $400 billion in 2006.

Obviously the theory was wrong—woefully so. People, whether they are money managers or individual investors, are not unemotional calculating machines, but rather humans who often make decisions spontaneously and emotionally, with sometimes serious mistakes.[4] In the late 1990s, the new economy stocks soared to levels out of all proportion to their underlying values, indeed to levels well beyond even the excesses of the 1920s.[5] If the NASDAQ Composite index, for example, was correct at 1,200 in April 1997, it surely wasn't correct at 5,000 in March 2000 and then correct again at 1,100 two years after that. (The rise and then almost 50 percent decline of the broader-based S&P 500, though less widely noted, was also stunning.[6])

Where were those rational investors during this tumultuous period? The crash of October 1987 may have had little impact on Main Street, but this time the damage was broad-based and severe. At one point retirees, endowments, and the rest of us had lost $8 trillion,[7] and the collective loss, measured in real (inflation-adjusted) dollars, is still huge.[8] Have scholars looked to see what the rational investors, the cornerstone of their analyses, were doing while this tsunami was under way? Was the smart money policing the markets, as the textbooks say? And if so, why then did the markets spin out of control? Perhaps these rational investors experienced the same huge losses as the rest of us. But if they somehow escaped, we should study the analytic tools, the investment philosophy, that enabled them to see through the speculative pyrotechnics that benumbed the rest of us.

Wait, wait, who are these "smart" investors, and how do they operate? Are they short-term traders? Are they simply better diversified than the rest of us?

It may not sound particularly brilliant, but there is little, if any, dissent from the proposition that, at the end of the day, the most efficient investment portfolio is fully diversified. And that's not just among economists; on Wall Street, too, we would be at pains to find an adviser who did not insist on it. Indeed, it has been suggested that for some retirement plans, we consider making full diversification a legal requirement.[9] A younger generation of economists has carefully scrutinized the various psychological and sociological biases that distort how investors make their decisions. Even this group, however, readily concedes that when attractive investment opportunities come to light, it is hard to believe they are not quickly exploited;[10] investors should, therefore, thoroughly diversify.[11] But is that how the smart money investors manage their portfolios? Or, conversely, do they focus on only a relative handful of carefully selected companies? *It would help to know.*

Particularly troubling is the assumption throughout the literature that the smart money—those who on Wall Street and in business schools, too, would be called value investors—are merely traders, focused on the very short term.[12] It is blithely assumed that value investors measure risk by the short-term volatility of a stock, and that having found a price discrepancy, seek to capture it before the underlying fundamentals change. Are value investors in fact fearful of holding a stock for the long term? *It would help to know.*

As the reader may have suspected, no one has looked.* It's a paradox; so much scholarly work is premised on the role of rational investors,

---

*Several years ago, Professor Lynn Stout tried to coax her academic colleagues to take a look at the poster-boy value investor, Warren E. Buffett, but none of them did. Stout, "How Efficient Markets Undervalue Stocks: CAPM and ECMH under Conditions of Uncertainty and Disagreement," *Cardozo Law Review* 19 (1997): 475, 491. To get away from the usual assumption that he is unique, I turned my attention elsewhere.

yet no one bothers to study them, seek them out, uncover what they are doing. There is the occasional reference to Warren Buffett, but no close examination. One recent academic paper concluded that "financial economists have been generally unable to identify *any* reliably 'smart' investors."[13] Gosh, perhaps they've been hiding. While there are casual suggestions in the literature that the performance of value investors during these "obvious market frenzies" should be studied,[14] no one has seriously done so.

So I decided to take a look. The conclusions are stunning. Yes, there really are rational investors out there. And no, during the remarkably turbulent five years from 1999 to 2003 they did not suffer the losses sustained by the rest of us. On the contrary, they beat the market averages by huge amounts. And they achieved those results by holding very undiversified portfolios, buying shares of a small number of companies. Whatever stocks they did buy, they were likely to hold for years to come.

The findings have big implications for every investor, armchair market savant, and day trader. And for academics, the results cry for further study . . . though this cry is likely to go unheeded.

A Simple Survey

To bring a group of rational/value investors out of the closet, I asked Bob Goldfarb, the highly regarded chief executive of the Sequoia Fund, to furnish the names of 10 true-blue value funds, those which, as they say on the Street, don't just talk the talk but walk the walk. The term *value fund* is often applied loosely. Morningstar, for example, will tell you that the Fidelity and Vanguard groups alone have over 20 funds it considers value funds. But as Bob picked over the Dover sole at his then favorite restaurant, La Caravelle in New York (alas, it has since closed), he ticked off the names of managers whom he knew as people who care deeply about what they do, investing only after painstaking research. (Had I prepared the list, I would have included Sequoia, but Goldfarb's 10 is Goldfarb's 10.) They are all mutual funds, except for Source Capital, a closed-end fund that invests much like a mutual fund. The funds are:

Clipper Fund	Mutual Beacon
FPA Capital	Oak Value
First Eagle Global	Oakmark Select
Legg Mason Value	Source Capital
Longleaf Partners	Tweedy Browne American Value

And so I set out to see what they were doing in the five boom-and-crash years of 1999 to 2003—to see if, given the enormous pressures to follow the crowd as the market soared, they had stuck to their principles—and of course to see if they had escaped the ensuing debacle.

I have no sense that the managers of these funds communicate with each other, except perhaps by reading what the others have been saying to shareholders or chatting at the communion of value investors at the annual meetings of Berkshire Hathaway. (Usually they zealously protect their good ideas, except as disclosure is mandated.) But their intellectual roots and their common model are derived from *Security Analysis*, by Benjamin Graham and David L. Dodd of Columbia University, first published in 1934 by McGraw-Hill. References to that bible are sprinkled everywhere, and some of them openly describe their first encounter with Graham and Dodd as an epiphany.[15] "[S]uddenly, investing made much more sense to me," said Jean-Marie Eveillard of First Eagle Global.[16] Go to the Oak Value web site (www .oakvalue.com), for example, and you will see an image of the cover of Graham's companion book, *The Intelligent Investor* (Harper & Row, 1973). Typically, value investors like Eveillard search with excruciating care for a handful of companies whose intrinsic value—that is, the discounted present value of their future free cash flows—can be calculated with some degree of confidence. They're looking to buy pieces (i.e., shares) at a substantial discount—say 30 to 40 percent—from the value an intelligent buyer would pay for the business as a whole. That's it—price, value, and what Graham and Dodd said time and again, the "margin of safety" that allows for the inherent risk in estimating future cash flows and the proper discount rate.[17] As Charles Munger, the vice chairman of Berkshire Hathaway, likes to say, if you're building a bridge intended for 10,000-ton trucks, you build it to carry 30,000 tons.

The *Fortune* 10 Test

The first test was quite simple. I looked to see if the funds had owned in the year 2000, when the market peaked, any of a group of very high-profile stocks that the editors of *Fortune* magazine had selected in an August 2000 article entitled "10 Stocks to Last the Decade."[18] The sub-head read "Here's a buy-and-forget portfolio," and the list represented the contributions of some "top stock pickers," as well as due diligence by the staff of *Fortune*. The 10 stocks were:

Broadcom	Nokia
Charles Schwab	Nortel Networks
Enron	Oracle
Genentech	Univision
Morgan Stanley	Viacom

These 10 stocks, which at the time had an aggregate market capitalization over $1 trillion, represented the cream of the ballyhooed new economy. For investors looking for the next General Electric, the *Fortune* 10 included some of the leading technology, media, and telecom stocks. They were the glory stocks of the fin de siècle bubble, and their high price-earnings ratios—only one was under 50—reflected the faddishness of the age, the fact that people were buying not because the shares were good value, but simply because their prices were rising. *Fortune,* swallowing the popular perceptions whole, said they were 10 stocks to let you "retire when ready."

What are the risks in assuming that market prices are rational? By year-end 2002, these 10 stocks had declined *on average* by 80 percent from the July 2000 prices quoted in the article.[19] That is, they had suffered a loss of $800 billion. (While the direction may have been wrong, one must acknowledge that an 80 percent loss is a major achievement.) Even after the market resurgence of 2003, the decline was still 50 percent. Investors who bought the list suffered what Graham called a permanent loss of capital, the sort that value investors obsessively try to avoid[20]—and that most investors never want to see, either.

None of the 10 funds, which were managing more than $20 billion in all in 2000, had laid a glove on the *Fortune* 10 stocks at any time during that year, with two interesting exceptions. Legg Mason Value owned stock in Nokia, though the stock represented less than 2 percent of its portfolio when purchased in 1996. Since the stock was sold in mid-2000 at a gain of 1,900 percent, it's hard to be too critical. And Mutual Beacon had *short* positions in Viacom and Nortel as part of arbitrages, meaning that it had bet against the stocks. That's it. Didn't every fund own stock in Enron back then? A lot did. But not these guys.

Why the Funds Didn't Bite on the Fortune 10

At a time when most of us were enthusing about Oracle, Enron, and the like, why were these value investors not joining the party? Their responses about why they were elsewhere are quite consistent, reflecting a willingness to make lonely judgments. Here are some samples:

> Clipper Fund: "[I]nability to perform a rational valuation. . . . [F]or example, we did not buy Enron because we could not understand its financial statements."★
> FPA Capital: "Ridiculous valuations."
> Oak Value: "At Enron, faulty disclosure and we didn't like management. At Broadcom, Nortel, Nokia, and Oracle, we didn't like the industry and price-to-value."

The others mainly contented themselves with the familiar Graham-and-Dodd response that the price relative to value was not attractive.

While these verbal responses enjoyed the benefit of hindsight, the funds' portfolio decisions at the time speak for themselves. As the year 2000 opened—the bubble did not peak until March—most of the funds were openly acknowledging to their shareholders that they were sorely out of step; on average, the group had for some time way underperformed the market, particularly in 1999, when they felt as if everyone else was getting rich. Over a long period, managers who trail the index are obviously not doing their job. Given the rapidity with which investors routinely cash out of cold funds and jump into hot ones, to underperform

---

★The lack of adequate disclosure at Enron was clear well before the debacle. An analyst from TIAA-CREF had complained about the deficiencies, only to be told: "We're Enron; we don't need good accounting." Roger Lowenstein, *Origins of the Crash* (New York: Penguin, 2004), 167.

even in the short run is for many funds a serious matter, known in the business as "tracking error." One of our group managers facetiously described tracking error as "professional misconduct vaguely comparable to dealing drugs."[21]

Even while agonizing over their tracking error and the fact that their investors were heading to the exits, the fund managers were vigorously reaffirming their investment principles. Envy of the crowd never caused them to lower their standards. In its year-end 1999 report, Mutual Beacon summed it up:

> During 1999, we stuck to our longstanding value and special situation approach. . . . [We] bought only when we saw substantial upside with relatively little risk. In our opinion, risk still matters.

Investors were telling Eveillard that value investing was dead ("You're obsolete"), and they withdrew huge sums. His eventual one-sentence response is classic: "I would rather lose half my shareholders than lose half my shareholders' money."[22]

Old Economy Stocks Were Still Cheap in 1999

Although tech, media, and telecom stocks soared in 1999, it remained a deeply bifurcated market, one in which many old economy stocks of traditional American companies could be bought at substantial discounts to intrinsic value. Indeed, although more stocks in the index were down than up that year, the soaring prices of stocks such as Cisco Systems, Oracle, Intel, and Yahoo! carried the S&P 500 21 percent higher. (It's not widely understood, but because the S&P 500 is a dollar-weighted index, as a stock's price rises, so too does its impact on the index.)

It might not have seemed a propitious time to buy stocks of any sort; and Professor Robert Shiller, in his timely book *Irrational Exuberance*, thought that even value stocks would be too risky.[23] For Graham-and-Dodders focusing as always on companies instead of markets or market indexes, however, it was a time of great opportunity. The First Eagle Global presidents, sounding like a latter-day Graham and Dodd, said to investors in their report for the year ended March 31, 2000:

For five years now, and particularly [the six months to mid-March 2000], smaller and medium-sized "value" stocks have been neglected, ignored, and—in our opinion—mispriced by investors . . . throughout the world.

While at the time it might have sounded like sour grapes to some, Longleaf Partners wrote to its investors:

The lackluster performance [up 2.18 percent for 1999 vs. 21.0 percent for the S&P 500] should not overshadow the fact that 1999 was one of our best years from a buying perspective. . . . History has proven that over time stock prices, although volatile in the short term, will converge with intrinsic business value.

Or as FPA Capital put it,

We strongly believe that the value style of investing is not dead, [merely] in a state of hibernation. . . . The last two years have been particularly difficult. . . .[24]

The Performance Test

The funds knew their model, and they were staying with it. (Who cares if you make money in the short term only to lose it in the long run?) They would soon be vindicated. The five years 1999–2003, one of the most volatile in history, make a fine test. Even after bottoming out in 2002 and racking up a substantial rebound in 2003, the S&P 500 index showed *negative* average annual returns of 0.57 percent.[25] If the stock market were the random walk described by academics, one would expect that for our 10 funds it would be a roll of the dice, a 50–50 outcome, with perhaps five performing better than the index and the other five worse. Given that they were selected for their investment philosophy, not their performance over any specific period, these funds should on average have done about the same as the index, except of course for the drag on performance of the funds' sometimes significant management fees.

But even allowing for hindsight, I found some things that pure chance, a random walk, cannot explain. The 10 funds all beat the index, not just as a group, but individually—each and every one of them did so. On average, they beat the index by a stunning amount, what economists like to call a five-sigma event, meaning a statistical marvel that pure chance cannot hope to explain. For the lay reader, a perfect game in baseball is a rare event; two such games back-to-back would be a freak— an occasion so rare as to be outside the bounds of mathematical probability. The 10 funds showed positive average annual returns for those five years of 10.80 percent, or about 11 percentage points *per year* better than the index—not quite 10 perfect games, but pretty close.

As one might expect, the average annual returns for the 10 funds varied considerably, but even the least successful outperformed the index, and by a significant margin. Table 2.1 shows the five-year 1999–2003 average annual returns.

Value funds are likely to outperform the index when the market is falling, or even treading water; the tracking error arises primarily in the years that stocks soar. The Clipper Fund, for example, suffered a loss of 2.0 percent in 1999, while the S&P 500 was rising 21 percent. Not surprisingly, Clipper saw big redemptions, as did FPA Capital and others. Clipper's senior manager, James Gipson, explained in his year-end 1999 letter to shareholders, "[W]e concentrated on avoiding the (currently large) potential for permanent loss of your capital." In a prescient moment, he

Table 2.1 Average Annual Returns, 1999–2003

Fund	Annual Return
Clipper Fund	11.90%
FPA Capital	15.29
First Eagle Global	17.02
Legg Mason Value	4.43
Longleaf Partners	10.94
Mutual Beacon	10.28
Oak Value	2.63
Oakmark Select	15.43
Source Capital	15.22
Tweedy Browne American Value	4.87
Average Annual Return for the Five Years	
Group Average	10.80%
S&P 500 Index	−0.57%

quoted John Kenneth Galbraith's observation on the 1929 market peak that "the end was at hand but was not in sight."

Were the results for the years 1999–2003 somehow an aberration, reflecting too small a test period? A couple of years after completing that study I was asked to do another, which I will discuss in detail in Chapter 4. But a summary here will be useful. Instead of using the *Fortune* 10 list as a comparison, I used as a test the 15 largest surviving large-capitalization growth funds. Table 2.2 shows the average annual total returns for both the five- and 10-year periods of the popular Group of 15 plus the Goldfarb 10 and the S&P 500.

For the five years, the Group of 15 underperformed our value funds by a stunning 18 percentage points *per year.* For the 10 years, going back to 1995, with the benefit of some better years in the mid-1990s, the group of large-cap growth funds did better, but even then they under-performed the value group, on average, by more than 5 percent a year. In bad weather, this group, like the *Fortune* 10, rocked badly.

What's the model? Safety lies in careful choices.

Some years ago, I wrote a book, *Sense and Nonsense in Corporate Finance*, setting out several strict criteria for selecting fund managers. The standards haven't changed much. Funds should (1) hold no more than 20 or so stocks; (2) hold their stocks on average for at least two years; (3) eat their own cooking (i.e., the managers should personally invest in the fund); and of course, (4) invest on Graham-and-Dodd principles.[26] Goldfarb's 10 funds come quite close to these very strict guidelines. Let's take a look at each of these four criteria in the context of today's market.

Table 2.2   Average Annual Total Returns for Large-Cap Growth Funds

	Average Annual Return	
	5 Years	**10 Years**
	Ended August 31, 2005	
Group of 15	−8.89%	8.13%
Goldfarb 10	9.83	13.49
S&P 500 Index	−2.71	9.85

Limited Number of Stocks

The average domestic equity fund holds about 160 stocks,[27] suggesting a good reason for the common academic criticism that fund managers as a whole should not expect to outperform the market index. Owning roughly one-quarter of all the outstanding stocks, mutual funds as a whole will inevitably mirror the index. Given most funds' fee structures and substantial transaction costs, they must in fact do worse.

The 10 funds in the study held at year-end 2003 only 54 stocks on average, barely one-third as many as the typical fund, and even that number is inflated by the geographically scattered, large foreign stock holdings of two of them, First Eagle Global and Mutual Beacon. Seven of the 10 had 34 or fewer stocks. Contrary to the advice of financial economists, investment advisers, and stock market writers, value funds seem convinced that safety lies in careful selection, based on in-depth research, not random or broad-based diversification.

The huge bonus of a concentrated portfolio is that you can buy a large amount of what you really like. As Munger said, when you find a really good opportunity, "don't buy just a little, back up the truck."[28] At calendar year-end 2003, the top five stocks in Legg Mason's portfolio accounted for 34 percent of the total. Others with concentrated top-five holdings included Longleaf Partners at 28 percent and Oakmark Select at 40 percent. Thus value funds need only a few good ideas out of the roughly 2,000 stocks of sufficient size—that is, those with market capitalizations over $1 billion. With so many choices, it's easy, as our group of funds did, to steer clear of the red flags that were flying high at Enron.[29] Highly diversified funds needed a reason *not* to invest in Enron. Those in our group needed a reason *to* invest. This very different approach naturally led to different results.

Indexing: 34 or 500. So where does that leave indexing? It's the obvious choice for the neoclassical economists who still believe in EMT, but its popularity doesn't stop there. Shiller, for example, recommended indexing, so as to diversify away "all risks."[30] To be sure, investors would have done worse than the index, if, say, they had put all their eggs in the "buy-and-forget" *Fortune* 10. (Better to forget than buy.) Indexing does have the advantage of avoiding the heavy management fees and other costs that afflict most mutual funds. But timing really matters. Markets are efficient much of the time and they're efficient in the long run, but they're not efficient *all of the time*. Measured in real dollars, stocks did not return to their 1929 level until 1958, and did not return to their 1966 level until 1992.[31] Indexers, far from escaping the *Fortune* 10, would have owned eight of them—all but the two foreign stocks, Nortel (which was in the index until sometime in 2001) and Nokia—and lots more like those eight highfliers that crashed and burned.

Underlying the insistence on indexing is an often casual assumption, or hope, that the irrationality—the overconfidence, trend chasing, and the like—operate only during the easily discerned market frenzies, or that perhaps these emotional biases might be self-canceling, leaving the smart money in control.[32] Alas, as former Treasury Secretary Robert Rubin is fond of saying, reality is always messier than the models.[33] The smart money was obviously overwhelmed, unable to control the markets in the late 1990s, but then again the same was true of the so-called Nifty Fifty of the early 1970s, the energy darlings of the late 1970s, the Southwest real estate bubble of the 1980s, and so on.[34]

An efficient market, as a popular finance textbook said, has no illusions;[35] *buy the index*. Because the wisdom is already in the price, the EMT model thus has no predictive or analytic value. But then neither does the newer discipline of behavioral finance.[36] Its focus is on the behavior of the investors who have been wrong, not the skills of those who are right. Lacking the highly qualitative, essentially judgmental tools of Graham-and-Dodd investors, their skills lie in hindsight analysis; hence they, too, fall back on indexing. Reality beckons; economists should get out more often.*

Neither of these popular academic models—EMT or behavioral finance—would have enabled one to do what the Goldfarb 10 did so successfully in the early days of 2000—that is, dig out and selectively pick up the good values in old economy stocks even while staying far, far away from the *Fortune* 10 and the like.

The Goldfarb 10's concentrated portfolios reflect the oft-repeated tenet among value funds that they invest from the bottom up,[37] company by company, with an almost insouciant disregard for macroeconomic trends and a disdain for the market predictions of the day. "Prediction

---

*Further, hopefully useful, analysis of the role of indexing appears in Chapter 9.

is very difficult, especially if it's about the future," said the Danish physicist Niels Bohr. The value investor copes with this amorphous, unquantifiable macroeconomic uncertainty by focusing on what's close at hand—a company's products and market position, the quality of the management, and management's identification with shareholder interests, profit margins, and balance sheets—rather than the prospects for global oil prices, war and peace, interest rates, currency fluctuations, and the like.

There is a note of humility—or is it humble arrogance?—as these value managers remind investors of their insistence on staying within a narrow circle of their personal competence,[38] a phrase borrowed from Warren Buffett. Bill Miller of Legg Mason Value likes to cite behavioral finance studies in commenting on market follies. And the scorn is palpable when he talks about the average portfolio manager's mistakes, such as trying to forecast macroeconomic events, trading too much, and, yes, owning too many stocks.[39]

Sitting on Cash Is Better Than Doing Something Dumb. For value investors who invest in companies one by one, what happens when prices are so high that they cannot find value—not even a few good companies selling at decent discounts to intrinsic value? Happily for our study, if not for some of these funds, the beginning of 2004 was just such a period. In the year-end 2003 report of Longleaf Partners, Mason Hawkins described an intensifying struggle, because "little or no margin of safety exists in the prices of those businesses that meet our qualitative criteria."[40] Others were saying much the same thing.

Some of the funds were holding very large amounts of cash. Back in March 2000, even while the market generally was peaking, the presidents of First Eagle Global had cheerily noted that "so many stocks [were] below their 'intrinsic' value."[41] Four years later, First Eagle Global was 22 percent in cash or equivalents, and the Clipper and FPA Capital funds were 32 percent and 37 percent in cash, respectively. The increased cash holdings were not due to any predictions of a market decline, but because they couldn't find anything cheap and worth buying.[42] The yield on Treasuries was pitifully small, but it was better than doing "something dumb."[43] As Seth Klarman of the Baupost Group said in the year-end 2003 letter to his investors, his (value-oriented) hedge funds

were heavily invested in cash solely as a "resu
search for bargains."[44](Italics added)

This state of affairs among value manag
In 1987, as stocks soared in the months bef
Graham-and-Dodders were doing precisel
good companies at reasonable prices, they l

Low Portfolio Turnover

According to Morningstar, the average domestic equity fund held the stocks in its portfolio in 2003 for an average of 10 months, equivalent to a turnover ratio of 121 percent, thus incurring the huge trading costs and taxes that funds are so reluctant to discuss. These expenses have a direct impact on shareholder returns, often doubling the funds expenses they do disclose.[46] However, at a fund that likes to "back up the truck" from time to time, the turnover will be far less. Our group had average turnover in 2003 of only 20 percent, meaning that they were holding their stocks on average for *five years*. This turnover rate may not be as good as the 3.6 percent turnover at the old Massachusetts Investors Trust, but it is far better than the rest of the pack.

These turnover figures speak volumes, not just to the costs imposed on investors but more significantly to the difference between taking momentary fliers and patiently selecting long-term buys. It is truly the difference between speculation and investing. (The Chinese word for speculation is "stir-fried stocks.") It is a commonplace of academic wisdom that information is costly and difficult to come by, so that investors, having learned something new and valuable about a company, quickly arbitrage—buy or sell—the stock so as to capture the new value, as if there were some precise figure, and then move on.[47] Those five-year average holding periods, however, tells us that these value funds are not looking to capture small differences. Warren Buffett put it succinctly: "You don't try to buy businesses worth $83 million for $80 million."[48]

How costly could the information be? Anyone can discern the holdings on the Internet for free, and these portfolios don't change that often. Oak Value's web site states flatly that in value investing there are neither difficult formulas nor inside or otherwise nonpublic information. Martin Whitman of Third Avenue Value Fund, too, says that the fund doesn't

or information; the trick is to use the publicly available
on in a superior manner.[50] Moreover, the funds' staffs are not
or the first 10 years of its 20-year existence, FPA Capital was
aged solely by Bob Rodriguez, and for the second 10 by him and
ree associates. The two international First Eagle funds—then over $14
billion in all—were managed with just seven staff analysts. The information is easy (too easy) to come by. Using the information selectively, dis-
criminating between the telling fact and the mind-numbing flow of
daily statistics, is the trick.

Value funds don't just buy and hold, of course. Legg Mason sold the
Nokia shares it once held at almost the precise moment the *Fortune* 10
list was being recommended for purchase. By then, according to *Fortune*,
Nokia's price-earnings ratio had reached the stratospheric level of 75.
Price and value were out of balance. And margin of safety, too, which by
then had evaporated for Nokia.

Implicit in their longer holding periods is the fact that value funds
define risk as business risk—profit margins might shrink, the flow of
new products might dry up—not the market fluctuation risk that still
consumes so much scholarly attention.[51] It is puzzling how much talent
is wasted on the effort to measure what is measurable instead of measur-
ing what matters.[52] Twenty years ago, when Buffett did a fund study
similar to mine, he noted that the managers of the nine funds under his
scope never bothered to calculate the beta of their holdings, the beta
being the popular statistical risk measurement based on a stock's short-
term volatility.[53] Bob Rodriguez explained this to some Wharton students and professors in 2004, saying that because of his fund's tight
investment concentration, he is able to define his investment time frame
as three to five years. And thus he is "willing to accept greater portfolio
volatility."[54] Or as Martin Whitman put it, "[T]he only risk that we ever
guard against is [business] risk. . . . We absolutely *ignore* market risk."[55]
(Italics in the original) The managers of the Tweedy Browne American
Value fund almost chortle as they recite the results of a study some years
ago that highlighted the fact that a group of highly successful value
funds had underperformed the market *one year in three*.[56] They live comfortably with the market's manic/depressive patterns; it's the long-term
results that matter.

Eating Your Own Cooking

It is obvious that fund managers should invest significant dollars of their own in their funds, so as to align their personal interests with their investors'. If we buy a loaf of bread, we'll know soon enough if it's a bummer, and we won't buy that one again. But investment funds are so complex, owning as they do many different stocks, typically flipping them in and out at a rapid clip. Even a full year's performance may be a poor gauge of a fund's long-term worth. Unlike that loaf of bread, a mutual fund is a product beyond the ken of most consumers. Managers' willingness to put their own dollars alongside the public's may be the single best marker for their credibility and integrity.

Agency costs is the term economists use to refer to the range of temptations for someone entrusted with other people's money. Back in Chapter 1, for example, we saw how sponsors of the investment funds of the 1920s dumped unwanted, even worthless, stocks into those funds, just one of the ways they abused their trust. It's an inherent problem, and no system of regulation can wholly cure it. Some fund families, such as those of Alliance and Fidelity, conceive of themselves as financial supermarkets for the masses, dicing their funds into ever smaller cubes, so that they can feature whatever style of fund—large-cap growth, health care, international—may be hot at the moment. It's all part of an effort to harvest more investor dollars rather than to manage them for investors' best advantage.[57] The sense of a fiduciary duty has largely dried up. I can recall a discussion some while back with the senior manager of a large brokerage firm family of funds, in which he said, quite candidly, that he was not trying to achieve particularly good results, just not to look bad, just to stay with the crowd, no matter what the values. It's the fear of that damn tracking error again—the fear of being out of step with the market or a benchmark of some sort, even for a short spell.

Some of the 10 value funds have made a point of commenting on their partners' personal investments in the funds they manage, including Longleaf, Clipper, First Eagle, Oakmark Select, FPA Capital, and Tweedy Browne. One would think all mutual fund managers would do the same, but as we will see in subsequent chapters, it's not how most managers play the game.

Several managers in our group have passed a further test of fiduciary duty, having closed their lead funds to new investors, rather than dilute the results for those already there. No manager bent on gathering assets would do that. As of year-end 2005, the following funds were closed: FPA Capital, First Eagle Global, Longleaf Partners, Tweedy Browne American Value, and Source Capital, the last one being of course a closed-end fund.* Of the funds then open, two of them, Clipper and Oakmark Select, had closed at times in the past.

Size impairs the object; it shrinks the number of companies with market capitalizations large enough to permit a fund to amass a meaningful position. What's important is not how much money you manage but how you succeed with what's there. Our select group seems to have latched onto that precept. They are a rare—too rare—species, as we will see in Chapter 7.

Graham and Dodd: Theme and Variations

The philosophy of these Graham-and-Dodd value investors reflects some of the same insights that underlie behavioral finance. Graham, for example, recognized that subjective factors and market prices influence not just speculators but also those committed to a purely investment program. A few excerpts may capture the distinctive spirit of it:

> One of your [business] partners, named Mr. Market, is very obliging, indeed. Every day he tells you what he thinks your interest is worth and . . . offers either to buy you out or to sell you an additional interest on that basis. . . . Often . . . Mr. Market lets his enthusiasm or his fears run away with him, and the value he proposes seems . . . little short of silly.[58]

> The merits of an issue reflect themselves in the market price not by any automatic response . . . but through the minds and decisions of buyers and sellers.[59]

> The margin of safety is the central concept of investment. A true margin of safety is one that can be demonstrated by figures, by

---

*In 2007, Tweedy Browne American Value announced that it would reopen.

persuasive reasoning, and by reference to a body of actual experience.[60]

Although their philosophy is similar, the funds in our group apply it in quite different ways. (Buffett came to the same conclusion in looking at his group of nine value funds in 1984.) Some focus on small-cap and mid-cap stocks, while others invest in large-cap stocks. One of the group follows a highly quantitative approach, which closely echoes the techniques used by Graham. Another one of the funds seeks out growth companies at reasonable, if not cheap, prices, and then stays with them over time. Several of the funds look for value overseas as well as in the United States. Another buys deep discount debt and does risk arbitrage.

At least one of the funds has moved much closer to the principles first enunciated by Philip Fisher in his celebrated *Common Stocks and Uncommon Profits* in 1958.[61] He was contemptuous of the constant attempts to forecast economic and market trends. For Fisher, value investing was more than a simple quantitative analysis, such as the price-earnings ratio or price–book value ratio. Unlike Graham, whose approach had been forged in the dark years of the Great Depression, Fisher believed that value investors could succeed by finding growth companies at reasonable, if not cheap, prices and staying with them over time. The fact that a stock might sometimes seem overpriced, he wrote, needed to be considered in the context of its long-term business prospects and growth potential. In words much like those of Buffett and Munger at Berkshire Hathaway years later, "If the job has been correctly done when a common stock is purchased, the time to sell it is—almost never."[62]

For value investors, there are thus many roads to heaven—many more than the easy quantitative tests, such as a low price-earnings ratio, that financial economists simplistically equate with value investing. For example, a company's price-earnings ratio may indeed be attractive, but the quality of the earnings—meaning the free cash flows available to pay dividends, expand the business, and the like—might be poor. A company might have, say, a strong balance sheet, perhaps even net current assets per share in excess of the stock price, but management may show signs of squandering the resources on ill-conceived acquisitions. The qualitative, judgmental aspects of how value funds operate constitute huge obstacles for the mathematical modeling so favored by economists and those money managers who think they can program a computer to do their job for them. (One suspects that few economists are comfortable reading and analyzing financial statements.)

Some years ago, Bill Ruane of the Sequoia Fund ventured a guess that value investing accounted for about 5 percent of all professionally managed money, but at least among mutual funds the figure is even less today. (Okay, it won't fall below zero!) The pressures on most managers are just too great. Whatever the precise number, it simply takes too much analytic effort, discipline, and independence of spirit to appeal to more than a handful. Why would such uncommon results ever be common? While their techniques vary, however, the group of 10 all stand on the common ground of patient, company-by-company analysis, always mindful that the stocks they are buying are part interests in a business. Apart from the intellectual challenge, two other factors ensure that the number of value funds will likely remain small: First, because value investors are in substance seeking to exploit inefficiencies in the market, the better opportunities would simply dry up if they numbered more than a handful. Second, few managers, or their management company bosses, can cope with the stresses and criticism entailed in being out of step with the momentum of the market. It's that damn tracking error.

David Swensen, the outstanding manager of the Yale University endowment fund, after reviewing some of these same factors, reached the same dour conclusion. Out of the thousands of stock funds, he said, "a mere several dozen merit the consideration of thoughtful investors. [For] the overwhelming number of mutual funds . . . [the] pursuit of profit overwhelms responsibility to investors."[63]

Value Investing: A Behavioral Finance Perspective

The younger, behavioral finance academics have convincingly demonstrated that perverse psychological and social factors—notably what they call herding or momentum investing—often distort the pricing efficiency of our markets.* And yet it happens with distressing

---

*The financial markets are the rare case where a *rising* price makes an object seem more attractive to buyers.

frequency and impact. Efficient market theory had argued that, yes, there are those folks out there who invest emotionally, without adequate research or analysis, and may push stocks' prices above or below their true value. That foolishness, however, would soon be corrected by rational investors who would seize on the opportunities for profit, bringing the prices back into line. What we have seen here strongly suggests that the few dozen value/rational investors on whom the efficient market model relies are not even remotely up to their assigned task. Let me briefly summarize:

- Not only do value investors account for but a small part of the market, but there are also some almost perverse factors keeping them small. When value investing is in vogue and prices are high, they are tempted to close a fund ("or two, or three" as First Eagle had intimated) to new investors, and when they are sorely out of step with a prevailing bullish mood, as happened in the late 1990s, they seem willing to see their pool of assets shrink rather than abandon their principles.

- For stocks that are priced too high, hedge funds may sell short, but mutual funds rarely do. Value funds, in particular, are content to sit on their hands, holding a bundle of cash, as some are doing even now.[64] Not much help for the market there.

- When a stock, or even groups of them, fall out of favor and are priced too low—ah, now value investors' eyes light up, but only if the market price is at a substantial discount to the intrinsic value. This group is very, very picky. Think of Ted Williams waiting for a pitch he can hit on the sweet spot. When economists speak of arbitraging price differentials, they are often referring to modest discounts that would not remotely tempt investors who have been disciplined to buy only when it's a very fat pitch. It's that margin of safety.

- Ultimately, the problem is the snail's pace of value funds' trading, only about one-sixth that of the average mutual fund. What the economic model requires is red-blooded activists, and these patient value investors think long-term, thus operating at an altogether different tempo.

- It's important to remember that value fund managers need investors who share their investment philosophy and are not distracted by the inevitable tracking errors or the market news media chatter. Scholars recognize that the individual investor tends to be an uninformed trend follower, but an equally intractable problem is the corporate chief financial officer (CFO) who hires vast numbers of managers and advisers simply to deflect any potential criticism of the near-term performance of the corporate pension plans. For a CFO, the trick is not to look bad.

Apart from throwing cold water on EMT, we have also addressed two serious errors in the economics literature: (1) the failure to look at the performance and profile of those rational investors who, in some ghostly fashion, populate the academic models, and (2) the failure to observe *directly* particular investors and their behavioral patterns, rational or otherwise. The economists' focus has been on markets, with no effort to listen to individual fund managers, hands-on. Polling large groups is not the same as looking at individuals and their performance. A one-by-one study is what was attempted here, and it was only by doing so that value fund managers' uniquely long-term perspectives could be confirmed. Buffett, as noted, did a similar study on the 50th anniversary of the publication of Graham and Dodd's *Security Analysis*. But otherwise we are bereft of much study or analysis in this area.

Why the academic oversight? Perhaps it's because the dramatic success of these value investors casts a long, long shadow on the temple of efficient market theory, and also on ancillary concepts such as the capital asset pricing model. While value funds' performance can be measured, their methods are highly qualitative and judgmental, focused as they are on the inherent uncertainties of business risk and value, not on readily quantifiable market data. Value fund managers make lonely judgments that may not be vindicated for years to come. Jim Gipson of the Clipper Fund commented, not without regret, "Intelligence is a necessary condition for success in this business, but it is not a sufficient one."[65] Patience, investment philosophy, temperament—these do not lend themselves to the algebraic formulas and computer models that are so popular in the academy.

The economic literature is also far more attuned to cases of over-pricing in the market—irrational exuberance—than to the sometimes egregious periods of underpricing. Manic, not depressed, markets are what excite scholars. Value investors, in contrast, tune out fairly quickly when prices soar; it is the opportunity to buy good companies at dis-count prices that stirs their juices. In the late 1970s, Buffett and other Graham-and-Dodders were salivating over the bargains in the market. I don't believe the academic community could grasp their enthusiasm.

What truly defines the Goldfarb 10 is their rare comfort with mak-ing lonely, out-of-step decisions. They are inner directed, willing to rely on patient, time-consuming analyses of business value, confident that whatever fads and fashions might then be afoot in the market will pro-vide the handful of opportunities they need and the margin of safety on which they rely. Almost everyone else—scholars, rating services, and most fund managers alike—measures investment risk by looking at the price volatility of a stock, numbers that are available at the click of a mouse but have zero use over the long run. Not so these value manag-ers, whose long investment horizons require that risk be measured by examining a company's market share, vulnerability to new competition, financial strength, management strength, and other subjective though analyzable factors. The reality is that sometimes there will be no attrac-tive opportunities—just as sometimes there will be no deals at the store for the shopper. One does not have to buy if the merchandise is over-priced or simply not attractive. David Winters, who had headed Mutual Beacon until 2005 and now runs the Wintergreen Fund, seems almost pleased to say that "at some moments in time we will continue to be out of step with investment fashions."[66] (To the question "What did you do at the office today, honey?" the answer is often "Nothing.")

Value managers knew enough, and had the strength of their convic-tions, to steer clear of Enron and the like, despite being sorely punished as many investors cashed out. Having a keen sense for market history and foibles surely helped. Jean-Marie Eveillard's previously quoted response to the French bank that still owned the First Eagle manage-ment company in early 2000 and was pressuring him to go with the market flow, says it all: "I would rather lose half my shareholders than lose half my shareholders' money."[67] In a profession not usually noted for such virtues, we've observed a group that demonstrated, under exqui-sitely trying circumstances, a keen sense of fiduciary duty and integrity. (Why else close off a successful fund to new investors?) My sense is that these qualities define their sense of self. It is bottomed, of course, on their confidence, born of experience, that while they may for periods be out of step with the market, they will be vindicated *over time*.

These value funds are a quite discrete segment. Not so for the second gap in the scholarly endeavor, which might be defined as the failure to examine the institutional structures and pressures that help to explain why the other 98 percent or so of the funds tend to be so short-term focused, finding safety—at least for the manager—in holding a great many stocks, rather than patient selection of a few. Funds trade at cyclonic speeds, turning over their swollen lists of stocks on average every 10 to 12 months. The transaction and tax costs of all this short-term trading are huge—huge, that is, for the investor, not the manager. Is anything much happening in the economy, or are the funds simply tilting with each new breeze in the market? In 2003, there were 30 days when the S&P 500 and the Dow Jones Industrial Average rose or declined by more than 2 percent.[68] In the first nine months of 2004, there was not a single such day, and even for this period as a whole those indexes barely budged. Given the apparent lack of major market developments, did the pace of trading drop off? Not at all.

The purpose of this analysis is to provide an analytic framework for investors, but it may also encourage a fresh, broader inquiry in the world of finance. I have obviously left some important issues on the table. Why are true-blue value funds so few in number? Is it simply too painful to swim against the crowd? To what extent do value investors outperform the market over longer periods of time than the five years we studied? Clearly it's not by 11 percent per annum. Is there any feasible means by which society could reduce the costly, wasteful short-termism that afflicts and distracts the market, or has the proliferation of derivatives and market news media rendered that an idle thought? For an intriguing behavioral puzzle, why have economists talked so often about rational investors but not bothered to study this intellectually astute, successful group?

The Goldfarb 10 were, of course, selected after the event—after the five years covered by the study. These 10 funds were not, however, a random selection, chosen out of thousands simply because they had performed well. It was plain, for example, that Goldfarb had not followed their performance all that closely. For example, he had included among his 10 the SoGen (short for Société Genérale, the French bank) funds, but several years had passed since they had metamorphosed into what is now the First Eagle group. When Buffett looked at nine comparable value funds in 1984, the 50th anniversary of the publication of Graham and Dodd, he confronted this same hindsight argument.[69] But like the Buffett Nine, the Goldfarb 10 had explicitly confirmed, as Buffett put it, their "framework for investment decision-making"*ex ante.* My group did so under the most exquisite circumstances, back in 1999 and 2000, when their funds were hemorrhaging cash as investors fled. And still they stayed the course.

Buffett and I both felt under pressure to counter the inevitable criticism that we had simply chosen, with 20/20 hindsight, some very successful managers. He spent a lot of ink explaining that he had been close to this particular group for many years and the likelihood of picking such outstanding managers in advance would defy the statistical odds of random chance. I used, of course, the *Fortune* list and the group of large-cap growth funds as yardsticks. While the markets were cheering Oracle and the like into the wild blue yonder, it turned out that these value managers had stayed far, far away from a list said by *Fortune* to be good for the decade. The value managers stayed the course, explaining their thinking along the way, even though they watched as investors fled.

I don't expect to dissuade the scholars and professionals committed to their theory, just as Buffett's efforts to do so were amusing but futile. In academia, a hands-on study has trouble competing with a good computer-driven model. Because it is futile, I am now turning over a new leaf; let this economic theory of rational markets go its own way, and henceforth I will go mine. After the 2005 World Series, a Chicago reporter said that no matter what, White Sox fans and Cub fans will never be reconciled. Here, too, why try?

Obviously someone out there was buying those *Fortune* 10 stocks, and it wasn't just Joe Sixpack. In Chapter 4 we will take a look at some more mainstream funds, a major group of large-cap growth funds selected essentially at random. Let's see what they were doing during this turbulent period, and how their investors fared. But first, let's take a broader view of the stock market, which you will see is a quite remarkable institution.

Chapter 3

The Anatomy of the Stock Market

There's a quick lift to be had by reading some of the articles explaining why so many investors, making decisions that may make or break their family's future, are such "dolts,"[1] simply chasing whichever stock has gone up lately or the one someone said would go up soon—happy to believe that this time it's a can't-miss opportunity. Had they been buying a car, of course, they would have checked the miles per gallon, made sure there were airbags for the kids, and taken a test drive. But not with stocks. Guaranteed, you will come away from those articles about investor foolishness feeling smarter and gifted with a rare talent to think independently of the crowd. And that includes the crowd on Wall Street, as well as your friends at the golf club. Of course, there is just the *possibility* that you will recognize some of this perverse behavior in yourself, but in either case, read on.

We explore here the nature of the stock market, which in fact is a very peculiar market, not at all like the ones we know from buying cars or even groceries. If General Motors suddenly increased the price of a Cadillac by 30 to 50 percent, buyers would back off, waiting until GM got its senses back, or simply go check the Lincoln or Lexus models and pricing. But that's not how it is with stocks. Hearing that a stock or fund, like the tech fund discussed in Chapter 5, has jumped in price sets off a buzz, an excitement to be part of the scene. There really is something special about the stock market, and we need to get a grip on the behavior of markets in order to understand why investors—professional and individual—behave as they do. Knowing our strengths and foibles will in turn help us better grasp the huge changes in the mutual fund industry in recent years.

Vaclav Havel, the hero of the Velvet Revolution that broke the grip of Communism in Czechoslovakia, and then its first democratically elected president, likes to say that "friends tell you the truth." So, is the industry a friend of investors, a really good friend, or perhaps not all that friendly after all? To answer that question, we need to understand first the stock market, and then in turn the public's strengths and weaknesses in dealing with the market. Simple!

The Stock Market

The stock market[2] is such a ubiquitous fixture—on the Internet, in newspapers, on TV screens in restaurants—that it may be easy to overlook the magic it works to the benefit of public companies and investors. Mr. Market permits long-term financing not just of hardwired plants and equipment, but also of research and development in medicine and technology of all sorts. A corporation issuing new stock is acquiring capital that is permanent and locked up, which it can put to work however and whenever it sees fit, without the pressure of having to repay, say, a bank loan that would mature in five or even 10 years' time. By the wave of Mr. Market's wand, however, what is long-term for the company has become liquid and freely marketable for the investor. Almost like money itself, stocks can be cashed out quickly, cheaply, and at quite continuous prices.

The market has other remarkable qualities. Insofar as it prices stocks accurately, in accordance with their long-term prospects, it allocates our savings to their most profitable—and some might say productive—uses. In late 2006, for example, Google could have raised capital inexpensively, because the roughly $500 price per share was over 40 times the company's earnings per share. Google's prospects for growth were so bright that relatively few new shares would have had to be floated to raise whatever fresh money Google needed. In contrast, the shares of Citigroup were then priced at only about 10 times Citigroup's earnings per share. In order to have raised a comparable sum, Citigroup would have had to issue many more new shares relative to the number already outstanding, thus diluting more significantly the earnings for the remaining shareholders. In this self-executing fashion, the so-called invisible hand of the market would have been offering, on attractive terms, inexpensive new money to the one, but not the other.

And there's more. Because stock prices tend, over time at least, to reflect a management's performance, investors are able to hold corporate executives accountable. Those executives, in turn, knowing they are being watched in the mirror of the market, are encouraged—nay, pushed—to confront disagreeable realities in detail, and *early on*. The old wisdom is that "you manage what you measure," and a stock price that has been going nowhere for years helps those bosses to overcome the very human capacity for denial. We all know about denial ("Well, yes, things are not going well now, but they will be better next year, or soon after that"). The stock market does not allow the CEO the luxury of endless procrastination.

It really is a bit of magic; think of the utter failure of the Soviet Union to manage these same challenges, delegating to a vast bureaucracy the power to decide where the economy should go, which enterprises should receive fresh funding, and who should run them. The invisible hand of the market stimulates more creativity and efficiency than any commissar could have imagined.

But nothing's perfect, not even the stock market. As we know, things went very wrong in the late 1990s, when a spectacular bubble overwhelmed (most of) our ability to think of stocks as an interest in a business. *Investment* decisions, like those of the value funds discussed in Chapter 2, should always be based on the price of a stock relative to its underlying value, after careful study of a company's prospects, managements, risks, and balance sheet. In the new economy madness, however, the market was dominated by *speculation,* in which the subtleties and nuances of a particular business and its long-term prospects seemed to fade from view. The focus, instead, was on the momentum of stock prices, whether this group or that group was rising, irrespective of anything else. Just the direction of the stock mattered. Up and up and up, like a balloon, was best. Follow the balloon . . . and go. Go, and it's likely to rise some more. Being in the new economy seemed to excuse us from the messy reality of whether this dot-com or that could really make it, or whether they even had things like revenues or were profitable business enterprises—pesky details like that.

Think of buying a Cadillac if GM had jacked up the price by 50 percent, buying not to *own* it, but because someone else might buy it, not from GM but from you, for an even higher price tomorrow. That was the state of affairs on Wall Street during those frothy years (and closely resembling the real estate market until 2007). Early in the year 2000, for example, the stock price of Cisco Systems peaked at $77 a share, Cisco having earned $2.1 billion in the prior fiscal year, equal to 31 cents a share. The earnings would grow by a nickel a share in 2000, but no matter how one pushed the numbers, the stock was selling for more than 200 times its earnings. Cisco, of course, was not some amorphous dot-com with no revenues and no real products or services, but a company with a solid business in computer network equipment. But even if the earnings in 1999 were to double, and then double again, and then again—no mean trick—at $77 a share, the stock still would have been priced at a hefty 30 times earnings. While Cisco was a legitimate company, the stock price was not. Cisco's earnings would, in fact, multiply five times, from 17 cents a share back in fiscal 1997 to 87 cents in 2005, but in December 2005, the stock, at $17 a share, was down by 80 percent from its peak.

There were other companies that lacked the substance of a Cisco, companies where the market could not have focused on earnings, because there were none. Even their prospects for earnings were poor. But back in those heady days, it was the dream that mattered; and for companies like Webvan, the online grocer, or the pet puppet company advertised during the Super Bowl, we believed the dream. It was a costly dream.

Many mutual funds, too, bought those high-flying stocks, thus reinforcing the cycle. A distinguished author (who happens to be Roger Lowenstein) summed it up well:

> Fund families such as Janus, Van Wagoner, and Putnam would stuff their portfolios with Cisco, Qualcomm, JDS Uniphase— the hottest stocks—which purchases would drive the stocks and thus the fund prices higher.... No sooner did word of their success filter out than their funds attracted more capital, which the managers used to buy still more of the favorite and already over-priced stocks and keep the cycle going.[3]

Those fund families were not simply riding the gravy train; they were pushing it. And of course they and their investors (but mostly the investors) paid a price for it.

Structure of the Stock Market

So, why is a share of GM so different from a Cadillac?[4] Why would we buy a stock *because* the price has gone up, while we would otherwise think it's a bummer to pay $70,000 for a car that only last week sold for $50,000?

Speculation, meaning how a *stock* will behave, as distinguished from investment or how a *business* will behave, has been an inseparable part of stock trading from its inception. The market was born in 1791, when trading began in the shares of two important corporations, the Bank of the United States, chartered by Congress but largely owned by the public, and the Bank of New York, chartered by the state. It took all of a year before a full-fledged mania bubbled to the surface. The scrip that would later be converted into shares of the Bank of the United States was issued in July 1791 at 25, rose to 280 in August, and fell to 110 in September before rising again. Referring to Lower Manhattan, James Madison wrote to Thomas Jefferson that "stock jobbing drowns every other subject. The coffee house is in an eternal buzz with the gamblers." Newspapers elsewhere began their two-centuries-long "assignment" of mocking the antics of New York speculators.

Bubbles burst, whether they are soap bubbles or investment bubbles, whether they happen in 2000 or hundreds of years ago. In 1792, a year after it began, the first of all U.S. stock booms crashed. By using other people's money, Martin Duer, who had been Alexander Hamilton's assistant at the Treasury, became one of the more visible players. Duer speculated heavily in the stock of the Society for Useful Manufactures and the Scioto Company, both highly speculative ventures. Like so many of his breed—and like the Janus funds and others 200 years later—Duer used each successive market gain to increase his holdings. Unlike today's mutual funds, however, which are essentially prohibited from buying on margin, Duer had leveraged his holdings. When the market collapsed in February 1792, so did Duer's paper empire. Unlike today, he was sent to debtors' prison. A colleague escaped by fleeing to New Jersey, then beyond the reach of the sheriff. Perhaps New Jersey was considered a fate so much worse than prison that no one thought to bother about extradition, if indeed it was possible.

By the end of the eighteenth century, much of the paraphernalia of stock market speculation was in place. Derivative securities? Yes. True, they were called "time bargains" instead of futures, but they were the most popular instrument at the New York coffee houses where the securities market of the 1790s coalesced. Booms and busts? As we saw, yes, and soon they were being called bubbles, even by the participants. When the Second Bank of the United States went public in 1818, the stock was bid up by speculators whose aim, according to the *New York Daily Advertiser,* was to "sell out as soon as the balloon is sufficiently inflated by puffing, and before the pressure of too much gas causes it to burst."[5]

All through the nineteenth and the early twentieth centuries, there flourished a whole panoply of colorful manipulative tricks—"fancies," for example, which, like the penny stocks of our era, were essentially worthless; today, almost all of them would be illegal under federal law. Federal law, you say? What is remarkable about the stock market today is that the trading of stocks is closely regulated, far more so than real estate and other assets. Why stocks? Why are stocks, more than other assets, the subject of intensive scrutiny, with an agency of the federal government, the Securities and Exchange Commission, overseeing how they are promoted and traded?

There are four distinct factors making the stock market quite unlike any other:

1. Securities are mere intangibles, easily created.
2. Security analysis is complex and difficult.

3. Stocks trade in an almost entirely secondary market.
4. Excessive liquidity lubricates the market too well.

Factor 1: Mere Intangibles, Easily Created

First off, securities are intangibles, mere pieces of paper, created at virtually no cost, rather than produced. They can be issued in unlimited amounts and printed with large or small numbers on them, because they are nothing in and of themselves, representing only an interest in *something else.* When Daniel Drew sold his controlling interest in the Erie Railroad to Commodore Cornelius Vanderbilt, Drew pulled a fast one on him. Acting before Vanderbilt could get his hands on the tiller, Drew turned around and issued enough new stock to himself to block a takeover. There are effective restrictions today against "watered stock," as it was called then, but what fascinated Drew was that stocks often trade with a vitality of their own, quite apart from anything happening within the company.

The annual trading in shares of the Harlem Railroad, a popular stock of the 1830s, was sometimes as much as 30 times the number of shares outstanding. Even the Second Bank of the United States experienced trading volume that exceeded three times its shares outstanding. With the traders chasing the buzz in the market, illusions became the reality, some of which centered on real companies, such as the Harlem Railroad, but many of them simply fancies, mere shells of, say, mining companies that had neither capital nor serious prospects. Anyone familiar with the computer stocks of the early 1980s or the Internet and other new economy stocks of the 1990s would recognize the speculative fever surrounding the canal, railroad, and banking stocks of the nineteenth century.

The pattern changes, but the temptation to peddle illusions never changes. Anyone on e-mail is getting spam tips like the one that came through my computer in November 2006. It seems it's China that's hot now:

RREF Price Settles and on the Rise! Time to Get In Is Now!

Red Reef Labs for New Manufacturing and Distribution Contract in China!

Company: Red Reef Laboratories Inc.

Symbol: RREF

Price: $0.352

Volume Expectations: Huge

. . . This one will climb hard. They have news coming out end of week and it is expected to push this up 300%.

/s Bonita Hartley

The stock had sold as high as $2.25 in October, but three weeks after that e-mail tip, the price had fallen by half, from 35 cents to 17 cents a share. Known as "pump and dump" schemes, the spammers buy the stock before touting it, then sell after the "gullible masses," as the *New York Times* calls them, take the bait.[6] Incidentally, the company's product, not mentioned in that e-mail, is a disinfectant, not nearly the second coming of the Internet or a cure for cancer.

Factor 2: Complexity of Security Analysis

If the first factor is that securities are only intangibles that represent something else, the second is that the "something else" is itself extraordinarily complex. As we saw in Chapter 2, the value of a common stock is the present value of a long-term, future stream of business income, which itself defies precise calculation. We do not know what a share of Exxon Mobil Corporation will be worth tomorrow, because we cannot predict with any confidence all the factors that may impact it—economic activity here and abroad, governmental actions, wars, tax rates, competition, research and exploration, much less the quality of the company's management years hence. If that seems daunting, remember that the quality of disclosure required of Exxon Mobil is extremely high and much better than we might encounter elsewhere.

These two factors, taken alone, help to explain the passion on the one hand and the loss of any resemblance to business values on the other, particularly in the new economy stocks of the 1990s—not just Cisco or Amazon but dozens on dozens of others. When we buy intangibles, we cannot kick the tires. Even if we could, their worth would be difficult to calculate. True, we cannot kick tires in the commodities market, but there is nothing very uncertain about the uses of a bushel of No. 2 soft red wheat. Supply and demand fluctuate, but we not only know what wheat is but we also know that at the end of the day its value is defined by its tangible end uses, such as a loaf of bread. In the stock market, at day's end, value is heavily influenced by perceptions, which in turn, as John Maynard Keynes said, are influenced by perceptions, which in turn are . . .

The common denominator of every hot potato of the nineteenth century and hot stock of modern times is the rush of investors to pay up for something today simply because it is selling at a higher price than yesterday. Hence the Cadillac dichotomy. In the tangible world of coffee beans, clothing, and cars, as prices increase, so too does our reluctance to buy. But in the perception-bound world of stocks, this basic economic concept of price elasticity is often stood on its head. As prices rise, appetites are whetted and the volume of trading jumps. Did the cash flow of WorldCom or Global Crossing turn negative, even as the stock price continued to make new highs? Except for a handful of money managers, working offstage, quietly digging into the messy details of the company's financials, no one seemed to care.

Thankfully, the federal securities laws narrow the perception-reality gap by requiring a high degree of disclosure. The laws work about as well as can be expected, given the enormous difficulty of reducing a complex business reality to a handful of printed words and numbers. Even the clearest disclosure snapshot, however, stops at the water's edge of today, leaving those future income streams still to be determined.

Given the enormous uncertainties created by factors one and two, Ben Graham preached, as we saw in Chapter 2, the importance to investors of a substantial margin of safety. Just as in the Greek legend, he wrote, when "the wise men finally boiled down the history of mortal affairs to the single phrase, 'This too will pass,'" so too did he, when "[c]onfronted with a like challenge to distill the secret of sound investment into three words, . . . venture the motto, MARGIN OF SAFETY."[7] Investors who insist on that safety factor will miss out on some successful investments. But with 10,000-plus stocks to choose from, they can afford to be selective and avoid the nightmare stocks, such as Cisco, that fell 80 percent—a magnitude of loss from which most investors will never recover—and still come out substantially ahead.

Factor 3: Trading in a Secondary Market

Stocks trade in what we call secondary markets, meaning that, unlike wheat, oil, or almost anything else except perhaps gold, stocks are not produced or consumed in appreciable quantities. They simply trade from hand to hand, so that investors—even value investors—are ineluctably drawn to ask, what would someone else pay for them next month or next year?

In grain markets, for example, the ultimate purchasers either consume the product directly or convert it into a product that will then be processed and consumed. These millers, bakers, and other real-world players on the demand side put limits on the range of speculative activity, just as farmers do on the supply side. No one would pay $50 for a loaf of bread. If prices rise too much, farm production increases and/or consumption declines; and if prices drop too much, farmers will switch acreage from wheat to soybeans or corn, speeding the process by which prices return to normal. Stocks are different.

To be sure, even if they are not "consumers" of stocks, prospective buyers may suspect that they should do a serious valuation. They ought to be thinking about the business in which they are buying a part interest, much as a bank would analyze a borrower's income statement. But because they expect merely to *resell*, investors are drawn to thinking in terms of the market. With only a minor payoff directly from the company—those in the S&P 500 are paying average dividends of less than 2 percent—financial analysis becomes primarily a guide to what the *market* will do. However confident investors may be as to the soundness of their valuation, success depends ultimately on the degree of interest shown by prospective buyers who, after having worked their way through all the same substantive uncertainties, realize that they, in turn, must also come to grips with the fact of being able to sell only to another trader—a month or a year hence.

The dilemma was captured by Graham and Dodd in the original 1934 edition of *Security Analysis*. The influence of analytic factors and fundamental values over the market price, they wrote, was only partial and indirect—partial in that they frequently compete with purely speculative factors and indirect in that "the merits of an issue reflect themselves in the market price not by any automatic response or mathematical relationship but through the minds and decisions of buyers and sellers."[8] Subjective factors influence the market and are in turn influenced by it. Even for those committed to a value-oriented program, market prices cannot be ignored, because they have a strong psychological impact on prices. Thus, Graham and Dodd concluded in an oft-quoted set of similes:

> In other words, the market is not a *weighing machine,* on which the value of each issue is recorded by an exact and impersonal mechanism, in accordance with its specific qualities. Rather should we say that the market is a *voting machine,* whereon countless individuals register choices which are the product partly of reason and partly of emotion.[9]

Factor 4: Excessive Liquidity

On almost any issue, we can take our pick of economists, even among Nobel laureates. On this issue, my preference is the late Professor James Tobin, who in a celebrated lecture expressed the fear that our securities markets are dissipating some otherwise useful talents and resources:

> I suspect that the immense power of the computer is being harnessed to this "paper economy," not to do the same transactions more economically but to balloon the quantity and variety of financial exchanges. . . . I fear that, as Keynes saw even in his day, the advantages of the liquidity and negotiability of financial instruments come at the cost of facilitating nth-degree speculation which is short-sighted and inefficient.[10]

The stock market is astonishingly liquid. The annual turnover was 14 percent back in 1960, meaning that traders and investors, as a group, kept their stocks on average for seven years. By 1984, when Tobin was writing, the turnover of New York Stock Exchange (NYSE) listed stocks, including trading away from the exchange, had quadrupled, to 56 percent. Today it is more than twice that. The turnover rate in 2004—meaning the percentage of all the listed shares that were traded—was 97 percent. Including, however, transactions in those same shares elsewhere, in other markets, the turnover rate in 2004 climbed to 120 percent, so that we were holding stocks for months, not years. Compare this with real estate. Ask yourself, for example, whether the homes on your block would be a better, more comfortable investment if they changed hands every eight or nine months. Even with the recent real estate frenzy and flipping scenarios, most homes are owned for many years; and those areas where homes were flipped have seen some suffering—in increased foreclosures and the like. Given the explosion in the marketplace of derivative securities—puts, calls, straddles, and lots more—the effective level of trading is astronomical.★ The brokerage commission for instituti-onal investors is now as little as a penny a share, a pittance compared to the standard commission of almost 1 percent of the transaction value that was obligatory before deregulation in 1975. Here, as in Britain after Big Bang, the demand for trading has proven to be quite elastic. (The economists would agree on that.) As transaction costs dropped, the vol-ume of trading exploded.

In a purely secondary market, however, liquidity is somewhat of a contradiction, existing only enough to maintain the illusion. In times of stress, when it really matters, there is liquidity for a few, and only a few. On Black Monday, October 19, 1987, when the Dow Jones Indus-trial Average fell by over 500 points, or 22 percent, total trading amounted to just 1 percent of the value of the outstanding shares. The other 99 percent were stuck; there was no liquidity for the crowd. It was like shouting "Fire!" in a crowded theater and then announcing, "Sorry, no one can leave without finding someone to take your place." What ignited the blaze that day was a clever but misleadingly named set of programs called portfolio insurance. This was not insurance in any sense, but rather derivatives purchased by pension funds that required brokers to sell stock index futures whenever the market as a whole dropped by some designated amounts. A few such programs might not have done much damage, but on Black Monday there was an avalanche; one set of sales triggered the next, and the next. Those com-puters had not been programmed to check what was happening in the real world or even whether there were any takers at reasonable prices for what they were dumping.

★There are over $300 trillion of derivatives of all sorts outstanding, measured by the value of the underlying assets: stocks, commodities, whatever. "Pension Funds Help Derivatives Market Surge to $370,000 Bn," *Financial Times,* November 18, 2006, 11.

Black Monday was obviously a rare event. But there is a second, and on a day-to-day basis particularly important, lesson in that crash. Yes, liquidity is a good thing; no one wants to be locked in. Better answers come, however, if we think less about how to get out than about how to make better decisions on the way in. Those who expect to sell out quickly and cheaply are far more apt to buy for speculative reasons, so they are likely to act as uninformed owners in between. On balance, they are less likely to know their companies. (People who rent housing for the summer do not take the same interest in the property as those who own it.) The cure devised by the Securities and Exchange Commission (SEC) and Congress for one aspect of people's tendency to invest impulsively, without adequate reflection—the penny stock problem—was to require a cooling-off period before buyers could commit, a response that has been useful though hardly a cure. And the primary remedy for the excesses laid bare by Black Monday was the so-called circuit breakers, which close the index-arbitrage market for short periods, thus giving the market a breather. Business thinking could then begin to displace the stock market thinking that overtakes Wall Street Chicken Littles from time to time.

Excessive liquidity impairs the social object. It fosters a climate in which investors need not concern themselves with the uncertainties of the long-term business realities, because at any time they have the ability to revise their commitment. As John Maynard Keynes summed it up, "Of the maxims of orthodox finance none, surely, is more anti-social than the fetish of liquidity."[11] Knowing that they lack the ability to sell on a phone call, it is probably safe to say that most homeowners take a more genuine interest in their homes' plumbing.

Taken together, these four factors present a uniquely perverse picture. We have an almost purely secondary market, a market where the wheat is seldom ground into flour and then sold and eaten as bread, but merely traded from one wheat speculator to the next, and where only infrequently do we enjoy the reality check of mergers or other events in which one buyer acquires the whole company and consumes, as it were, the "bread" of its operations and cash flow. There is, indeed, something quite tangible underlying those stocks, but the analysis of the company, and where it is heading, is devilishly difficult and inevitably uncertain. Think of an oil company: What will the Middle East or the price of oil look like 10 or 20 years hence? We just don't know what the future holds, but it's hard for us to live with that. "Our psyche," an economist said recently, "abhors the darkness of ignorance,"[12] the unsettling passivity of leaving things as they are. We turn to the market seers, who *pretend* to know what's going to happen, which provides some comfort. The dizzy pace of trading amplifies the problem still further, creating a palpable pressure to focus on Mr. Market, as if it were a conscious being that could offer advice. (You've heard it: "Never argue with the tape.")

Nothing about the stock market prepares us to be as patient and disciplined as we need to be. Warren Buffett said to this author some years ago that he typically read about 500 annual reports a year. He did not, of course, *buy* 500 stocks a year; but instead he filed away in his prodigious memory snapshots of the handful of companies that, at some price, might interest him. He had, for example, studied the business of Coca-Cola for years, not to mention having been one of its loyal customers. It was not until 1988, however, that he acted. The price of sugar had risen, and the market, fearing a squeeze on the company's profits, drove down the price of the Coke stock. Recognizing that the problem was transient, he pounced—investing $1 billion at a time when Berkshire Hathaway's net worth was only about $3 billion.

The traders and other professionals cared only about the short-term market response to a rise in the price of sugar. Whether they drove the Coke stock below its business value was, to them, irrelevant. But by year-end 1990, the stock price of Coke had doubled, and by the mid-1990s doubled and doubled again. Similarly, institutional investors with an equally short-term time frame pushed the market over the cliff on Black Monday.

Traders and professionals are one thing, and their twists and turns give us insights into the behavior of markets. Main Street Americans are a different story. We will see in Chapter 6 why they're in the stock market, how well they cope with the challenges, and what they need from mutual funds. Only then can we take the full measure of how well mutual funds fulfill their mission.

Chapter 4

Investing at Warp Speed

T he value investors and funds we examined in Chapter 2 are a commendable group, but when the day is done, they account for no more than a minuscule part of the professionally managed money, or of the overall stock market. Their focus is on absolute returns—are we making money and how much?—quite unlike most fund managers who focus on relative returns, judging themselves by how well they perform compared to a narrowly defined index of their peer group. In addition to providing us with valuable insights, those value funds are useful as a yardstick or benchmark for stock funds generally. But if we want a good understanding of what most mutual funds are doing, we need to look elsewhere.

First off, let's do a brief sketch of the mutual fund universe. It has grown dramatically in recent years. At the beginning of 2007, there were about 4,800 equity mutual funds, with total assets of $6 trillion. These stock funds accounted for more than half of the $10+ trillion in mutual funds as a whole, which include also bond and money market funds.[1]

Stock funds have grown more than 20 times over since 1990, when their total assets were only $250 billion. Stock funds now own one-fourth of all common stocks, versus only 8 percent in 1990.[2] Over 90 million people now own shares of stock funds.[3] The remarkable growth is a reflection, no doubt, of a pervasive anxiety about corporate pension plans and Social Security, a sense that people had better take care of themselves or they could be left out in the cold in their so-called golden years.

Now let's take that $6 trillion in equity funds and break it down into three broad sectors: first, the great preponderance of actively managed funds; second, the basic index funds, such as the S&P 500, accounting for about 10 percent of the total; and then finally, the third and smallest sector, the assets managed by those few true-blue value investors. It's clear that over 85 percent of all equity funds are managed energetically, and while their particular styles will vary, there is the common thread that they keep a keen eye on what the market is doing, so as to keep pace.

Years ago, if a friend said that she had invested in a mutual fund, it would have meant that she owned a large-cap blend fund, which, like the Massachusetts Investors Trust in Chapter 1, held shares in a variety of major companies, some of which would be, say, steady-as-she-goes financial companies, such as banks or insurance companies, while some would be industrials, and perhaps some retailers. The managers would decide where the dollars went, depending on the opportunities. That was why your friend had invested in the first place, to be relieved of that burden. Forget it; that's history. Look at any major fund family today, say T. Rowe Price, and one sees an array of funds in the nine style boxes (small-cap value, large-cap growth, mid-cap blend, etc.) that the industry has uniformly adopted. Mutual funds of the sort your friend had in mind, large-cap blend, constitute only a minor part, about 10 percent in market value, of all the domestic stock funds offered by the T. Rowe Price group.

Sell It All Every Year?

The average mutual fund turns over its portfolio at 100 percent or more a year. Let's call it "investing at warp speed," admittedly an oxymoron, since churning stocks at such a pace can hardly be considered "investing." Being alien to a world that spins so wildly, I called Don Phillips of

Morningstar, who helped set up a baseline group of large-cap growth funds, the 20 largest in assets at year-end 1997. That would, we thought, provide a representative sample.

By 2005, there were 15 survivors ("Group of 15").[4] As one might expect, over a period of time two of the funds had drifted, as they say, from growth to blend, fairly common as a fund grows in size and the managers focus simply on staying abreast of the broad market index. Two others, with mediocre records, had been quietly merged into other funds. (A fifth, being essentially the twin of another fund, was dropped from the study.) Given the usual survivor bias—the losers are gone— the Group of 15 should have performed rather well. In fact, the results were quite ghastly. But like rubbernecking a car wreck, we can enjoy eyeballing the victims, and tut-tutting that the passengers weren't wearing seat belts.

For the five years ended August 31, 2005,★ the Group of 15 experienced (on a total return basis, which includes dividends and other distributions) an average annual *negative* return of 8.89 percent, versus a *negative* 2.71 percent for the S&P 500. (See Table 4.1.)[5]

Over the same five years, and again on a total return basis, the 10 value funds we studied in Chapter 2 enjoyed *positive* average annual returns of 9.83 percent. The reader is no doubt quick with numbers, but let me help. These 15 large-cap growth funds underperformed the Goldfarb 10 during those five years by an average of over 18 percentage points *per year*. This adds up to real money in my book. Only one of the 15 had even modestly positive returns. Now, if you go back 10 years, a period that includes the years when growth stocks were very much in vogue, the Group of 15 did better, averaging a positive 8.13 percent per year. All in all, it was a daunting 10 years, first soaring, then plummeting. Even for that 10-year period, however, they underperformed the value group, on average, by more than 5 percent *per year*.[6] With a good tailwind, those large-cap funds were not great—underperforming the S&P 500 index by something under 2 percent per year—and in stormy weather their boats leaked badly.

★This study, with the arbitrary cutoff date, was prepared for a speech given before the New York Society of Security Analysts in December 2005.

Table 4.1   The 15 Survivors

Group of 15	Average Annual Return	
	5 Years	10 Years
	Ended August 31, 2005	
American Century Growth Investors	−8.71%	+6.24%
American Century Ultra Investors	−6.91	+7.01
American Funds Amcap[3]	+1.98	+11.69
Consulting Group Large Cap Growth	−9.40	+7.21
Fidelity Advisor Equity Growth	−8.84	+6.87
Fidelity Growth Company	−7.91	+9.65
Harbor Capital Appreciation	−8.21	+8.66
Janus Growth & Income	−3.34	+12.72
Janus Twenty	−9.79	+11.35
Mainstay Capital Appreciation	−11.33	+4.75
Massachusetts Investors Growth Stock	−9.53	+9.48
RiverSource (formerly AXP) Growth	−12.93	+4.81
RiverSource New Dimensions A	−6.77	+8.05
Vanguard Growth Index	−7.31	+9.28
Vanguard U.S. Growth	−15.43	+4.13
Average Annual Return for the Five Years		
Group of 15	−8.89%	+8.13%
S&P 500 Index	−2.71%	+9.85%

DATA SOURCE: Morningstar.

Table 4.2 shows the average annual returns for the Goldfarb 10 for the same five- and 10-year periods.

By mid-2005, these value fund managers were struggling to find stocks at prices that offered the requisite margin of safety—the market price discount from a company's intrinsic or enterprise value—that is their trademark. Half of the Goldfarb 10 were holding one-sixth or more of their assets in cash, a level of reserves matched by only one of those 15 growth funds. Portfolio turnover for the value funds had on average been one-fourth that of the growth funds.

So much for averages. The reader may remember that I said that I would stop dueling with economists. Not being an economist, I find it more useful to look at individual funds one at a time, reading annual reports—bottom-up if you like. Averages often conceal as much as they reveal. Indeed, as we saw in Chapter 2, while the market *on average* was sky-high in the late 1990s,

Table 4.2 Goldfarb 10 Average Annual Returns

Goldfarb 10	Average Annual Return	
	5 Years	10 Years
	Ended August 31, 2005	
Clipper Fund	+9.53%	+13.89%
FPA Capital	+16.38	+15.41
First Eagle Global	+17.49	+13.47
Legg Mason Value	+0.65	+15.38
Longleaf Partners	+10.19	+12.79
Mutual Beacon	+8.67	N/A
Oak Value	+3.95	+10.77
Oakmark Select	+11.78	N/A
Source Capital	+15.38	+15.87
Tweedy Browne American Value	+4.26	+10.33
Average Annual Return		
Goldfarb 10	+9.83%	+13.49%
S&P 500 Index	+2.71%	+9.85%

whole sectors of old economy stocks had been ignored and were selling at bargain prices, which the computer-based studies missed.

Massachusetts Investors Growth Stock Fund

At first I picked three of the 15 growth funds for a closer look. The first was the Massachusetts Investors Growth Stock Fund, chosen because of its unusually long history. Founded in 1932 as the Massachusetts Investors Second Fund, it was, like its older sibling, Massachusetts Investors Trust, truly a *mutual* fund, in the sense that it was managed internally, supplemented by an advisory board of six prominent Boston businessmen.[7] That structure was remarkable, both because the managers were accountable directly to the investors rather than operating as a subsidiary of, say, a bank or an insurance company with distinct and often conflicting interests, and because the existence of an advisory board reinforced the sense of a civic service. In 1969, when management was shifted to an external company, now known as MFS Investment Management, the total expense ratio was an extremely modest 0.32 percent.

I am confident that the founders of the Massachusetts Investors Trust would no longer recognize this second child, which has become a caricature of the "do something" culture. The expense ratio, though still below its peer group, has tripled. But it's the turbulent pace of trading that would have puzzled and distressed the founding fathers—along with the shocking lack of candor. At year-end 1999, having turned the portfolio over 174 percent, the managers said they had moved away from "stable growth companies" such as supermarket and financial companies and into tech and leisure stocks, singling out in the year-end report Cisco and Sun Microsystems—each selling at the time at about 100 times its earnings, a fact not mentioned—for their "reasonable stock valuation." The following year, while citing a bottom-up, "value sensitive approach," the fund's turnover soared to 261 percent. And in 2001, with the fund continuing to remark on its "fundamental . . . bottom-up investment process," turnover reached into the thin-air level of 305 percent. That the managers seemed to lack a sense of direction is reflected in the fund's performance, which for the years 2002 and 2003 fell short of the S&P 500 by a cumulative 12 percent. It is difficult to conceive how, even in 2003, well after the market as a whole had leveled off, the managers of a then $10 billion portfolio could, in effect, have flipped it almost three times over, selling in all $28 billion of stocks and then reinvesting the $28 billion proceeds in others.

For the five years ended in 2003, turnover in the fund averaged 250 percent. All that senseless trading took a toll. Each 100 percent in annual portfolio turnover increases the costs by almost 1 percent of a fund's assets, reflecting the brokerage fees but also the significant effects of market impact, meaning that the managers' purchases push the market up even while they're buying, and then down when they sell. These are quite hidden costs, not broken out by the funds or included in their calculation of expenses.[8] Then, too, there is the tax burden of all that buying and selling, which is passed through to investors. For the five years ended August 2005, average annual returns were a *negative* 9.5 percent. Over the 10 years then ended, which included the glory days of the new economy, the fund did better, almost matching the index, though still trailing our value funds by 4 percent a year. Net assets, which had been a modest $1.9 billion at the kickoff date in 1997 and had risen to $17 billion in 2000, fell to about $8 billion in the fall of 2005. The management company,

Massachusetts Financial Services (MFS), thus enjoyed a fourfold increase in assets under management, with commensurate increases in fees, despite the roller-coaster performance of the fund. (In 2006, when the fund would show a 7.5 percent total return while the market index was earning 15 percent, the expense ratio was increased yet again.[9])

If the reader is feeling some sympathy for the passengers in this financial vehicle, hold on. Investors, and I'm using the term loosely, in the Massachusetts Investors Growth Stock Fund had for several years running been spinning their holdings in and out of the fund at rates approximating the total assets of the fund. In 2001, for example, investors cashed out of $17.5 billion in Class A shares and bought $16 billion in new shares, leaving the fund at year-end with net assets of about $14 billion. Having attracted, not investors, but speculators trying to catch the next new thing, management got the shareholders they deserved.

In fact, there's a story beneath all that churning by shareholders. In 2004, MFS settled charges brought in 2003 by the SEC and state authorities charging that 11 of its funds had engaged in either (1) so-called directed brokerage, meaning that instead of obtaining the best executions for their portfolio transactions, the funds had paid inflated trading commissions to brokers who helped market the fund, and/or (2) market-timing abuses, which the funds had assured investors they would not allow. In both respects, of course, the managers were enriching themselves at shareholder expense. A fund management company could itself pay a broker a fee for helping to sell its funds, but MFS and other fund complexes chose instead to pay the brokers extra dollars on purchases or sales of stocks in their funds, thus transferring these marketing costs to investors. MFS was also one of some two dozen fund families that engaged in market timing, a practice whereby a fund manager would allow favored clients to buy or sell fund shares at closing prices based on events that took place well after the market had closed. The fund sponsor received in return a payoff in some form of side deal or another.[10] The settlements included a $225 million pool to compensate the affected MFS funds; in addition, the president and chief executive officer of MFS resigned. MFS thus became one of the 23 fund managers that within a short period were implicated in the market-timing scandals.

With new management in 2004, one might have expected more candor. In fact, investors in the Massachusetts Investors Growth Stock

Fund would have had to be, well, research analysts to unearth from that year's annual report what had transpired. The only useful disclosure of the charges and penalties was on page 54, buried in the footnotes to the financials.[11]

To get some historical perspective, I read a speech given in 1954 by the then chairman of the Massachusetts Investors Trust, Dwight Robinson, reflecting on the role of its management. Dwelling on the Prudent Man Rule, he stressed the importance of investing clients' funds as men—they were of course all men—would their own funds. There should be full-time management, "at very low cost," "invest[ing] for the long haul without consideration of . . . fluctuations of the market." Reflecting that same long-term perspective, turnover rates for open-end funds in the mid-1950s were generally about 5 percent, meaning that they held stocks on average for 20 years.[12]

Full-time management, Robinson said. The most senior portfolio manager of the Growth Stock Fund had day-to-day management responsibilities not just for that fund but for eight other investment funds,[13] and the 11 trustees of MFS were overseeing more than 65 funds.[14] But then, it would be asking too much of Sun Life Financial, the Canadian financial conglomerate that purchased MFS in 1981, to be thinking of trusteeship in the sense used by Robinson. Jack Bogle, in *The Battle for the Soul of Capitalism,* stresses that of the 50 largest fund groups, over 40 either are themselves publicly owned or are part of large financial conglomerates. At best, their loyalties are torn between those who invest in the management company and those who invest in the funds. Managers, he said, have gone from stewardship to salesmanship.[15]

Some recent shareholder reports of Sun Life send a perverse message to the MFS management and, indeed, to the rare Growth Stock Fund investor who searched the corporate hierarchy to see where the money went. Assets under management (AUM) are what seem to matter. Yes, for the third quarter of 2005, the AUM of MFS increased by $7 billion. As of year-end 2004, with $75 billion under management, Sun Life noted proudly that MFS was the 11th largest retail mutual fund company. As for those highly publicized regulatory investigations, Sun Life acknowledged that they had "hampered . . . [r]etail sales of many large fund groups, including MFS." Not a word to suggest that sales might have been hampered because investors realized they had been cheated.

Intending to do a hands-on look at two other funds, I selected, first, Fidelity Growth Company Fund, because it was then the largest among the Group of 15, with $25 billion in assets, and second, the American Funds group's Amcap Fund. The Amcap Fund was intriguing because it was the one fund in the group with even modestly positive returns during the five-year period ended in 2005, but also because both its low portfolio turnover and its substantial cash holdings gave it a quite decent resemblance to our Goldfarb 10 value funds. In both cases, I stopped, however, as it became apparent that their respective managements are excessively focused on growing assets, whatever the ultimate effect on performance.★ Each of these families manages $1 trillion or so in its funds or other accounts.

The American Funds group includes three large-cap growth funds; one of them, the Growth Fund of America, has now grown to $190 billion in assets, and still has not closed. It is said to be a composite of 11 separately managed accounts, which arguably should be, but are not, broken out for the public to see how each of the "funds" is doing. (The 11 managers obviously are not equally talented.) One is left to speculate as to how such an enterprise is managed. What happens, for example, if several of the 11 hit on the same idea? Clearly they cannot all buy the stock without impacting the price substantially. As for Fidelity, it manages over 20 large-cap growth funds.† What's the point of it, except to accumulate assets rather than focus one's best skills in a single, more modest enterprise? Stewardship versus salesmanship: The tension between the two is palpable.

A proper sense of stewardship entails thorough research, careful selection, and patient investing. And it requires that the managers show their commitment by investing side by side in the funds they control, not just in the management company, whereby they profit from quantity, not quality. Those three large growth funds, among the largest of the

---

★The American Funds group made aggressive use of pay-to-play (i.e., paying brokers to market their funds to investors who would assume that the "advice" they received was unbiased). David F. Swensen, *Unconventional Success: A Fundamental Approach to Personal Investment* (New York: Free Press, 2005), 275–279; see also Chapter 8, infra.

†Morningstar described Fidelity as a "marketing construct," noting that its board of trustees oversees 300 funds (FDGRX stewardship report, August 10, 2004).

Group of 15, owned as of August 2005 an average of over 180 stocks. Longleaf Partners, First Eagle Global, Oakmark Select, and others of the Goldfarb 10, discussed in Chapter 2, talk up front and candidly about their personal stakes in the funds they manage. Not so these large-cap funds. The contrast is all too clear.

Investing Blind

One cure for investing at warp speed would be the index funds, which account for one-seventh of the assets of all equity funds, including the increasingly popular exchange-traded funds (ETFs). One would think index funds would all be the same and fairly plain-vanilla, but they, too, now come in a range of different flavors. There is an emerging markets index fund and a health care index fund and many others; the choices look like the ice cream counter at Ben & Jerry's. Broad market index funds, like the Vanguard 500 Index Fund, account for about three-quarters of all indexed mutual funds, or about $400 billion in all out of the $6 trillion in the universe of stock funds.

The rational investor, the hypothetical sort who inhabits those academic journals, might buy the Vanguard 500 Index Fund and stay put, year after year. In fact, the number of investors doing just that has been growing. Over long periods, the S&P 500 gains on average about 10 percent a year, and for a patient investor those long-term results are what matter. Add to that the huge savings on management fees, expenses, and taxes, and simply capturing the market return becomes quite attractive. As we will see in Chapter 6, investors typically don't do nearly so well. The passions of the crowd are so contagious that investors wander from this sector to that, hoping to catch the latest wave. It's difficult to resist the impulses and market chatter of the day. Or as Graham and Dodd said some 70-odd years ago, the market is not a weighing machine but rather a voting machine, "the product partly of reason and partly of emotion."[16]

Unfortunately, however, a buy-and-hold index strategy has several shortcomings:

First, timing still matters, because price and value matter. In real dollars, stocks did not return to their 1966 level until 1992. And as we know, the S&P 500 fell by almost half when the 1990s bubble burst, and did not recoup the lost ground until 2007. An index fund investor would have needed patience, and rather a lot of it. Much of the shortfall in the index stemmed from the fact that the S&P 500 is weighted by market capitalization, so that in the late 1990s index investors were buying more of the sky-high new economy stocks and conversely proportionately less of the good value stocks of the old economy—whether they knew it or not. That weakness inevitably encouraged promoters to create, and brokers to sell, a large variety of new index funds based on a range of factors other than those market caps.[17] Having been told that plain vanilla was no longer the right way to go, investors were back where they started—forced to pick and choose, guessing which way the wind would blow next. The reality is that there are no shortcuts. And why should there be? For Joe Sixpack, indeed for Millionaire Murph, we're talking about a handful of decisions that over a lifetime can make or break his retirement, and his family's security.

Second, we're emotionally not capable of walking past a financial Ben & Jerry's. Buy the market index? Which market, which index? With the dollar said to be at risk, investors are currently buying global funds, or single country funds, or perhaps...Truly passive investing is, well, just too passive. "Hi honey, what did you do at the office today?" "Well dear, actually nothing." "But honey, weren't you looking for some alpha?" ("Alpha" is Wall Street and B-school jargon for beating the market as a whole, even by a few basis points. Okay, a basis point is 1/100th of a percentage point.)

In a word, while our large-cap growth funds demonstrate that an investor can do worse than indexing, it remains true that an intelligent investor can do better. Invest in 500 stocks, chosen without so much as a glance at their business or managements? Keynes, as so often happens, said it best: "[T]o suppose that safety-first consists in having a small gamble in a large number of different directions . . . as compared with a substantial stake in a company where one['s] information is adequate, strikes me as a travesty of investment policy."[18]

We will take another look at index funds in Chapter 9 while discussing how reasonably thoughtful investors, not just the experts, can make sensible decisions about their personal investments, in light of the issues raised here and throughout this book. For now, it's time to do a close-up analysis of one of the major management companies, to see what's in it for the managers as they accumulate their AUM—to see, in short, how they deal with the inherent conflict between the interests of the investors in their funds and the investors in the management companies. Where, for example, do the managers keep their personal dollars? What's the impact of taking a management company public? It's curious, but no one has bothered to look. So, let's have a look.

Chapter 5

Greed Is Good

*The Appeal of a Publicly Owned Fund
Management Company*

I t's not new, but Paul Samuelson, the first American to win the Nobel Prize in economics, may have had it just right when he explained in 1967 why he invested not in a mutual fund, but in a fund management company:

> I decided there was only one place to make money in the mutual fund business as there is only one place for a temperate man to be in a saloon, behind the bar and not in front of it . . . so I invested in a management company.[1]

The vast majority of fund management companies are either privately owned, Fidelity being the most prominent, or owned by financial conglomerates, such as insurance companies or commercial or investment banks. But there are a handful that trade publicly, thus allowing us to see how well the barkeep is doing. Remember, the saloon gets paid whether the customers enjoy themselves or not. The following list highlights the 10 major ones, with their market symbols and market capitalizations (market price times the number of outstanding shares):

Top Publicly Traded Fund Companies, Market Capitalization as of February 2006 (in Billions of Dollars)

Alliance Capital	AC	$ 5.1
Ameriprise Financial	AMP	10.7
Eaton Vance	EV	3.7
Federated	FII	4.2
Franklin Resources	BEN	24.2
Janus	JNS	4.7
Legg Mason	LM	14.8
Nuveen	JNC	3.4
T. Rowe Price	TROW	9.7
Waddell & Reed	WDR	1.8

T. Rowe Price

Would Samuelson still be right to pour the drinks, rather than drink up? I decided to look at T. Rowe Price Group (TROW), which has essentially confined its business to money management, making it a good case study. TROW has also escaped the recent mutual fund market-timing scandals, so when we examine TROW's business we should be looking at the fruits of managing money, not of *mis*managing it.

TROW has maintained high standards in other respects as well. The Price funds are all no-load funds, meaning that an investor can buy into one without paying the typical 5 percent sales charge that funds use to induce brokers to recommend their offerings rather than someone else's. Also, TROW levies so-called 12b-1, or marketing, fees only on limited (designated as Advisor or R) classes of shares. Many of the Price funds deserve good marks for not churning their portfolios, as happens all too often in the industry. Some of the mid-cap and small-cap Price funds also get credit for having closed to new investors once they grew to a size such that further growth would impair performance. Best of all, perhaps, among

the large-cap growth funds I examined most closely, the management fees
and expenses have been kept well below those of their peer group. At the
Growth Stock Fund, founded in 1950 and the oldest of the Price group, the
management fee is 0.56 percent and the total expense ratio 0.74 percent of
the assets. Except for the Vanguard funds, which enjoy an at-cost organiza-
tional structure, that's about as good as it gets.

About as good as it gets . . . so how good is that? If the reader suspects that Price is also operating on anything like an at-cost basis, well,
not quite. While TROW, the management company, may have relatively
clean hands, it is still wildly profitable. This is what we call a scalable
business, meaning that as the assets under management (AUM) and
therefore the fees grow, the profit *margin,* meaning the profit per dollar
of revenues, increases because costs do not increase commensurately. The
following list sets forth the growth in assets under management, net revenues, net operating income, operating profit margin, net income, and
stockholders' equity from 2001 to 2005.[2] Over the four-year period, the
operating profit margin, already a very healthy 31 percent in 2001, soared
to 43 percent in 2005; costs increased, too, but obviously they did not
keep pace with revenues.

TROW Financials (Dollar Amounts in Millions)

	2001	2005
a. Assets under management	$156,000	$270,000
b. Net revenues	$995	$1,512
c. Net operating income	$311	$655
d. Operating profit margin (c÷b)	31 percent	43 percent
e. Net income	$196	$431
f. Stockholders' equity	$1,078	$2,036

Profitability

For the year 2005, TROW enjoyed a net profit margin on revenues
(e ÷ b) of 28 percent *net of taxes.*[3] It's difficult to think of many legal
businesses with comparable returns. But good as that profit margin may
be—and it is better than Google's!—it understates the company's true
profitability. To get a better grasp, we should subtract from net equity

(item f) two significant items: (1) the intangible assets (the $665 million of so-called goodwill of businesses TROW had acquired), which, while they may have to be charged against future earnings, will not require a cash outlay; and (2) the $1 billion of excess cash equivalents and invest-ments (what the company calls available liquid assets[4]), meaning cash and investments not integral to, or needed in, the operations of the busi-ness. At year-end 2005, the company had shareholders' equity of $2,036 million, but when we deduct the bulk of those two items, we see that the company had net tangible *operating* assets—assets needed and used to run the business—of less than $500 million. TROW's net income in 2005 of $400 million (net of the interest on the excess cash) thus rep-resented a return on those operating assets of 80 percent. And remem-ber, that's *per annum*. Here is a company, with net operating assets of less than $500 million, that was valued in the stock market at almost $10 billion.

For the reader unaccustomed to financial analysis, let's suppose you found a bank that paid out year after year 80 cents for every dollar you depo-sited, and that the 80 cents was after all taxes had been paid. Would that strike you as a Ponzi scheme, the sort your dad warned against? But in this case it's a quite reputable business.

How to Make 80 Percent a Year without Breaking the Law

There are several factors contributing to the success of this legit scheme, no, not separate, distinct causes but factors that, taken together, produce an institution—and a culture—that is prepared to extract an unseemly profit from its customers. First, as noted, managing money is a scalable business, meaning that as assets under management (AUM) grow, costs increase less rapidly than fees, so that profits increase at a disproportion-ately rapid rate. Second, TROW's customers, like those of other financial institutions, typically have neither the expertise nor the time to work their way through the barrage of marketing pressures and Wall Street bab-ble to make skillful, carefully considered investment choices. The Securi-ties and Exchange Commission (SEC) has failed to overcome a state of ignorance by failing to require adequate disclosure and regulation—early on and in plain English.*

Investors hurt themselves by bringing to their portfolio decisions an attitude of childlike trust, even of naïveté. Indeed, when one considers the fierce attention that consumers devote to the cost, and to the quality, of their weekly groceries or, say, to the purchase of a new washer and dryer, their nonchalance when it comes to mutual fund cost and quality is remarkable. Perhaps, and this might be a third factor, the investors assume that TROW, being a financial intermediary, will rise above the minimal standards of honesty that one expects from ordinary commercial enterprises. But even if they get beyond blind trust and begin to research their fund choices as they do their car purchases, they may still find themselves unaware of the conflict of interest that may doom their investment—even if everything looks good. No matter how low the turnover or how clean the fund managers, at the end of the day TROW, a publicly owned company, owes a competing loyalty to its own shareholders. This creates a profound, abiding conflict of interest, for TROW and almost the entire fund industry. And, finally, though mutual fund boards are supposed to ensure that the fund investors (the customers) are not the losers in this conflict, those boards are weak and disinclined to confront their managements. Besides, for the board of directors of the management company, its first duty is to the TROW shareholders. The prince may wish to take care of the people, but as long as his father is king, he will always be in a position of subservience to the king.

Running a mutual fund is, as we said, a scalable business, in the sense that the cost to manage $10 billion is not proportionately more than to manage $5 billion. TROW is one of the 10 largest fund management groups.[5] At year-end 2005, it was managing $270 billion in assets, of which $170 billion was in the 80 Price mutual funds, and the balance in other portfolios. The in-house mutual funds are the most profitable part of the business; while they constituted 63 percent of the total assets, they

---

*In November 2007, the SEC proposed a new short-form mandatory prospectus as a supplement to the statutory version. Under the prospectus, however, delivery of this more concise version could still be witheld until after investors have bought and paid for their shares. *BNA Sec. Reg. & Law Report*, 11-19-07, @ 1773.

produced in 2005 approximately 75 percent of the total advisory fees.* A key factor in this profitability is that the business is not capital intensive; the company needs some computers, furniture, and fixtures, but its largest expenditures are for people, including the well-paid suits who manage TROW, and for advertising. Its capital expenditures in 2005, net of depreciation, were about $10 million, or about one-eighth of what it spent on advertising. The rest of the cash flow comes right down to the bottom line, meaning it is available for dividends, to buy back stock, or to buy other fund management companies, as it has done in the past.[6] In 2004 and 2005, TROW did not choose to do much of anything with its cash flow, and as a result its bank account grew by $500+ million. Incidentally, this Midas-like accumulation has been achieved without leverage; the company is debt-free. Yes, Samuelson was right, more so than he then knew! Over the four years from 2003 to 2006, TROW stock rose 240 percent.

Size matters. TROW has grown fast. In 1995, when TROW managed just $75 billion in assets, its net after-tax profit margin was only 17 percent.[7] Ten years later, in 2005, when it was managing three and a half times as much, its net profit margin had surged to 28 percent. The reports to shareholders routinely mention that the industry is competitive, and so it is, but in marked contrast to the usual workings of the marketplace, the competition never induces management companies to seriously shave their fees. The huge economies of scale are simply not being passed on to the public[†]—not at TROW, not elsewhere. In recent books, David Swensen and Jack Bogle have thoroughly described the failure of stewardship; according to Bogle, the total costs to equity fund investors have actually risen more rapidly, one and a half times as rapidly,

---

*The advisory fees for fund shareholders typically exceed those for institutional investors, such as public pension funds, often by a wide margin. See generally, Freeman and Brown, infra n. 40, 627–637. See also SEC, *Public Policy Implications of Investment Company Growth,* H.R. Rep. 89-2337 (1966), 126.

†A General Accounting Office study, looking at the fund industry as a whole, noted an inability to measure economies of scale; and while the researchers had access to some data for 18 publicly traded advisers, the report basically ducked behind bland generalizations ("generally profitable and . . . profitability . . . increasing"). *GAO, Mutual Fund Fees: Additional Disclosure Could Encourage Price Competition* (Washington, DC: GAO, 2000), 10–11, 33, 44. Examining a single, representative publicly owned adviser, TROW, overcomes that hurdle.

as the industry's AUM.[8] Morningstar, the Chicago-based fund rating firm, was so right when it described the TROW business as a castle surrounded by a very "wide moat."[9]

Thus a 1961 report commissioned by the SEC commented even then that the fees "simply do not reflect the economies of scale":

> The fees paid to investment advisers have no substantial relation to the cost of performance of the service or its results, they do not reflect the economies of scale, and are obviously not the product of arm's-length bargaining. They sometimes resemble a toll levied on the investment company as a result of the strategic position occupied by the investment adviser.[10]

Conflicts of Interest

When Willie Sutton, the bank robber who achieved a degree of celebrity in my youth, was asked why he chose banks to rob, he replied, "That's where the money is." Remember, it's the management company that typically sponsors and creates a fund, but the corporate structure is unique. The fund has shareholders—you and I—and a board of directors. But the adviser that manages the fund is almost invariably a business entity independent of the fund, with its own separate board of directors and shareholders.[11] Where do the insiders at TROW keep their money? To paraphrase Sutton, where the profits are, in the management company, with only token investments in the funds they direct. A fund's management fee is based on the AUM, not fund performance. It's obvious, therefore, that the corporate officers and managers will be mostly, and even obsessively, consumed with attracting more assets. The picture would be different, of course, if they invested some real money alongside the public—that is, in the funds that TROW sponsors. Then they would be worrying night and day about performance—just as the investors do. A few fund managers do stand alongside their investors. The officers and trustees of the several Oakmark funds have collectively invested over $240 million in their funds, but such examples are rare.[12]

And it surely didn't happen at TROW. Brian Rogers, for example, is the chief investment officer of TROW, age 50, an officer of eight different funds, and in 2006 was to be elected to the board of some 25 funds in all. Yet, according to a proxy statement for the funds filed in April 2006, at year-end 2005 his holdings in those funds were modest, and his aggregate holdings for all Price funds appear to have been roughly $1 million. (It's possible that the holdings are larger, but the disclosures, while legally sufficient, are inadequate. TROW refused a request from Morningstar for better information.[13]) By contrast, Rogers, who is an officer and director of TROW, owned beneficially at year-end 2005 over 900,000 shares of the management company's stock, worth more than $65 million at the then market price of $75 a share. In addition, he held a further stake in the management company, thanks to options to acquire an additional 790,000 shares. The stock and options were in addition to his cash compensation, which in 2004 was over $4 million.

Edward Bernard, also an officer of TROW and also 50 years old, who was in 2006 to be elected to the board of all 80 Price funds, presented a similarly disconcerting picture.[14] TROW disclosed only that Bernard owns over $100,000 in each of nine funds and lesser amounts in others, and that the total of his investments in all funds overseen or to be overseen was over $100,000. This iota of information is hardly sufficient; while we don't know the total, we have no reason to believe that Bernard has enough money in the funds to constitute a serious vote of confidence in any of the funds' strategies and to make him more mindful of trading costs and taxes. However, in TROW, the management company, where the SEC does require better disclosure, we know that Bernard owned at year-end 2005 over 290,000 shares of TROW stock, worth some $20 million, plus options for 560,000 additional shares.

The importance of the options cannot be overstated, for they greatly tilt the interests of the executives further in the direction of the management company. At the year-end stock price, Rogers' options were already in the money, as they say, for $25 million, and Bernard's for $15 million, and these totals will escalate with every dollar that the stock rises. These grossly disproportionate stakes—nominal holdings in the funds managed, which they seem shy about disclosing, and outsized stakes in the stock whose performance will track the flow of fees to TROW—are typical of the other senior managers as well. At year-end 2005, TROW had options outstanding, some then exercisable and some not, for almost 23 million shares, with an in-the-money value of over $700 million.[15] Wow, a $700 million gain for the executives with no cash investment. I guess Willie Sutton was looking in the wrong place.

The aggressive use of options, representing 17 percent of the 132 million shares outstanding, caused a generally laudatory Morningstar analyst to downgrade his appraisal of the fair value of TROW stock by $6, to $61 per share in 2006.[16] The executives are so greedy they are even taking advantage of their TROW stockholders by taking a level of options that is truly indecent. This is a well-established business, not a high-tech start-up with a genuine chance of failure and in which the executives are running a personal risk. But even if investors in TROW stock have reason to feel slightly chiseled, they are in a much better place than investors in TROW-sponsored funds, because management's interests are so clearly aligned with the former. They have hardwired their incentives so that, as the assets grow, so do their personal piggy banks.

Have the insiders been reading Samuelson? Probably not. TROW stock more than doubled in the three years from 2003 to 2005, and that may be as much economics as they need to know.[17] How have investors in the funds fared? Is it possible for the managers to accumulate such wealth without delivering stellar, or at least superior, returns to investors in their funds? Table 5.1 reports on five Price large-cap growth funds, chosen as representative because their aggregate assets are among the largest of any category in the Price family, and because one of them, the Growth Stock Fund, created in 1950, was the original Price fund. This table sets forth the asset size and the average annual performance, plus the performance of the S&P 500, as of and for the five and 10 years ended December 31, 2005, all on a total return basis.

Table 5.1   T. Rowe Price Large-Cap Growth Funds

	Assets under Management ($Millions)	Average Annual Performance	
		5 Years	10 Years
Blue Chip Growth	$ 9,100	−0.53%	+9.11%
Capital Opportunity Fund	88	+1.26	+5.61
Growth Stock Fund	14,500	+1.38	+9.92
New America Growth Fund	877	−0.26	+5.49
Tax Efficient Growth Fund	67	−2.06	+0.14*
S&P 500 Index		+0.54	+9.07

*Since inception date, July 30, 1999, compared to +0.59 percent for the S&P 500 for that period.

Grow the Assets

The performance figures are plainly mediocre—for the 10 years, two of the funds did slightly better than the market index, with three falling short by a significantly wider margin. One can make sense of such unimpressive statistics only by recalling that TROW's stated goal is to deliver not so much superior performance as "consistent style discipline"— meaning its funds will attempt not to exploit the occasional mispricing of stocks that market trends produce, which is the real challenge in managing money, but to mimic those very trends.[18] As the table shows, that is precisely what they have done. There is nothing to warrant outsized option grants; remember, it's not a star system. But then, as we saw, the executives aren't being paid for their funds' performance. As their reports bring out, the performance that matters to TROW is the performance relative to an index, be it the Lipper Large Cap Growth index or whichever one is deemed relevant.[19] (In 2007, the American Funds Group, a major fund complex, saw its institutional business "showing signs of unraveling," the *Financial Times* deduced, because its returns in international markets for the prior three years "fell" [sic] to 23.2 percent against the relevant Morgan Stanley index return of 24 percent.[20])

Pension consultants and financial advisers, themselves concerned about the potential for criticism, insist on this style consistency and thus the ability to stay close to the benchmarks by which the brokers and 401(k) plans will in turn be measured.[21] Are real estate or tech stocks, for example, priced too high? It doesn't matter—just track the benchmark, up or down—for that sector. TROW focuses, therefore, on assuring those financial intermediaries of the growing availability of a menu of mid-cap value, large-cap growth, and other carefully compartmentalized offerings coupled with Advisor Class and R[etirement] Class shares offering 12b-1 fees for the brokers and others who market the Price funds.★[22] For the fund sponsor the presence of these numerous, clearly delineated fund

---

★The additional expense burden for those Advisor and R Class investors is considerable. In the Price Growth Stock Fund, for example, while the total expense ratio for the basic Investor Class is a commendable 0.73 percent, for the Advisor and R classes it is 0.94 percent and 1.18 percent, respectively. See Growth Stock Fund, Semiannual Report, June 30, 2005, 14.

styles offers the same marketing advantages that General Motors used to reap by segmenting its brands—at the cost of ensuring mediocre returns to the fund investor.

Underlying the effort to grow the assets is the structural conflict between the publicly owned management company and the funds it manages. Thus, TROW focuses on gathering assets, extensively advertising and marketing to enlarge the funds it controls, as distinct from managing smaller sums well. Advertising expenses in 2005 were $86 million, up 45 percent over 2003. The management company presses to put the best face on its funds, so as to continue accumulating assets and just as quickly to redeploy them in the market, even when, as in the late 1990s, stocks in the tech-media-telecom industries had reached irrational levels. For existing investors, however, adding new investors not only doesn't help, it has serious adverse effects. As a portfolio grows in size, the universe of potential investment choices rapidly shrinks. According to Jack Bogle, a $1 billion fund could expect to find as many as 2,500 stocks of sufficient size to accommodate a meaningful investment. However, for a $10 billion fund, the universe would shrink to as few as 250 stocks.[23] Fund size works against investors in still another way. As a fund grows and it begins to buy larger positions, it will have a greater impact on prices—pushing them higher even while accumulating a position.

Bob Rodriguez, the very successful manager of the FPA Capital Fund, which he has closed to new investors twice, once in 1995 and again in 2004, explained that researching and choosing a quality portfolio requires that one be selective; a portfolio of 30 or 40 individual stocks is roughly the upper limit. This, in turn, puts an effective limit on the amount of assets that a value investor can hope to deploy— otherwise the average invested position would reach an unworkable level of 10 percent of a company's outstanding shares.[24]

How much does the manager care about the welfare and the success of his investors? Section 36(b) of the Investment Company Act explicitly affirms the fiduciary duty owed by the management of a fund to the investors. Commendably enough, TROW has closed some of its small- and mid-cap funds, though like other fund groups it may have then opened similar, look–alike funds to meet the demand. At the large-cap growth funds, however, the size and therefore the fees have been allowed to run. The largest of these funds are really closet indexed, quite unlike funds that are built selectively from the bottom up with the patient addition of stocks one by one, wherever they may be. These unwieldy pools of assets are essentially designed to mirror the Standard & Poor's 500 stock index, not so much to perform well, but rather to stay close to the market trends and more critically not to *under*perform. The Price Growth Stock Fund, to use the clunky jargon of academics, now has an R-square rating of 95, meaning that 95 percent of its movements will track those of the market as a whole. It's as if on 19 days out of 20 all you're getting is the index, which an investor could get at far lower expenses and lower taxes in an index fund. In other words, TROW isn't contributing anything of value.*

Who's Watching the Store?

Who is the watchdog who will arbitrate these conflicts? In theory, the independent directors of the funds are supposed to exercise energetic, unbiased oversight, but that seems unlikely here, or elsewhere in the industry. First off, typically each of them sat on the board of all 80 Price funds that existed in 2005—plus 30-odd others also managed by TROW.[25] Their compensation for serving on a given board averages roughly $1,500 a year. Here an insidious economy of scale works against the investors. Though each director's financial stake in any one fund (again, less than $1,500) is trivial, his or her compensation from sitting on *every* board, over $100,000, is substantial indeed. Thus, each director has a far greater interest in remaining in TROW's good graces, thereby assuring the continuance of his or her six-figure sinecure, than in the fate of any particular fund or of the investors.

Are the board meetings serious, or do the boards rubber-stamp the dictates of the insiders? One can't be sure, of course, but various of the funds' boards meet all on the same day, which by sundown must leave their eyes glazed and fingers reaching for a single malt. The

---

*One incidental benefit from this closet indexing is that the managers become more passive, so that turnover declines, as it did in 2005 for the Growth Stock Fund, to 36 percent.

independent directors' holdings in the various Price funds at year-end 2005 were trivial and scattered. In most funds, their holdings were zero. Instead of investing side by side, they were bringing up the rear. The boards do review, we are told, the management contracts of each of the 80 Price funds, but as a former head of the SEC's Division of Investment Management recently said, "We delude ourselves if we think true negotiation [of the advisory fee] is going on."[26] Given the sheer number of funds, with highly diverse portfolios, one would hope at least that these nominally independent directors are closely questioned at the annual shareholders meetings of the funds. Oops, sorry, the Price funds have generally dispensed with shareholder meetings.

These economies of scale, working for TROW's benefit, not the investors', crop up in surprising places. Much as the independent directors sit on an absurdly large number of boards, the portfolio managers play on more than one team. It has become commonplace. The chief economist of the Investment Company Institute, the industry's trade association, recently explained that team management is popular because fund complexes have been creating marketing and brand identification more around the fund and the fund complex than around the manager.[27] Star managers are out; obviously there would not be enough stars to man a diverse $270 billion portfolio; but beyond that, stars might one day quit, forming funds of their own, taking clients and assets with them. The team concept is safer . . . and much less costly. TROW seems to have pushed the limits, however, in the case of the two major growth stock funds, the Blue Chip Growth Fund with $9 billion in assets and the Growth Stock Fund with $14 billion. While each fund had a team of 12 managers, eight of them *worked for both funds.*[28] And of the 10 largest holdings in each fund, accounting for 24 percent of the total assets in each, eight appeared in both.[29] The managers sometimes wear two hats at other mutual fund families. However, at a firm like Oakmark, the critical difference is that there is full, up-front disclosure. Not so with these TROW funds. Other business corporations are required to disclose their managers' divided loyalties. That is particularly important here. To the extent these two already large funds are, in effect, being managed as one $23 billion fund, the cost of buying and selling very large blocks of stock will be higher if they are to acquire meaningful positions in a stock. There will be, therefore, a growing pressure to trade less often, and simply to track the market index, a pressure that will be more burden-some than investors could possibly have suspected.*

T. Rowe Price is considered an honorable family of funds. As Morn-ingstar's analyst put it, "you would feel good about your granny invest-ing in the Price funds."[30] Maybe his grandma, but not mine.

The Greed Factor

Going public enabled the Price fund portfolio managers to be com-pensated, in effect, two different ways. First, they are paid for managing a fund, as such, and it is commendable that at the Price funds, com-pensation is in part based on the performance of the funds over an extended period relative to a peer group. (By contrast, until recently, Janus group managers were rewarded for the fees generated—that is, the assets gathered.[31]) Second, Price managers get the rewards, largely tax-deferred, from owning shares in TROW and from receiving, year by year, big stock option grants. The compensation in shares exceeds the performance pay by orders of magnitude. As Morningstar noted, the paychecks are moderate, while the option grants have been "particularly lavish."[32]

Once the management company has gone public, the ability to rake in unseemly amounts of stock and options becomes more than human flesh can resist. As a fund grows, the *percentage fee* charged by the manage-ment should decline, given, as we said, that costs do not rise commensu-rately. In a fully competitive industry, the savings that accrue to size would be passed on to the customers in the form of lower prices. (Think Wal-Mart.) Once, that was also true in mutual funds. Go back 50 years, to the early days of TROW's first and still most visible fund, the Growth Stock Fund, and the management fee was typical of many funds, large or small, namely 0.50 percent a year. The Fidelity Fund charged the same, as did the American Mutual Fund,[33] both being the original venture of what today are two of the largest families of funds, the Fidelity and

---

*For the statisticians out there, according to Morningstar the two funds had identical market-risk factor (R-squared) measures, and almost identical turnover ratios.

Table 5.2   T. Rowe Price Growth Stock Fund Fee Schedule

Year	Assets under Management	Annualized Fee Formula
1955	$4 million	0.50%
1965	$129 million	0.50%, dropping to 0.40% on amounts over $50 million
1975	$797 million	0.50% up to $50 million, 0.40% next $100 million, 0.35% next $850 million, 0.30% excess over $1 billion
1985	$965 million	0.50% on first $50 million, then scaled down to 0.30% over $1 billion
1995	$2,067 million	0.59% on all assets
As of February 2006	$14 billion	0.56%

American groups. Table 5.2 sets forth at 10-year intervals the fee structure, as gleaned from the annual Wiesenberger reports and Morningstar, for the Price Growth Stock Fund from shortly after its modest beginnings.

In the early years, as the fund grew, the fee rate fell dramatically, as one would hope to see from managers with a sense of fiduciary duty. They added breakpoints at various net asset levels, thus allowing the investors to share in the reduced expenses resulting from the economies of scale. But, whoa, then in April 1986 the management company went public, the game changed, and they got greedy. In May 1985, anticipating the public offering, the managers added an upside performance fee that kicked in if the fund outperformed the market index.[34] In 1987, however, even those helpful breakpoints were eliminated, and the entire fee structure increased. Perhaps because the management still felt a twinge of fiduciary responsibility, there was added a downward adjustment if the fund *under*performed the index. All in all, however, the result was clear; indeed, the CEO boasted on page 1 of the 1987 annual report to the TROW shareholders of the now "higher fees earned on [the Price fund] assets."[35]

Where were the independent directors of the Growth Stock Fund, while the management was shamelessly feathering its own nest at the expense of investors in the fund? Under the Investment Company Act, they have an obligation to bring independent judgment to bear on the conflicts of interest inherent in the role of the fund adviser. The SEC has been quite clear on this:

> The failure of a board to play its proper role can result . . . in excessive fees and brokerage commissions, less than forthright disclosure . . . and inferior investment performance.[36]
>
> [There is a] crucial challenge [to] establishing an appropriate balance between cooperation *with* the management and oversight *of* the management company. . . . [T]oo often the proper balance has not been achieved.[37] (Italics in the original)

Once TROW went public, it was predictable that the management fee would go up. If TROW was to produce a decent return on capital, say 12 to 15 percent, for its new, public shareholders, the managers would either have to cut their personal take-home pay—heaven forbid—or take back from investors in the Price funds the economies of scale that had previously been shared with them. The choice was easy. The percentage fee went up, even beyond what it had been when the Growth Stock Fund was in its infancy and struggling with a mere $4 million in assets.

The total, all-in expense ratio at the Growth Stock Fund, consisting of the management fee and various administrative costs charged by TROW (but not the trading expenses), jumped from 0.52 percent in 1985, the year before TROW went public, to 0.57 percent in 1986, then to 0.67 percent in 1987 and 0.77 percent in 1988, an increase of almost 50 percent in just three years' time.[38] TROW prospers while fund investors pay more. As a consultant commented to the *Financial Times*, "It's a luxury of the investment management industry that once you're a larger firm with a cachet brand, you don't have to cut prices."[39] Yes, the Price funds do have a cachet brand. Incidentally, the current management fee of 0.56 percent of assets may seem small, but it adds up to over $70 million, roughly $30 million more than if the 1985 fee scale were still in effect. And that $70 million is without regard to the dollars earned on the almost look-alike Blue Chip Growth Fund. All these fee increases were approved by the so-called independent directors, and under the prevailing law, that approval is essentially binding.[40]

Candor Becomes a Casualty

I can almost hear someone saying at this point that it's a free market, investors have lots of choices among the 4,000-odd equity funds, and if they don't like what they see at T. Rowe Price, they should take their marbles and go elsewhere.[41] Sunlight is the best disinfectant, and the burden is on the investor to read the disclosures carefully. That would be all well and good, perhaps, if the disclosures were clear, but in fact they are poor in several important respects.

Neither the prospectus nor the periodic reports to fund shareholders reveal precisely how much—perhaps one should say how little—the managers have invested in the funds they control. Minimal disclosures (such as TROW's revelation that a manager owned "more than $100,000" in a fund), as well as the extent to which managers work at competing funds, do appear in the blandly titled Statement of Additional Information (SAI), filed with the SEC. The funds' reports to investors don't give a clue as to what interesting stuff one would find there. And if you were to download from the SEC's EDGAR online service a copy of the 2006 SAI you would be confronted with a 230-page document, with tightly meshed data for all 80 funds. Is it even a little bit realistic to think that anyone—whether a college physics professor or a nurse or a carpenter or even an attorney—has the time to sort through all this for *any* fund in which they might invest? Is it realistic to think that anyone—whether they are an attorney or a car mechanic—will understand most of the language and, more important, what it means to their investments? If the disclosures necessary to understand an investment demand this kind of time on the part of the buyer, and if the background information is so convoluted that even highly educated people would have a tough time following it, can we say we have truly free market conditions? It seems more like a rigged system, countenanced by government regulators, that gives the fund companies a distinct advantage over their existing and prospective clients.

Even if you do read the disclosure documents, even if you do understand them, they do not so much as hint at the huge stakes the officers and directors hold in the management company—holdings that testify to their success in proliferating additional funds and aggregating assets. Would an investor in a Price fund like to know that the manager has only a modest investment in the fund, as compared to, say, tens of millions in stock, plus large stock options, in the company that manages the fund? Some of TROW's *subsidiaries* are casually mentioned in the fund prospectus investors receive—but not TROW itself! Having no reason even to suspect its existence, the investor is not given a peek behind the legally separate but functionally entwined corporate identity to see the enterprise as a whole. Lawyers call it piercing the corporate veil, but here it is a tightly woven shroud. Candor always suffers in the face of conflicts of interest.

Form over Substance: Shame on the SEC

The contrast with the disclosure required of publicly owned business corporations is striking. At General Electric, the compensation, conflicts of interest, stock options, employment contracts, and the like of the executives and directors are disclosed in great detail, and then broadcast in the press. To be sure, the shareholders of TROW are informed of the executives' compensation. It is only the investors *in the Price funds* who are kept in the dark. Why does the SEC not insist that fund shareholders, too, be given equal access to this oh-so-relevant information? If GE had agreed to pay its senior management a collective 1 percent of GE's assets, it would surely be of concern to the GE shareholder that the CEO had a perverse incentive to grow the assets and make acquisitions regardless of profitability, and the SEC would insist on piercing the corporate veil to see how that affected the take-home pay—and stock options, if any— for each of the senior officers personally. Has it occurred to no one at the SEC that 90 million fund shareholders suffer from that very abuse and are entitled to the same disclosures?

It is now commonplace for a fund management to operate as, or as a part of, a publicly owned corporation. It was not always thus, and the history is revealing. In the industry's early years, from the 1920s into the 1950s, funds were run by small, private firms that strove to make a decent profit managing money. The SEC did not permit managers to *capitalize* that profit by selling shares of the management company to outside investors. When in 1956 the managers of a successful California fund, Insurance Securities, sought to sell control of the management company at 25 times the net asset value of their shares, the SEC argued that, because of the fiduciary relationship, the "excess value of the management contracts" were an asset of the fund itself and thus could not be sold by the management company. Any such sale, it argued, would encourage trafficking in management contracts "without regard to the best interests of [the fund]." Well said, but the Ninth Circuit rejected the SEC's argument.[42] In 1971, the Second Circuit took a more stringent view, laying down a prophylactic rule forbidding an investment adviser from receiving personal gain from the transfer of an advisory contract.[43] But the damage had been done; the gates were open. In 1975, knuckling under pressure from the industry, Congress amended the Investment Company Act to provide definitively that:

> An investment adviser . . . may receive any amount or benefit in connection with a sale of securities of or . . . any other interest in, such adviser. . . . (Section 15(f)(1))

Today few of the major fund management companies are privately owned. The transfer is subject to approval by the fund's board of directors, and one would hope that the board would not casually accept whichever buyer happened to be high bidder. Think about it; just because the buyer paid top dollar does not make it the right choice. On the contrary, it may be the one that is most avidly intent on accumulating the maximum AUM and harvesting the economies of scale. Except for a handful of instances, however, that approval has been routinely given.[44]

The Failure of Candor Runs Deep

Fifty years ago, Arthur Wiesenberger, a brokerage firm that published an annual "compendium" of data, plus valuable insights, about the various investment companies, said in its 1955 edition that mutual funds were the means of bringing organization to the investment problems of people in all walks of life:

> Those who earn and save money rarely have the background, time or facilities to study and interpret the complex developments that cause changes in the prices of stocks and bonds. The [mutual fund] enables them . . . [to enjoy] the same diversification and continuous supervision as the largest [investor].[45]

The fee structure back then was modest, and perhaps because funds were more content to hold their stocks and less intent on trading in and out of them, the industry seemed more in tune with its mission of trusteeship. Its investors, too, were less peripatetic. The annual investor turnover rate in equity funds was an almost irreducible 16 percent.[46] (In other words, investors stayed with their funds for an average of six years.) And the shares that the funds owned, stocks in leading industries such as oil, chemicals, steel, utilities, and merchandising, seem, at least in retrospect, to have been delightfully stable compared to the corporations engaged in the fierce global competition of today.

Interestingly enough, Ben Graham, the dean of security analysis, who surely was no friend of conventional Wall Street wisdom, was also giving mutual funds two thumbs up, at least for the investor of small means wishing to obtain an interest in an adequately diversified list of stocks. The well-established open-end companies, he wrote in 1949, "are competently managed; they certainly make fewer serious mistakes than the typical small investor. [And] the expense[s] involved in buying these shares are little, if any, in excess of the commissions on very small lots" bought in the open market.[47]

Graham's advice remained constant right through the 1959 edition of his best-selling primer, *The Intelligent Investor*, but by the time the 1973 edition appeared, he had become more skeptical. Many of the fund companies, he argued, had created a large and bewildering variety of choices for the investor, growth stock funds, income funds, and specialty funds for chemicals, aviation, and the like. In effect, he said, the funds had shifted the burden of selection back to the investor, now forced to make choices not too different from those offered in direct investment.[48] And in the years since then, the bewildering variety has only gotten worse.

The investor's chief problem, Graham said, is likely to be himself.[49] In 1970, there were 300-odd mutual funds for both stocks and bonds; there are now about 4,800 equity funds alone. But instead of providing guidance and stewardship, the fund companies are exploiting the public's lack of patience and sophistication, recklessly breeding new variants of funds to (they hope) attract investors chasing whatever is the flavor of the day. And investors are taking the bait. In the 1950s, they held their funds on average for six years. In 2002, when the market had in fact bottomed out and was headed for a resurgence, the redemption rate was as high as 40 percent if we include not just outright redemptions, but the switches from fund to fund within a given family.[50]

It almost seems that the fund companies are telling each other, "Perhaps if we keep investors switching, they will never quite come to grips with the fact that so many of our funds are mediocre." Sadly, TROW is not immune. TROW had created just four stock funds in the 30 years from 1950 to 1980, but in the 25 years since then, it added at least 80 more.[51] In addition to the growth stock funds already mentioned, TROW boasts a flock of technology funds, as well as health funds and more conservative entries combining stocks and bonds and permutations of all of the above, plus others aimed at every specific size (small-cap, mid-cap, and so forth) of stock.*

While Granny needs to know a fund's expense ratio, what will matter most to her is candor with respect to what's happening to her money, particularly at a time, such as the late 1990s, when speculation was driving stock prices to levels unsupported by earnings, revenues, or indeed anything tangible. Candor is not easy to define. At the very least it means full and accessible disclosure of the hard facts, such as the expense ratio, the turnover, the total return, and the like. For fund managers thinking about their professional responsibilities, it should also contain a qualitative element, something to show they care about the folks whose life savings they are guarding. They should be drawing on their experience, and their knowledge of what's happening from day to day in the market. In the 1990s this would have meant talking openly about the palpably growing risk inherent in the celebrated so-called new economy.

For the Price Science and Technology Fund (PRSCX), the largest of TROW's technology offerings, the end of 1999 and the weeks that followed were a critical juncture. The fund's total return, which had been a superb 42 percent in 1998, soared to an unbelievable 101 percent in 1999. And attracted by those returns, the fund's assets, which had been

---

*The aforementioned GAO report, describing the industry as a "monopolistically competitive market," suggested that these highly differentiated products help to deflect competition on the basis of the fees charged to investors. GAO, *Mutual Fund Fees* (2000), 56, 61.

$3.5 billion at year-end 1997, swelled to $4.7 billion at the end of 1998 and then, as $3.6 billion (net of redemptions) of fresh money came in, to $12.2 billion at the end of 1999. If not Granny, then her grandson, needed some straight talk: "What's going on? Should I just relax and enjoy the ride? And just what sort of stocks are we riding, and has their potential really doubled or just their price?" The investor certainly would have liked to hear the manager's view—his straight, unhedged opinion of whether tech stocks, based on their valuations, were still the place to be.

But an investor who looked for guidance in the PRSCX annual report would have been disappointed. The message from Charles "Chip" Morris, the portfolio manager, quickly noted that the fund had enjoyed another year of outstanding returns. He then explained that the fund had, however, lagged the relevant Lipper index, which had risen 114 percent, "because of our comparatively conservative fund profile." Conservative? This science and tech fund in fact contained nothing in the science sector; it was entirely invested in the tech-media-telecom sectors that were then trading on the thin ice of financial mania. The five largest holdings, comprising 20 percent of the total fund holdings, in order of size, and their approximate price-earnings ratios were:

Company	Price-Earnings Ratio
Oracle	85
Yahoo!	Infinite (no earnings)
Analog Devices	40
Cisco Systems	100
Microsoft	60

Whatever a "conservative fund profile" might have looked like, PRSCX was not even in the ballpark. Rather, it had been racing to stay a step ahead of the crowd and, more importantly, the Lipper index, by trading stocks at a reckless rate of 128 percent a year, an endeavor that could produce successful results only in a steadily rising market. Chip Morris's cash reserves at the end of 1999 were 3 percent of assets, meaning that if any of the hot money in his fund was withdrawn, he would have to start selling stocks to meet redemptions.

Chip was really more a cheerleader than a manager, and—what the investor was not told—a rather young one (37 years old) to be managing $12 billion. What the 1999 annual report did talk about was "the

outstanding . . . extraordinary . . . accelerating growth . . . robust demand"
across the technology landscape. "Science and technology stocks [were]
the place to be . . . almost the only place to be." Chip had never seen a
bull market like it. Come to think of it, Chip hadn't really seen a bull or
bear market—at least not with managerial responsibilities. He would
have been only 25 during the 1987 crash, having just joined T. Rowe
Price as an analyst that year.

Almost lost in the excitement were a couple of comments to the
effect that investors might want to be sure their exposure to tech stocks
was consistent with their long-term objectives. But just what might
their exposure be? Lest a reader go to bed anxious, Morris closed by
saying he had attempted to dampen the risk by concentrating on "lead-
ership . . . companies with solid economic foundation[s]," and that if the
sector pulled back, he was prepared to reposition the fund more aggressively. In other words, he had no answer. The manager of TROW's Price
Science and Technology Fund had no idea, or expressed no idea, whether
tech stocks were a good investment. That—although he didn't expressly
say so—was the investor's responsibility.

While Morris was in over his head, PRSCX was part of the TROW
family of funds, one with a reputation to protect. In the TROW year-end
report to its own shareholders, the management dwelt instead on the Science and Technology Fund's "outstanding performance." And then, in
March 2000, precisely as the market peaked, it added to the PRSCX Fund
an Advisor Class of stock, which includes an annual 12b-1 fee, the fee that
unconscionably sticks investors with the cost of finding more assets—for
the manager to induce brokers and other intermediaries to put yet more
of their clients' money there.* This was done at a time when PRSCX was
already bloated with $12 billion in assets. This Advisor Class brought in
$1.3 billion of fresh cash in the remaining months of the year.[52] In August
2000, TROW created still another tech fund, the Developing Technolo-
gies Fund (PRDTX), to catch whatever small-cap tech stocks were still
on the table. Hey, investor, TROW was not even remotely thinking about
you. It was thinking about keeping its style consistency and about proliferating products, the better to attract more assets. Of course, it was not alone;

---

*PRSCX was among the first of more than two dozen Price funds to add an
Advisor Class.

according to Jack Bogle, during the market bubble, the "industry created 494 'new economy' funds—technology and telecommunications funds, and aggressive growth funds dominated by those sectors."[53]

Two years later, early in 2002, Chip Morris, by then almost 40, having aged if not matured considerably, decided it was time for a change. No wonder; in 2000 and 2001, the fund had lost 34 percent and 41 percent, respectively. That's a cumulative loss of 61 percent. The report for the year 2001 began by saying it had been "a terrible year for the stock market," though in fact the market index had declined by only 12 percent, not 41 percent. Net assets of the fund fell to $5.2 billion. Meanwhile, Morris had still been looking for upbeat trends; the fund's annual portfolio turnover in 2000 and 2001 was 134 percent and 143 percent, respectively. Except that there were no upbeat trends, just a deep pit . . . and no candor.

As Good as It Gets?

This continued spinning of portfolios, in a frenzied effort to keep the champagne on the table, speaks to a mind-set, perhaps an entire culture, that has lost its way. Remember, the Price funds are not some renegade group. These are no-load funds, the management fees have been modest relative to the industry, and TROW escaped the market-timing scandals that beset many major fund families. Commentators tend to speak well of Price funds.[54] But if this be a reasonably representative *good* fund complex, then it is ultimately bad news. Something snapped after TROW went public. What had begun as a top-notch firm soon lost the sense of trusteeship that had previously defined its character.

The overriding concern is the failure of the TROW managers to put their primary emphasis where it surely belongs, on whether clients were making or losing money. They focused instead on their *relative* performance vis-à-vis a Lipper index of like-style funds, which in turn are collectively playing the same asset-style game. So, too, the reckless proliferation of funds, and the sometimes ferocious trading of stocks within those funds. Ultimately, it was not the management fee but rather the failure to pursue their clients' best interests rather than their own, and to do so with candor, that hurt the most.

TROW, if given the opportunity, might respond to my criticisms that it is simply producing the products that the market demands; if it does not, others will (a time-honored cop-out). The marketplace has changed dramatically, TROW might add, and while the statute imposes a fiduciary duty, the day-to-day reality is that the preponderance of investors rely on brokers and consultants in choosing from among the thousands of funds. Those consultants, and institutional investors such as pension funds and endowments, require systematic rules and consistent styles for portfolio asset allocation in order to simplify their own choices.[55] Don't blame TROW for the state of the markets, the industry, and asset allocation strategies. Okay, let's accept that TROW cannot change the nature of the business. That said, what is inescapable is that TROW has put profitability of the management company ahead of performance of the funds' investors. Someone might then say to investors, caveat emptor. But shouldn't average investors be told about the caveat? (Shouldn't they be told openly by the funds, instead of by me after shelling out for a book?)

This is quite unlike the marketplace our parents or grandparents knew, and we need to examine the changes.

Chapter 6

The Investor's Dilemma

Long on Life Expectancy, Short on Income,
and Searching for Guidance

Increasingly abandoned by employers who are freezing or dumping
their pension plans, left with the responsibility and risk in managing their modest savings, engaged in an almost futile effort to provide for retirement at a time of growing life expectancies even as real
wages stagnate, seeking advice on investment funds from the omnipresent experts who blithely run with the bulls and growl with the bears, as
if that helped—welcome to the dilemma of working Americans.

A Crisis of Moral Imagination

Years ago, at least in the 1950s, it seemed easier for investors to cope with
the stock market. People bought on the basis of the dividends, and dividends
were steady. The Fidelity Fund, for example—yes, Fidelity had only one

fund in 1954—had a dividend yield of about 4.5 percent. Massachusetts Investors Trust was paying about 4 percent, and given its portfolio of industry leaders, the shareholders did not need to look much beyond that. Earnings might be subject to interpretation and even manipulation, but dividends are . . . well, they're real money, an anchor to windward. My mother adored the $9 annual dividend that AT&T paid like clockwork, and I'm sure she never thought about whether Ma Bell's earnings were going up or down. We can't do that today. The S&P 500 has a dividend yield of just 1.8 percent, barely half the rate of inflation.

It is tempting to don rose-colored glasses when reviewing the past and think that life, including investing, was easier then; but history tells us otherwise. Looking back over a 30-year period, 1925–1954, one Wall Street firm, Arthur Wiesenberger, charted the market price of $1 of dividends—that is, the amount of investment in the Dow Jones Industrial Average needed to receive a $1 payout. (See Figure 6.1.) Dividends were fairly steady, but our emotions were all over the map: enthusiasm (1928), then panic (1932), more enthusiasm (1935), then worry (1937), followed soon by more confidence and then worry. The price one would have paid for that average dividend dollar went as high as $33 in 1928, as low as $10 in 1932, up to $36 in 1936, then back down to $14 in 1938, and so on.

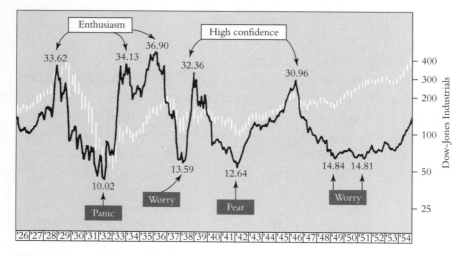

Figure 6.1 Market Value of $1 of Dividends
SOURCE: Arthur Wiesenberger, *Investment Companies 1955*, 15th Annual Edition (New York: Wiesenberger & Company, 1955), 15.

Think about it: In the depths of the Depression, blue-chip companies were paying a 10 percent annual dividend—but nobody was buying. Investors were either themselves depressed, or broke, or most likely some of each.

More people are familiar with stocks and funds today. As the 1980s opened, fewer than 5 million households owned shares in mutual funds, compared to 55 million today. Their comfort level may be no higher today than it was then, but circumstances have forced them to think about putting something away for retirement. As recently as 1985, 30 percent of all private-sector workers were covered by defined benefit plans, under which their companies promised that, on retirement, they would receive a pension, typically measured by their years of service and terminal pay. The beauty of these plans is that Terri and Rick don't need to know anything about the stock market or mutual funds. The burden is on the employer to put enough money into the plan to pay the promised benefits. Markets up, markets down, the guy in the shipping room *knew* that a lifetime of work at, say, DuPont would be rewarded by a lifetime pension. Just do your job, and the security would be there. It was DuPont, right?

At least, the guy thought he knew. DuPont announced, late in 2006, that shortly it would accrue pension benefits for its existing workers at just one-third the old rate; and effective in 2007, new hires would not be covered at all. (Those new hires would also be dropped from the health insurance plan, but that's another story.) The announcement noted that the company would save about $46 million after taxes, adding that the "changes reinforce our commitment to help employees provide for a secure retirement."[1] Huh, reinforce what? As has happened across corporate America, DuPont is replacing traditional pension benefits with so-called defined contribution payments, under which the company would match employee contributions to a 401(k) plan, topping out in DuPont's case at 6 percent of the salaries of those who elect to participate. (Regardless of the workers' contributions, DuPont will contribute an additional 3 percent of salary for each of them, or potentially as much as 9 percent in all.[2])

Will these contributions be enough to provide for a secure future? That depends. In 401(k) and other defined contribution plans, the worker has to grapple with two major issues: (1) how much he or she will need to save today to provide for a decent retirement income years later, and (2) how best to achieve the necessary future income. This means that when our DuPont employee is, say, 35 years old, working hard and focusing on career and family, that he or she will also have to get a handle on life expectancies, the average annual returns on stocks and bonds, and the impact of inflation. Employees also need to have an eye for risk—such as the risk that the stock market will tank just when they're ready to hang up their cleats. Remember the relief when they first came home, years ago, announcing that they would have lifetime security with DuPont? Gone, leaving that empty feeling. Knowing that the company, with its $2.4 billion of annual earnings, stood to gain an additional $46 million surely did not provide workers much solace.

The percentage of private-sector employees covered by pension plans has now fallen below 20 percent, and will continue to decline. In the wake of the market crash of 2000–2002, companies woke up to the peril of underwriting their pension promises. Not only are they more wary of the market risk, but there is the problem that people are living longer. (Some of us may not see that as a problem, least of all the chief financial officer of DuPont who, in addition to a $500,000 pension, received a $2 million retirement bonus.[3]) Most companies that have offered pension plans have been far smaller than DuPont, but of the 112,000 pension plans that once existed, 80,000 have been frozen or terminated. Many of the corporate plans still in effect are significantly underfunded, by amounts estimated in all at hundreds of billions of dollars.[4]

When Pat O'Neill retired after 35 years as an aircraft mechanic at United Airlines, he felt pretty good. He had, as he said, "a work ethic, and . . . was very loyal to the company. . . . I knew I had a good retirement. Check would come every month, and we'd be able to kick back, enjoy life . . . no more working midnights . . . and spend quality time with each other."[5] Having taken retirement, he probably assumed that while United had already filed for bankruptcy, it would not affect his "guaranteed $3,000 monthly pension check," which would be paid out of the pension trust fund. Not so; United unloaded its pension funds, by then $10 billion in the hole, onto the federal Pension Benefit Guaranty Corporation (PBGC), which insures failed pension plans. The PBGC cut Pat's monthly checks by one-third, and he now finds himself hauling trucks to make up the shortfall. (United's CEO won't have to go "trucking," except on a dance floor; he got special protection for his retirement benefits.)

It's too late for Pat, but even now that United has emerged from bankruptcy, workers there, as they have elsewhere, are seeing that their financial futures are cloudy at best, and that they are increasingly on their own if they are ever to kick back and get that quality time. They're learning that mutual funds, in or out of 401(k) plans, are the key. That's why they're exploring the various types of funds, how much they'll need to sock away, and new concepts, like risk and return.

The heart of the problem, in the United States as well as elsewhere in the world, is the otherwise good news that people are living much longer, which needs to be seen in the context of a declining birth rate. By 2030, when the baby boomer generation will have retired, the economy as a whole will have to support twice the current number of retirees, with only 18 percent more workers.[6] Until recently, corporate managements shielded their eyes—and their workers' eyes, too—from the problem, using complex accounting fictions, which, for S&P 500 companies alone, puffed up their collective balance sheets by $240 billion. Now, with a new mandate from Congress—the Pension Protection Act of 2006—the financial reporting will be clarified, and more strict funding required. Translation: As managements face reality, more of them will skinny down their plans, à la DuPont, or freeze them entirely.

Companies have switched workers to 401(k)-style plans, with 40 percent of American workers now covered by them.[7] Managements realized that the 401(k)s would cost far less than the old lifetime pensions—in fact, only about half as much, or about 6 to 8 percent of payroll. If, as usually happens, not everyone signs up for the plan, the cost might be as low as 2 to 3 percent of payroll. Happily, under the new 2006 statute, employers will be allowed to enroll employees in a 401(k) plan or individual retirement account (IRA), unless the employees, who tend to let these things slide, take affirmative steps to *opt out*.[8] The effective participation rate should, therefore, rise. DuPont will be among those adopting this automatic enrollment.

According to a Fidelity spokesman, these plans should be good for workers:

> Now before I get too deep into this, let me say . . . [y]ou're in the driver's seat of this 401(k), OK? You're the pilot. You're going

to make all the decisions. So what we're looking at here, these are just suggestions. . . . Everybody needs to have an investment strategy. Maybe you like high tech, health care, or the electronics sector. . . . Call 1-800-FIDELITY. . . . [We're] going to charge you for this service. There is a fee.[9]

Not so fast, says Professor Alicia Munnell, director of the Center for Retirement Research at Boston College, and a former member of the President's Council of Economic Advisers. From her long experience in and out of government, she argues that these 401(k)s were never intended to be the "mainstay of people's retirement," for which they are poorly designed:

> Everything has gone wrong. The individual has to decide whether to join the plan, how much to contribute, how to allocate those contributions, how to change those allocations over time, decide what to do when they move from one job to another, think about what to do about company stock. . . . And then the hardest thing, [what do they do] when they get to retirement and somebody hands them a check? How do you figure out how to use that over your retirement span?[10]

The numbers bear out her sense of foreboding. Someone making, say, $50,000 a year needs to replace about 75 percent of that income to maintain their standard of living in their golden years, or about $37,500 a year. Some expenses will have gone down then, but others such as medical costs will, despite Medicare, almost surely go up. Social Security replaces on average about 35 percent of preretirement income,[11] or $17,500 for the worker with that $50,000-a-year job, leaving the retiree to find another $20,000 a year to fill the gap. Retirees can fill it by drawing on their private capital, but to do that and not risk running out, they would need to have saved about $500,000, which 95 percent of all Americans never come close to. The consultants say that retirees can prudently withdraw from their funds about 4 percent a year. They will be tempted, of course, to withdraw more than the 4 percent, but there is a trap in that. The trap is that a 65-year old man's life expectancy is about 18 years and a woman's is 22 years, so as hard as they struggled to accumulate those dollars, they may not be able to maintain their living standards if they live "too long."

Some will continue working after reaching retirement age, but after that, there's no defense against the cost of living except Social Security, digging further into their home equity, or slinging burgers at Wendy's. On a combined employer-employee basis, people should have been putting into their plans 14 or 15 percent a year of their salaries—for 30 years running! More often, companies and employees think they're doing fine if they put away 10 percent—and most people consider these retirement contributions as savings so that they tend not to save otherwise. This inevitably leads to the unhappy scenario whereby some workers use their plans as rainy day funds, to pay for a down payment on a house, or for the kids' education. Many workers cash in their plans when they change jobs, even with the hefty penalties and taxes. With real wages stagnating and household debt rising, we should be sympathetic, not critical.[12]

National Semiconductor might be a role model for how best to promote 401(k) participation. Instead of the common dollar-for-dollar company match, it provides an additional 50 cents, or $1.50 in all, for each employee dollar. That really grabs workers' attention, raising participation rates at National to 90 percent or more. The company also makes an unusual effort to educate its staff, with mandatory attendance at focus group meetings. But National Semiconductor is . . . well, unusual. For most of the 40 percent of Americans covered by mutual funds in these 401 (k)-style plans, managements seem too preoccupied with shareholder and executive welfare to think much about those further down the ladder. A quarter or more of the eligible workers don't join a plan at all,[13] and the median value of these retirement accounts is a sadly inadequate $35,000.

Long on life expectancy, short on income—and yet, in the richest nation in the world, there's no sense of social or moral outrage. Some of the companies that trimmed or froze their pension plans were broke, but many, like DuPont, were anything but. One would like to see at least the long-term workers assured of a retirement with dignity. Standing the concept of loyalty on its ear, however, one Kodak executive rationalized, over a wine-tasting dinner with me, that workers actually prefer the uncertainties of a 401(k), because unlike a pension plan, their 401(k) plans, and thus their mutual funds, are "portable." As long as the market was steadily rising, many no doubt did prefer a 401(k). But since 2000, the cold shoulder has been cold indeed.

Should there not be at least some shared sacrifice by the senior management, as was notably absent at United Airlines? Sorry, companies freely do whatever the labor market and the law permit, and they do it in a characteristically corporatist style: bureaucratic, impersonal, legalistic, mediated by complex institutional rules.[14] Scholars have written reams about shareholder value in an effort to stem the excesses of executive greed. One strains to hear any allusion to the "value" of those who toil or any sense of shared pain. This is, indeed, a crisis of moral imagination.

How the Other Half Lives . . .

If this picture of 401(k) participants seems frightening, they are, however, among the more fortunate of the now-graying baby boomer generation. Companies are not obligated to provide a retirement program, and half of all American workers are not covered by one, whether a pension or a 401(k)-style plan. Nothing. They have Social Security plus whatever equity remains in their home, if they own one, after subtracting a rising level of debt.[15] No doubt some of them are saving for retirement on their own, but statistically they are in the minority. The total of *all* financial assets held by the median American family, in a bank account, retirement account, or wherever, is a meager $30,000.[16] It's hardly surprising that, as that Kodak executive observed to me, some workers pass up even health care to buy the car they need to get to work.

Knowing that the savings bank will never get them to where they need to be, people have increasingly turned to the stock market. Contrary to the Fidelity adviser's script, those who venture out solo are in a financial no-man's-land. Successful long-term investing is not easy. There are so many complex factors, some of which are quantitative, such as sales, earnings, and cash flows, while others are qualitative and depend on a host of unknowns and unmeasurables, such as how our economy and world events will evolve. At the end of the day, most of us, like Terri and Rick, have neither the time, the patience, nor the training to be successful stock pickers.

Recognizing the problem, many of us turn to mutual funds hoping to simplify the process. This is reasonable, but not necessarily simpler. The industry proliferates funds even as we breathe, so that the choice between Franklin Templeton's Foreign Fund, International Fund, World Fund, and Foreign Smaller Companies Fund may escape Rick and his wife (or indeed me). Beyond that lies the intrinsic difficulty that funds are essentially opaque, *more difficult to analyze in many respects than individual stocks.* To pick a stock, one can begin, as suggested by Peter Lynch, the celebrated former manager of the Fidelity Magellan Fund, by picking a company whose products or services we personally know and respect. That's not hard. How about Johnson & Johnson? Procter & Gamble? Even Starbucks, where you have to wait for that latte? Of course, you still have to do some homework, or as Lynch said—in bold type, hoping someone might heed the message—**"Investing without research is like playing stud poker and never looking at the cards."**[17] People, he concluded, spend hours deciding whether to switch to Charmin toilet paper, but then invest significant bucks in Procter & Gamble without reading the annual report to see how much the Charmin contributes to the company's earnings.

We need to do some checking, but at least we're on familiar turf with Starbucks and P&G, where that ounce of homework would begin to provide helpful answers. *Not so with a mutual fund.* The average fund has 150 or more stocks, no one of which will account for more than 2 to 3 percent of the total. It would be a waste of time to check any of them. How about checking the fund manager? No help there; the major fund families rarely talk about their managers, preferring to focus on "asset classes," as if somehow the fact that a fund is, say, a small-cap blend fund is enough to tell us how well it will do compared to a large-cap growth fund or the market index. (Funny, some of us thought managerial skill was the critical factor in picking a stock fund.) That leaves the investor to check a fund's expense ratio, which is important, but low fees won't matter much if the stocks in the fund's portfolio collapse. Has the reader perhaps noticed that we don't hear much about the funds that perform badly? Check their ads; the fund sponsors almost invariably single out the recent winners. The poor performers are systematically merged into others—lost, gone from view and from the historical record forever.

Everyone Agrees: We Are Frightfully
Poor Investors

Tenure has been won at distinguished universities and whole careers built on the reams of evidence that the Terris and Ricks have barely a clue about skilled, patient investing. There is a thriving discipline, behavioral finance, with journals devoted to the latest insights and the fine points of how the Terris and Ricks so often get it wrong.[18] (Though some studies indicate that Rick gets it more wrong than Terri.) Allowing for some overlap, the more common errors and shortcomings include:

- People switch in and out of stocks and even funds far too often. Forty years ago, investors redeemed their mutual fund shares at a rate of 5 to 7 percent a year,[19] meaning that they kept them for 14 years or more. Now redemptions run 20 to 25 percent a year, sometimes more, meaning that holding periods have collapsed to just a few years. All this switching brings heavy tax and transaction costs.
- The information available to mutual fund investors is not all that it should be, but it is useful. Alas, people don't read even what's there, perhaps because the stuff is impenetrable or just comes too late, after the decision has been made.
- People are impatient decision makers, and in money management, impatience produces notably bad decisions.[20] Why should anything this important lend itself to quick analysis? Bill Nygren at Oakmark Select, one of the funds discussed in Chapter 2, brazenly tempted his investors with an impatience quiz, using several short questions likely to produce quick—and wrong—answers. (The questions and answers are set out at the end of this chapter.) Think of a stock or fund that has fallen, and how we almost impulsively jump to get rid of it, so that our mistakes won't sit there, staring at us. But wait, maybe the original concept is still sound? Forget it, out it goes. Impatience, impatience.
- Another error is overconfidence and the demonstrated tendency of many investors to be optimistic, to believe that bad things happen only to the other guy, and to make decisions without considering all the consequences if they are wrong. The problem is not unique to the stock market. Pro football teams, for example, often give up

too much for the number one pick in the draft, being overconfident of their eye for talent.[21] In 2004, the New York Giants traded four high draft picks to the San Diego Chargers in exchange for the top overall choice. Three of those four Chargers went to the Pro Bowl in 2007. The Giants' top pick, Eli Manning, has not yet come close.

- Perhaps most important, there is a visible contagion of ideas, or "herding," as it is called by scholars. On Wall Street, it's called momentum investing. Warren Buffett says that the five most dangerous words in business may be "Everybody else is doing it."[22] In 2005, real estate funds were hot; in 2006, everyone just had to be in an international fund.

- These so-human traits promote the most basic error of all—the fatally wrongheaded tendency to focus on how the *market price* of a stock is performing (and at this very moment), rather than how the underlying *business* is performing. Stock prices are not a perfect mirror of business reality, but for investors who are impatient, short-term focused, impulsive, and overconfident, market prices are easy to find on CNBC or the Internet.

True, there is a different school of financial economists who argue that, in the final analysis, it doesn't much matter if Terri and Rick know when and what to buy or sell, because the "smart money" will make sure that whatever they do, the market price will be what it ought in fairness to be. For this group, any actively managed fund is a waste of fees, time, and money. The best approach, they say, is an index fund, in effect a little bit of everything; then just sit back and relax. But even they have nothing good to say about people like Terri and Rick—nice folks, but they are not the ones we rely on to get the prices right.

And Now a Word from Pogo . . .

A Boston-based consultancy illustrated the shortcomings of fund investors with the story of a hypothetical couple, Quincy and Caroline, who began to invest in the market in 1985.[23] The husband, Quincy, followed the market assiduously. He sold after the market fell in October 1987, when the outlook seemed to be grim, and reinvested when courage was back in style. Each bit of bad news would induce him to sell, and then later, feeling confident, he would buy back. Caroline, whose investment was separate, allowed the market to take its course, up and down. At year-end 2005, after 20 years had elapsed, Quincy's original $10,000 stake was worth a meager $21,000, while Caroline's $10,000 had grown to . . . $94,000. Quincy's mood changes were, of course, a veritable catalog of the principles of behavioral finance, particularly the tendency to follow the crowd. Scholars also call it a feedback loop, meaning that the behavior of the group influences others to behave in like fashion, which influences still others to do the same.

That consulting firm, Dalbar, concluded that the average equity fund investor had, over the 10 years through 2005, earned annualized returns of 5.8 percent versus 9.1 percent for the S&P 500. The common cause of this shortfall is those falling markets that sneak up on us unpredictably. By the time we get ready to act, the damage has been done. Feeling remorse for having allowed the family's savings to shrink, we assuage our guilt and cash out some losers. In real life as well as that fable, a Caroline would have been rewarded for her patience.[24] Dollar estimates of these self-inflicted wounds vary widely. What is clear is that the more volatile the market, the more likely we—or most of us—are to get it wrong.[25] As Pogo said, we have met the enemy and he is . . . us.

But if we stopped there, the story would be woefully incomplete.

What Pogo Forgot

Investors' performance is awful, but perhaps, just perhaps, that's because the professional advice they get is so awful. Don't blame Terri and Rick, if by and large they are simply following the experts. Too often, what they hear is not intelligent, carefully researched insights, but rather what economists call noise, the clucking of hens in the financial barnyard. Let's put the criticism where it belongs, not on the innocents who are stumbling, however well intentioned; rather, let's point a finger at the fund managers and other professionals who have self-serving agendas, in pursuit of which they pretend to know what so often is unknowable, or which requires more patient digging and thought than they are able or willing to give.

While no one knows where Mr. Market is going next month, the experts always have an opinion. No TV anchor ever asked an analyst at, say, Merrill Lynch where stocks were headed, only to receive a puzzled look in response. A Belgian economist, Paul De Grauwe, provided a tasty explanation of all this—what he called the Belgian chocolate theory of financial markets.[26] When we see that Godiva chocolates are expensive, he said, we infer that the high price reflects high quality and a much richer taste than the chocolate that costs less. Somehow it's also true that when we see the stock price of, say, Google rise, we infer that there must be some good developments driving it. There is one critical difference, however. The chocoholic can immediately check the quality of Godiva. The investor in Google cannot.

Now enter the fund managers, analysts, economists, and media. They may not know any more than the next person, but they always have a story: Interest rates are holding steady, investment banking revenues will grow, some reason why energy or international is the place to be. At the end of 1999, the hottest story was how long the new economy would persist. The correct answer would have been that we simply did not know. But, as De Grauwe observed, "our psyche abhors the darkness of ignorance," so we turn to the seers who are paid to know. We need to dispel the shadows; and given the inherent ambiguity of how to invest, we need the validation of someone telling us what to do.[27] It's uncanny how predictably the wise men return from their huddle, only to announce with great solemnity that whatever has been happening . . . will continue to happen. To suggest anything else would require them to exercise independent judgment, to stick their necks out, which they are loathe to do.

Two factors are at work: First, if we already knew the events that would produce a change in direction, the changes would have begun; but of course we don't know. Second, and perhaps more important, the economists, advisers, and financial analysts have thoroughly absorbed John Maynard Keynes' dictum, which few of them have read: "Worldly wisdom teaches that it is better for the reputation to fail conventionally than to succeed unconventionally."[28] You'll not be criticized if you stay with the crowd. Keynes' insight was borne out in our study of the Goldfarb 10 in Chapter 2. Those managers' sturdy adherence to Graham-and-Dodd tenets of value investing, particularly the precept of a margin of safety, cost them dearly. They saw money being made elsewhere as new economy stocks soared, but still they refused to go with the crowd.

Many of their investors fled, so that the managers' personal incomes shrank. The French owners of the management company for what are now the First Eagle funds said that they had calculated to the day when their last investor would have left. In the long run, we now know, the managers of those funds were vindicated, but the long run can be very painful indeed. Keynes wasn't really advising us to be conventional, but only a very few of us have the intellectual and emotional gift to stray from the crowd.

Of Bubbles and Swans

The contagion of ideas, herding, momentum investing—call it what you will, but it fairly screams out during the bubbles that emerge from time to time and will continue to emerge. Contagion also screams in panics. As we saw in Chapter 3, there was no news to explain why blue-chip stocks collapsed so suddenly on Black Monday in 1987, given that interest rates had been rising for quite some time. These episodes have occurred throughout history. Just to take some examples: the junk bonds in the late 1980s, the biotechs in the 1990s, Third World debt (e.g., Russia, Brazil) in the late 1990s. There were the energy darlings of the late 1970s and the Southwest real estate bubble in the early 1980s.[29] Told of whatever snippet was supposed to justify the then mania, David Dodd (of Graham and Dodd) said the four most dangerous words in the English language, "This time it's different."

These episodes paled, however, alongside the new economy bubble of the late 1990s, a so-called "black swan,"[30] meaning an event of such a magnitude or character that no one could have foreseen it. Nor could anyone discern the day it might end. It did end, of course; indeed, it exploded, and investors suffered a severe, in many cases permanent, loss of their savings. As the fall of 2007 unfolded, the broad market index, the S&P 500, was hovering near, but still shy of, its peak level early in 2000; and the NASDAQ index, which tracked so many of the exciting telecom, media, and tech stocks of the day, had reached only half its peak. The losses were not just the easy profits of investments made early on. Too many of us jumped on the bandwagon—as happened in the Massachusetts Investors Growth Stock Fund we examined in Chapter 4—shortly before the music stopped. As for those who retired or were given redundancy notices early in the current decade when their retirement portfolios were depressed . . . well, better not to ask. The bubble of the late 1990s, therefore, is a good episode in which to see if Terri and Rick were being any more foolish or shortsighted than the wizards of Wall Street: the fund managers, the analysts, and the media pundits.

Where was the "smart money" when the bubble was peaking? By early 2000, if not before, prices had reached irrational levels; and it was clear enough that investors intent on hanging around for the proverbial last drink were on treacherous ground. For the cognoscenti on Wall Street, the telecoms remained a must-own,[31] even though bandwidth prices were already in free fall. Global Crossing, which had plans to build a transoceanic fiber-optic cable, was valued by the market at $45 billion. Two years later, by January 2002, it was in bankruptcy, soon to be followed by WorldCom and the like. (The insiders at Global Crossing did not wait for that fateful moment; they sold early and often.) Once reality has set in, it is hard to recapture the magic of a moment when it truly seemed as if the old rules no longer mattered. In 1999 alone, however, the NASDAQ climbed by 86 percent, and Merrill Lynch, catching the evangelical fever, announced that "The Internet revolution is . . . perhaps putting more of us in touch with the meaning of life."[32] By the end of that year, the S&P 500, at 1,469, was priced at 29 times its earnings, about twice the price-earnings ratio it would enjoy during a very good but still sane year, 2006.

History can be a nasty teacher. Yes, the bubble did collapse, but for the moment let's focus on what the analysts, the funds, and the media were saying as 1999 wound to a close.

The Analysts

Stock prices moved up . . . and up . . . seemingly inexorably. Analysts fell into line, cheering the market onward, perhaps because they, too, believed that the world was being made anew. Remember, however, it was in their self-interest to believe. Their firms were underwriting the hot stocks, and cheerleading their firms' products is what analysts are paid to do. One analyst who misunderstood his role at Merrill Lynch told investors to *sell* Amazon, which had no earnings but was priced at twice the value of Barnes & Noble, which had profits and vastly higher revenues. Amazon then tripled and he was out the door, replaced by someone from another firm who was predicting that Amazon would go still higher, much higher. A lack of profits in that era seemed almost to be a plus, because no metric of profit existed to anchor the stock to any ratio or price at all.[33] Another analyst, Mary Meeker at Morgan Stanley, exhorted investors to buy up stocks at whatever the price. By then, it was enough that others were buying. All that mattered, she said, was "Bull Market."[34] There was a euphoria, emotions were surging, and balance sheets and earnings were no longer important. Another analyst, at Prudential Securities, also saw the market itself as a divining rod of where the market was headed. Comparing Norfolk Southern and Cisco Systems, he mocked the notion of buying the former rather than the latter, a hot tech stock. During the ensuing year, however, Norfolk Southern rose by one-third and Cisco fell by almost two-thirds.[35]

Mutual Funds

Many of the fund families were busy buying up the hot tech-telecom-media stocks of the day, confident that their purchases would drive up the prices of both those stocks and their own funds, thereby attracting still more investors to their products.[36] Newspaper surveys of the top-performing funds let investors know who had the hot hands, treating funds such as the Jacob Internet fund as heroes of the day.[37] (We will return to the Jacob fund shortly.) But lest the good news escape Rick's notice, the funds engaged in vigorous advertising programs to catch some of the unattached money still out there. As the number of funds grew, so too did the need to advertise, to distinguish one firm's products from the thousands of others. Very few ads provide significant information, such as expense ratios or portfolios, but they do influence people's choices, and not always to the good. One study found that, if anything, advertising frequency is linked to poor performance thereafter.[38]

A quite systematic analysis of over 6,000 ads placed during the years 1994 through 2003 in *BusinessWeek* and *Money* magazines by four major firms—Merrill Lynch, Fidelity, T. Rowe Price, and Schwab—reinforces these conclusions.[39] Merrill Lynch, for example, produced six distinct campaigns featuring mottos that highlighted the Merrill brand, such as "a tradition of trust" and "the difference is Merrill Lynch." But the themes changed with the times. In 1999, the study found, the images were much hipper and more modern than before, and then in 2000–2001 the theme was simply "be bullish." One of these "bullish" ads showed a Merrill bull wired as a semiconductor board; the earlier theme of protection was gone. Not until *after* the market had declined did the theme of protection return, with notes of "ask Merrill" to emphasize the uncertainty in the world. In the case of T. Rowe Price, the share of ads for growth stock funds rose as the bubble peaked, then disappeared after the decline began. T. Rowe continued to advertise funds after the bubble burst, but switched to funds connoting safety such as bond funds and foreign funds.

A similar study, done several years earlier, found that the fund management companies advertising in *Barron's* and *Money* focused on those that had performed well above their benchmarks in the preceding year, but, on average, the funds in the ads posted results significantly below those benchmarks thereafter.[40] The advertised funds did perform well in one respect: They attracted significantly more new money than the control group. Good for the managers, yes; good for you and me, no.

The firms were obviously selling what could be sold, not what might have been helpful. They were pandering to investors' foibles, not giving them the advice or data they might use to get a grip on the mania on Wall Street. The pattern of these ads persists to this day. Schwab says to "Talk to Chuck," stressing the element of personal attention, with no data of any sort. There is a profound conflict of interest, however, in how Schwab picks its recommended funds, all of whose sponsors pay Schwab to get on the preferred list. Known by various names, such as "revenue sharing" and "pay to play," the only oblique reference is deep in the small print boilerplate at the bottom of the page. And Fidelity, fully aware that international stocks had for several years been bubbling up, was recently boasting of its three foreign funds' performance and announcing the creation of still a fourth.[41] Not a word of caution from Fidelity to put this sector's record in perspective, and certainly no mention of its performance in whatever sectors had been lagging. Only: "The world is your oyster," Fidelity said.

The Media

Terri and Rick were also getting doused by the stream of advice that the popular magazines feature each year as the calendar winds down. Major magazines, such as *Business Week, Money,* and *Fortune,* boast of having gathered investment insights from an array of analysts and other professionals, as well as their own editors. In effect, they were synthesizing for Terri and Rick all the then-current wisdom. Think how fortunate Terri and Rick were to have such a collection of experts at their disposal. And what better time to check that advice than year-end 1999, when the bulls were running? Those three magazines were also running hard, with issues bloated by mutual fund ads. Let's see which mutual funds in particular topped their recommended lists.

Fortune was running the hardest. It was a "new era," the writers said, and to select the new heroes, they first identified "four sweeping trends . . . [and] the stocks best positioned to capitalize on" those trends. They did their "own due diligence by poring through financial statements, talking to companies," in order to pick 10 "winners over the coming decade."[42] One could sense where they were headed by the managers of the hot funds they consulted, the Janus fund and the Franklin Biotechnology Discovery fund. Among the stocks, four were seen as positioned best: Nokia, Nortel, Enron, and Oracle, whose lofty price-earnings (P/E) ratios ranged from 114 for Nortel to a "modest" 51 for Enron. (The latter turned out to be a meaningless figure, because, as we soon learned, Enron's earnings were phony.) The high P/Es, however, did not seem to be a problem: This was a "buy-and-forget portfolio."[43] There was not a moment's hesitation. As we noted earlier, the 10 stocks on the *Fortune* list had, within 18 months, fallen by 80 percent *on average*, which arithmetically is a very difficult achievement. (Don't try it; you won't succeed.)

Four mutual funds were also selected, they being ones that would "punch up your portfolio (and still let you sleep at night.)"[44] The top two on the list were the Invesco Telecommunications and the Invesco Leisure funds, so it was clear where *Fortune* thought the future, plus a soft pillow, lay. The Telecommunications fund had gained *on average* 57 percent a year over the preceding three years, and was said to be on its way to another good year. As it turned out, the Invesco family of funds would soon be in deep trouble over market-timing abuses. In the settlement, it paid $325 million, one of the largest such penalties paid by any of the funds that had deliberately allowed Canary Capital and other scoundrels to steal from their investors. (Like Enron, Invesco had dished out a huge sum to put its name on a sports stadium, which may be a negative indicator of sorts.) Executives left abruptly, and by December 2003, Morningstar, in a rare note of censure, concluded that the Invesco funds didn't "deserve investors' money."[45] By then, it was too late. Investors could not have done worse if they had skipped that issue of *Fortune* altogether.★

Money published in its January 2000 issue its "best recommendations for 2000 and beyond." First it set the table for these predictions in its December 1999 issue, where it cheered and gurgled over some of the 66 "stunning" funds that had shown triple-digit (100+ percent) performance sometime during 1999. Three domestic funds were highlighted, with profiles and photographs of the managers: the Amerindo Technology, Internet, and Firsthand Technology Innovators funds, which over a year's time had gained 290 percent, 301 percent, and 235 percent, respectively. Young Ryan Jacob had dropped out as manager of the Internet fund in July 1999, and so the article focused on his new Jacob Internet fund, where by cautious pruning of the industry lists, he expected to show gains of 100 percent "on the high end, 30% on the low!"[46] Modest fellow, but he was truly cautious alongside Amerindo's Alberto Vilar, who predicted that if "you're out of [dot-coms], [y]ou're in a horse and buggy, and I'm in a Porsche."[47] The article closed with a brief plug for the Nevis fund, up 260 percent that year.

Before long, Vilar was sitting not in his Porsche but in jail, unable to make bail, charged with absconding with investor funds. The Jacob Internet fund, not so cautious after all, fell by 91 percent in the ensuing two years, having at one point frantically turned over its portfolio 10 times in a single year.[48] A hemorrhage of that magnitude was truly newsworthy, but by then *Money* had moved on. Like the others, why look back?

★Investors in the Leisure fund who stood fast through 2006 would have come out moderately well, assuming they were patient during 2001–2002 while suffering a cumulative loss of 26 percent. The Telecommunications fund was merged into its sister Technology fund in 2003, which had suffered cumulative losses in the preceding years of 77 percent and has not done much since then.

As for the Firsthand fund the magazine had featured, it lost over 50 percent during the next three years. By 2006, withdrawals and losses had reduced its net assets over 90 percent to $28 million.

A month later, in January 2000, *Money* went on to produce a definitive list of recommendations, the result of speaking with fund managers, economists, consultants, and even "futurists" (astrologers, perhaps?). The conclusion was that telecoms and health care would be the strongest sectors. Noting "the possibility of a near-term pullback," *Money* suggested that readers space out their purchases, but keep on buying.[49] The two funds on the "buy" list were the T. Rowe Price Science and Technology fund, one of *Money*'s "top 100" funds that year, and the Invesco Health Science fund. The T. Rowe fund, as we saw in Chapter 5, had been a triple-digit gainer in 1999, but soon sustained a loss of 61 percent in 2000–2001. The Invesco fund, which lost 40 percent during 2001–2002, switched managers, abandoned its role as a no-load fund, and emerged finally as the AIM Advantage Health Sciences fund, with a 5.5 percent front-end sales load. As for Nevis, in 2004 the managers settled fraud charges brought by the Securities and Exchange Commission (SEC). The management had achieved its too-good-to-be-true results by secretly funneling into the fund hot new issues—initial public offerings (IPOs)—the gains from which could not be sustained, of course, but which served to attract new money into the fund. Without those IPOs, its gains for the year 1999 would have been 38.7 percent, instead of the bully 286 percent it reported. It, too, was soon merged out of independent existence, never to be heard from again. Once the tide had washed out, we could see, as Warren Buffett likes to say, who's been swimming naked.

That same issue of *Money* recommended, of course, not just funds but also stocks. Even now, years later, it is painful to see which ones the experts had singled out as good for the year "2000 and beyond." One of them, Broadcom, also on the *Fortune* list, soon lost over 90 percent of its value. The list included such other highfliers as Lucent, Qualcomm, and Duke Energy, each of which lost, at one point or another, 70 percent or more of its value. (None of the three have regained their peak prices.)

For the subscriber to *Money* who somehow missed these two issues, the phrase "blissfully ignorant" acquired a new and poignant meaning.

BusinessWeek did the most extensive analysis of what the new century would hold, a 67-page special report entitled "Riding the Bull into 2000." Readers caught the basic thrust early on, with an "All Systems Go" prediction of double-digit gains for the stock market again in 2000, and "the Internet—which is fueling it all—just picking up steam."[50] Looking ahead, *BusinessWeek*, like *Money*, relied on Alberto Vilar and Ryan Jacob for bullish predictions on where the dot-coms were headed.[51] Chiding the prior year's experts for having "lowballed" the economy, *BusinessWeek* asked, "Have they learned their lesson?"[52]

BusinessWeek tossed in a Harris poll of a broad group of investors, who in fact had the only keen sense for the risk in a market that had gone manic. Half of the investors who had an opinion realized that the stock market was somewhat or very overpriced, and 75 percent of those with an opinion responded that Internet stocks were overpriced. Too bad, but this cautious comment was pushed to the back of the issue.[53]

In fact, it is hardly fair to pick on *BusinessWeek*, *Fortune*, and *Money*. The same crowds of experts riding the same horses, focusing on the momentum of stock prices, could also have been seen on CNBC and in the pages of the *Wall Street Journal* and *USA Today*.[54] Why would respected journals and TV casually promote stocks with little or no earnings, surely aware, in some deep recesses of their collective experience, how difficult it would be to predict the winners of the dot-com competition? Anne Ackerley, a managing director at the fund family Black Rock, laughingly said to me that one should think of Jim Cramer on CNBC, and inferentially of the rest, as providing not serious advice but entertainment. It's true, *Money* and the others do make easy reading; and at the end of the day, that is their business, attracting eyeballs, because it's the eyeballs that attract advertisers. They look to the likes of Vilar and Jacob because they give good quotes, not good advice. They are recognizable. This is the same publishing formula proven by *People* magazine, drawing on about the same level of expertise. Besides which, the nature of the business is such that it creates a vicious circle: A hot manager with hot performance attracting investors is like a magnet, and everyone wants to interview him or her. One media outlet does the profile, gets the interview, and then the rest have to follow or they look like idiots for not profiling the new hot fund in town. When your job is to attract eyeballs to attract advertisers so you can keep your job, you don't stop and say "Hey, maybe we shouldn't profile that Vilar guy" when everyone else is selling magazines or catching television viewers.

Memories are short; no one remembers today what *Business Week* predicted in December 1999, so the annual ritual continues. *Fortune*'s "Investor's Guide 2007" featured "30 hot stocks and mutual funds." *Business Week*'s year-end 2006 cover story was entitled "Stocks, Mutual Funds, Real Estate, the Economy: Where to Invest 2007." Inside was the same warmed-over advice from economists, plus tips on how to "juice up your portfolio," all the usual stuff—hey, sit back, kick up your heels, and enjoy the read.[55]

At the end of the day, this cacophony of hollow advice from all corners serves only to aggravate the difficulty we have in making considered choices from among the soaring number of funds being tossed at us—in 2005–2006 alone, over 600 brand-new funds in a bewildering variety of flavors came onto the market.[56] Set adrift by employers who had stripped away our retirement security, then burned in the bubble, and now desperately in need of direction, we have turned for guidance to professional advisers, and particularly to major brokerage firms, such as Merrill Lynch, Schwab, and Edward Jones. People don't want to read prospectuses (the information is too dense or too late)[57] or to make the choices (there are so many, where to start?). And so we go to a broker or planner to have it explained to us, for the choices to be winnowed, to get some relief from the seemingly overwhelming burden. And it *is* overwhelming— particularly if you work eight-plus hours a day, have a family to tend to, and maybe even enjoy some leisure activities. When, pray tell, does one have time to become an investment expert? When does one have time even to begin to analyze all the fund literature?

For all these reasons, the funds' ability to sell direct to the public has largely dried up, with the result that the major retailers now have a choke hold on the industry. A registered representative at a brokerage firm cannot keep abreast of more than 20 to 30 funds, so management prunes the list for him or her. Which funds will survive the cuts? The fund sponsors were soon told that, to stay in the game, to reach the public, they would have to pay. As we will see in Chapter 8, there has been, in fact, a river of big money—some legal, some not—coursing through every vein in the industry, which, like the River Styx, is invisible to the unsuspecting eye.

Like the Styx, it leads to no good. Those brokers and other retailers to whom investors have turned are but the last link in the extended chain of people and dollars by which the larger fund sponsors try to gain preferred shelf space for the myriad products flowing from their drawing boards—products that are then assigned to teams of managers of often indifferent experience. Indeed, marketing expenses may exceed all the expenses combined of managing and administering a family of mutual funds.

It's an intricate, complex picture, and we need to step back from Main Street investors in order to grasp the larger dimensions of an industry that is wildly profitable but ethically has lost its way. The root of the problem is that deep conflict of interest, one that has been there from day one but has grown more acute over the years: Is the public's bottom line suffering as the industry relentlessly pursues its own?

Are You a Patient Investor?

Try this quick test.[58]

1. A bat and a ball cost $1.10 in total. The bat costs a dollar more than the ball. How much does the ball cost?
2. If it takes five machines five minutes to make five widgets, how long would it take 100 machines to make 100 widgets?
3. In a lake, there is a patch of lily pads. Every day, the patch doubles in size. If it takes 48 days for the patch to cover the entire lake, how long would it take for the patch to cover half the lake?

Answers

1. The ball costs five cents. The bat costs $1 more, or $1.05.
2. It takes five minutes. If five machines make five widgets in five minutes, then effectively five machine-minutes are required for each widget. Making 100 widgets with 100 machines will also require five minutes.
3. It would take 47 days for the patch of lily pads to cover half the lake. If 100 percent of the lake is covered on day 48 after doubling in size that day, then it must have covered 50 percent of the lake on day 47.

Chapter 7

The Industrialization of Mutual Funds

In 1969, Joe McGinnis's *The Selling of the President 1968* was published.[1] His expose about the 1968 Nixon campaign shocked our innocent spirits, because it revealed that presidential candidates were being marketed like soap. We have long since grown accustomed to the idea that commercialism runs the show in politics, but what about mutual funds—those repositories of 401(k) (read retirement) monies and savings? Oh, we know, for sure, that Franklin Templeton, Fidelity, Alliance Bernstein, and so on are in it for the money. But I suspect that when we invest in a fund we harbor the conceit that it exists because it might be useful—advantageous—to us. That fund will be different, and distinct from the next; otherwise, why would it exist? And when we seek advice, either from a fund family or from an adviser, such as Schwab or Merrill, at the moment we step into our broker's office we are hearing what is meant to be good for us, right? They're really thinking about what we need, how best to serve us.

That is what the advertisements suggest—some kindly gent, old enough to know a little something and to have seen it all, but not too on in years to have lost his nerve, guiding us through the thicket of financial confusion to the very fund that was intended for us, personally, all along. Television commercials offer images of people achieving their retirement dreams, of sending their children off to college. These visuals are powerful and they assure us that the fund families or advisers care about us. Their goal is to help us realize the full potential that investing can provide for our future.

Wake up—that's not what's happening. In truth, the mutual fund industry has become wholly commercialized. It is driven by huge corporations, each bent on selling as many different products as possible, to maximize their market share. The funds themselves are mostly as distinct as various brands of detergent.

The total assets of stock funds have grown from $250 billion in 1990 to over 20 times that today, almost $6 trillion.[2] And as the industry grew, there has been a consolidation at the top. The top five complexes now account for 38 percent of all mutual fund assets.[3] Each of the majors, Fidelity, Black Rock, American Funds, and Vanguard, manages in one pocket or another about $1 trillion. A number of others, such as Legg Mason, JPMorgan, T. Rowe Price, and Franklin Resources, have hundreds of billions under management. Legg Mason has acquired the funds previously managed by Citigroup. Black Rock now manages the funds that had been run by Merrill Lynch and is looking for more deals overseas.[4]

Bigger is better . . . for the industry. As they grow in size, however, these fund complexes become more removed from you, the investor, more dependent on seeing their funds as standardized products reliant on the tools of mass marketing that had so shocked us on reading about the 1968 presidential election. None of these so-called advances in the industry were conceived for your benefit.

We saw earlier that for some serious value funds there are three words, a mantra written in capital letters, that define the group:

Margin of Safety

The future is inherently uncertain, and to avoid significant losses, these managers insist on buying stocks at a discount from the estimated value of the business. Theirs is a nice concept, but they're a tiny part of the industry, one likely to appeal only to the tiny segment of the public ready to think long-term. It is clearly not something on which to build a megabusiness.

For essentially all other funds, particularly those like American Funds, Black Rock, or Fidelity, that are already large and bent on growing larger, the defining three words would be:

Economy of Scale

The very first mutual fund, Massachusetts Investors Trust, had soon recognized that, as the fund grew, revenues were outpacing expenses. And so the trustees, good fiduciaries that they were, drove their fees down, and then down again, as the fund gained size. But that is not a model that would appeal to fund executives today, seeking as they do to capitalize on the industry's explosive expansion.

How the Marketing of Mutual Funds Came to Look like Soap

Think of Unilever, the soap company. It has some products the public has known for a long time, and then others that, with good marketing—capitalizing on strong brands—we begin to see that we need. How about an air freshener? Hmmm, Grandma never bought one, but maybe we'll put one in the guest bath. Mutual funds now operate much like Unilever. The fund complexes are not simply satisfying our requirements; they are creating them—products with consistent standards, and recognizable brands that provide the buyer with a sense of comfort—all of which is reinforced by heavy investments in marketing and advertising, plus support for the retailers who are the critical link in reaching the public. Which fund should you buy within the family of funds? It doesn't really matter to the company; that's why they continually add new products, whether distinct from one another or not.

Sound like soap? I work in Manhattan, where supermarkets are small and the chains parcel out shelf space jealously, giving to any one brand only some of the stock-keeping units (SKUs) that the suppliers would like to put there. But even in Manhattan, in an Upper West Side market, I found 12 varieties of Dove soap:

> Calming night, energy glow, cool moisture, exfoliating, sensitive skin, nutrium, white, beauty bar, pink-rosa, silkening moisture, unscented, and fresh reviving.

Not only are we given the option of different kinds of soap, but there are also different sizes to choose from, and we can get our soap in solid or liquid form. The more options, the greater opportunity for the soap company to capture the maximum shelf space and visibility. These are old tricks, and for Dove it works. (I learned about SKUs in an earlier incarnation, when I was president of a major supermarket chain. Without us, Unilever could eat their soap, but of course no one had to spell that out. The suppliers knew darn well that if they wanted better, more visible shelf space, it came with a price tag, mostly in the form of price promotions, but sometimes as trips to nice conferences in the Bahamas, flying in their private jets.)

Now let's turn our attention to mutual funds, specifically the large-cap growth funds that Fidelity has produced. According to Morningstar's analysis, there are 24 in all. As you will see, they are designed to capture lots of shelf space. Fidelity knows full well that no broker will stock them all, but that's okay. Any retail adviser, such as Schwab or Smith Barney, will find at least some Fidelity large-cap growth funds to feature:

> Advisor Consumer Discretionary, Advisor Diversified Stock, Advisor Dynamic Cap Appreciation, Advisor Equity Growth, Advisor Fifty A, Advisor Growth Opportunity, Advisor Large Cap I, Advisor New Insights, Advisor Strategic Growth, Asset Manager 85%, Blue Chip Growth, Capital Appreciation, Contrafund, Export and Multinational, Fifty, Growth Company, Independence, Large Cap Growth, Large Cap Stock, Magellan, Nasdaq Composite Index, OTC, Select Consumer Discretionary, and Select Leisure.

The Fidelity Advisor funds differ from some of their look-alikes (e.g., Advisor Fifty vs. Fifty) because they have the front-end sales charges the brokers feed off (no load, no broker, because there's nothing in it for them). Even allowing for the inevitable duplication created to capture retail shelf space, however, one senses a crisis of imagination in the design of these products—soaps and funds alike. Has anyone ever said about Dove, "No, I don't think 'beauty bar' or 'silkening moisture' would be right for me, but yes, give me the 'sensitive skin,' please"? Do you jump to buy a Fidelity Independence fund because you know that it will be better over the long term than the Advisor New Insights fund? Soap and funds alike, the labels are marketing constructs, devoid of substance, no matter how you shake them. It can't be helped. The basic idea of soap is to get clean. The point of investing is to grow assets within reasonable limits of risk. Neither is all that complicated. To maintain and grow market share, to capture those economies of scale, Unilever has expansive product lines. I doubt the company bothers to keep a running count of the total number of SKUs in all its warehouses.

So, too, with Fidelity, operating in a $6 trillion stock fund market, one that is growing faster, and with better profit margins, than soap. But the labels are no more meaningful than the one for "silkening moisture." The Advisor Fifty fund would seem to have a distinct pedigree. It limits its portfolio to 50 stocks instead of the more typical 150 to 200, which suggests that because the manager will exercise care to select a choice portfolio, the fund will enjoy very low portfolio turnover rates. That's a sensible assumption, and it's what we saw in the value funds examined in Chapter 2. Alas, even when Fidelity has a good idea, it is overwhelmed by the pressures of marketing. True, there were only 46 stocks in the fund, but the annual turnover rate was an absurd 226 percent, meaning that those "carefully picked" stocks came and went on average about every five months, all at great cost to investors. The only plausible explanation is that Fidelity's need to stay trendy, and thus marketable, overcame its supposed buy-and-hold strategy, turning a fund seemingly built for patient investors into yet one more version of the latest in soap. According to Morningstar, the heavy trading had, *after taxes*, reduced the five-year average annual returns of the Advisor Fifty fund by about one-fourth—from a nominal 8.64 percent to a mediocre 6.61 percent.[5]

As much as we may lament what has happened to soap (or politics), managing money was supposed to be different. It's a profession, for one thing. If Terri doesn't like the "beauty bar," she'll know soon enough, and she's out only a buck or so. With a mutual fund, the investment is in the thousands of dollars, and the choice between one fund and the next can make a big difference in people's ability to retire comfortably, send children to college, or pursue other dreams. The other key distinction, of course, is that Terri won't know for years to come whether her hopes for retirement are likely to be realized.

Much like other industrial companies, Fidelity moves managers around. With soap, Terri won't care. If the guy running "calming night" is transferred to "beauty bar," who would even know? At mutual funds, however, the managers matter a whole lot; otherwise, Terri might as well have bought a low-cost index fund and dispensed with those actively managed Fidelity funds altogether. Did Terri know that the talented manager at the Independence fund was shifted to a larger fund elsewhere in 2006, and that according to a Morningstar analyst his replacement, Bob Bertelson, had posted "an extremely poor" record in his prior managerial assignment?[6] For Fidelity, of course, it was just a normal part of managing a $1 trillion enterprise, in this case moving a good manager to a larger account. Sadly, the 2006 annual shareholder report of the Independence fund casually mentioned the change in managers only in a *footnote* to a discussion of the year's performance; the chairman's letter to shareholders made no reference either to him or to his history. Perhaps Bertelson, too, will shortly move on; he has invested in the fund between $100,000 and $500,000, for which Morningstar gives the fund "no credit for manager investment."[7] I assume the fund's board of directors was satisfied with all this; but then again, they may have failed to study the matter carefully, given that they sit on over 300 other boards at Fidelity.[8]

Fidelity is a marketing company, not an investment company. As I write, in 2007, Fidelity, faced with declining market share and a very mixed performance of its funds, has hired more analysts, so that overall it appears to have roughly one analyst for every two funds. It has also switched to teams of managers, much like the American Funds group. Always sensitive to those economies of scale, however—and thus eager to reduce costs—it has begun outsourcing to India, not just back-office support, but also some of the research function.[9] (The cost savings for analysts run on the order of 80 percent.) Those analysts in Bangalore may have great computer skills, but I doubt that they make many personal visits to companies whose stocks are in the funds' portfolios. And just as Unilever has diversified its revenue base, so, too, has Fidelity. It now operates the biggest brokerage firm in the United States, as well as a bank. Your mutual fund is obviously not as important as you might have thought—at least not to Fidelity.[10]

Franklin Resources—A Study
in Economies of Scale

The Fidelity parent company, FMR Corporation, is privately owned, but Franklin Resources is publicly owned; of the publicly traded management companies, Franklin is the one with the largest market value. Paul Samuelson, the Nobel economist, who knew that management companies were a better bet than their funds, would have liked Franklin. It operates some high-profile funds, including the Franklin, Templeton, and Mutual groups; the total assets under management are $550 billion—equivalent to a $16,000 investment for every man, woman, and child living in California. Over the 10 years ended February 2007, the stock price quadrupled. With a market capitalization of $30 billion, the stock is priced at five times its book value, but after deducting from book value the company's intangible assets and the bundle of excess cash, it is priced at a stunning 20+ times net *operating* assets. This means that investors are putting a huge premium on Franklin's ability to fend off competition and to maintain its growth. Over the five-year period ending in 2006, Franklin's revenues doubled to $5 billion—not too shabby, but as those economies of scale kicked in, the operating income more than tripled, to $1.6 billion. Wall Street has bid up Franklin's stock for very good reason.

This growth in revenues and profits reflects an intense focus at Franklin on marketing and distribution, the outlays for which, in 2005–2006, exceeded all the various expenditures for management of the funds. To put it bluntly, if you happen to be an investor in a Franklin fund, they spent far more money to hook you than they did taking care of your money once you were on board. Not surprisingly, an industry veteran describes Franklin as a "sales organization—they're really good at it. The sales and marketing people are the most important people there; they're different from investing folks." Another expert went even further. Franklin's fund managers are *not* important to the organization, he said. Thus, they're "paid less than the marketing guys."

Because this business is not capital intensive, cash just piles up at Franklin. Together with investment securities, the cash totaled roughly $4 billion, or about four times the $1 billion in net tangible assets needed to operate the business. The cash hoard would have been higher still, except that the company spent almost $1 billion in fiscal 2006 to repurchase shares of its outstanding stock.

The entire industry is insanely profitable. While Franklin's stock price was quadrupling, its peer group was doing even better.[11] As for passing on those economies of scale to investors in the Franklin family of funds . . . fugget about it. Remember that conflict of interest between duties to the shareholders of the funds and those of the management company? From 2002 to 2006, the assets under management at Franklin roughly doubled, and so did the revenues from management fees and other charges, such as distribution and servicing fees.[12] (A fund investor should not overlook those "other" fees, which at Franklin are a full 40 percent of the total.) Even as the assets doubled, the employee head count rose less than 20 percent, a telltale sign of why Franklin seeks growth. The economies, however, were kept for the shareholders of Franklin, rather than passed through to the investors in the funds paying the fees that flow through to the management company and its very different shareholders.

In 1996, Franklin purchased the Mutual group of funds. Mutual back then was a case study in the inherent profitability of the business. Because it had essentially no marketing costs, its operating profit was 85 percent, thus boosting its cash flows.★ Franklin paid a full price—10 times cash flow—and one that made sense only to a buyer intent on growing the assets.

Michael Price, who unloaded Mutual onto Franklin, regards the industry today as a "marketing machine," adding that while the advertising and marketing dollars could be "turned off in a blink," the sponsors are reluctant to do so; operating margins would soar, and then so, too, would pressures to reduce fees.

★Like other fund complexes, Franklin bloats its reported revenue by including ancillary fees, such as underwriting and distribution, the effect of which is to drive the reported operating margin down to a "respectable" 30 to 32 percent, rather than an otherwise 50 percent or so that would create pressure to reduce management fees. It's a way, as one observer said, "to blow smoke in the eyes of the SEC and the analysts," and to keep the boards of the funds happy, lest they suggest fee reductions.

The key, Price added, is to think of a fund "as a product, not someone's savings."[13] Seen as a product, the business becomes less personal, which makes it easier then to accumulate assets relentlessly, without having to worry about Terri and Rick. Other industry veterans strike the same note. Tim Melvin, a Maryland broker, was blunt, saying the industry is a "marketing machine . . . that just preys on" the investor.[14] Indeed, Franklin was one of the major groups guilty of those market-timing abuses, which, in substance, allowed some big clients to steal from everyone else in the funds.

Soaps are a product; no one will be surprised when "cool moisture" is no longer on the shelf. But mutual funds come and go at a pace that perhaps exceeds even soaps. Hundreds of new funds are born each year; and during the five years (2002-2006), an astonishing 28 percent of all general equity funds closed their doors or were merged into others.[15] Caveat emptor: If a fund family's overall performance record looks really good, take a fresh look—the ones with a poor scent likely have been taken off the shelf. Dead product performance does not get reported or reflected in the overall family performance records.

Industrialization

For a fund complex, it is no longer practical to scrutinize the universe of stocks for the rare few issues that would meet the stringent standards of a value investor. That would require the sort of individual attention to product that would not be in keeping with an assembly line. As manufacturers, fund complexes are more concerned with making sure their products achieve a "style consistency," as the managers like to say, so that a corporate 401(k) plan consultant, a broker, or a financial adviser will know precisely what the fund is about. "Silkening moisture" has got to smell like silkening moisture. The manager of, say, a small-cap growth fund must not allow it to suffer "style drift." The broker—the institutional customer, that is—does not want two funds in the same style box. The manager must, therefore, *absolutely must*, stay fully invested within that box, one of the nine such "styles" created by Morningstar that have become the industry standard. These nine styles are usually visualized in the schematic shown in Table 7.1.

Table 7.1   Mutual Fund Styles

	Value	Blend	Growth
Large–Cap			
Mid–Cap			
Small–Cap			

In addition to the nine styles—large-cap value, small-cap growth, and so on—there are various industrial and global "sectors," so that a major fund family will also offer technology, financial services, real estate, international, energy, utility, and health care funds. The fund family will then fragment these sectors by creating, say, a small-cap international fund. It truly does resemble Unilever grappling with Procter & Gamble for shelf space.

Retailers, That's Where the Money Is

Underlying the pressure to create these distinct, consistent products have been several dramatic changes in the industry, primarily the fact that most individual investors, and almost all corporate 401(k)-style sponsors, have turned to consultants, planners, and brokers—one form of adviser or another—to create the overly diversified portfolios that are the order of the day. Direct sales from funds to the public are now a minor factor. These advisers then allocate assets according to fairly rigid sets of criteria, parceling out the dollars, first between debt and equity securities, then among the styles, plus several of the various sectors. It simply would not do for the manager of that small-cap growth fund, seeing that growth stocks had become pricey, to put a significant part of the fund into value stocks or cash. That is not his role. It's up to the consultant to decide how much to allocate to energy or Malaysia, value or large-cap stocks, and if the six or 10 managers in his portfolio go off their designated tracks, his consultancy will have become meaningless, because his allocations will have been rendered meaningless.

The fund families are keenly aware that an overwhelming majority of the public—70 to 80 percent of those who find their funds outside of plans, such as 401(k)s sponsored by their employer[16]—rely on these advisers. If Terri decides to take money out of her savings account to buy shares of a mutual fund, it's more than likely she will call the local office of, say, Merrill Lynch or Schwab. The Janus family of funds, for example, gathers only 5 percent of its total sales directly from the public, Third Avenue only 10 percent.[17] Catching the trend, the American Century group recently announced plans to switch some quite visible funds from no-load to the load lineup, thus increasing the overall number of its load funds from 26 to 39.[18] For fund managers, these brokers and other advisers have become the true customer, the ones on whom attention and money is lavished.

Alas, Warren Buffett doesn't stay awake at night wondering if he needs to put more money into large-cap growth stocks, and neither should Terri and Rick, who are trying to sock away something so their daughter can go to college. They want it to be safe, and over time to grow. Whether it's in mid-cap or large-cap stocks is of no concern to them or, for that matter, to the college. Those nine styles are a marketing construct, one that enables a Fidelity to market a product the broker can then use as a building block to rearrange a client's chips every several months from one style to another.

The Death of Security Analysis

This asset allocation is all the rage these days. What does large-cap growth mean? Typical translation: stocks of large companies with high price-earnings ratios. But so what? What is there about this group that will allow them to move in sync, and thus make a useful counterweight to small-cap value or mid-cap blend?

In fact, it's a myth. There is no substance to this concept of a large-cap growth fund. Look at the Fidelity group, and you'll soon see that their performances are all over the lot.

Let's return to the Fidelity Advisor Fifty, a large-cap growth fund. The portfolio contains companies with large market capitalizations and, to satisfy the growth requirement, stocks with high ratios of market price to earnings or to book value. Given, say, their high price-earnings ratios, one might think that some of the stocks are just expensive. In fact, some of the stocks don't seem like a good fit in a growth stock fund or, indeed, as complements to one another. Since when did beer become a growth business or, for that matter, Hertz, an auto leasing company?* No matter, Morningstar's data show that it was quite comfortable desig-nating the Advisor Fifty fund as large-cap growth.

Will a broker who uses this fund as one of his eight or 10 choices have had time to examine the portfolio and to recognize that beer and auto leasing are part of the mix? Probably not. According to a 2006 study by Financial Research Corporation (FRC), very little effort is spent by financial advisers on analyzing stocks either individually or within a fund.[19] They're reading computer selection screens focused on the funds' three- to five-year performance records, not financial state-ments of the companies within those funds. Bottom line: It's the com-puters and the benchmarks that define growth stocks, not analysts trying to find companies with strong market positions, shrewd managements, and shareholder-friendly boards.

Few people in this business seem to be using their brains. When Morningstar refashioned its rating system in 2002, it commented that it had moved away from seeing funds as "stand-alone" investments. Instead, given the increased emphasis in the marketplace on the role of funds as components in a portfolio of funds (like one more ingredient in a pie), it had now become "important that funds within a particular rating group be *valid substitutes for one another.*"[20] (Italics added) Valid substi-tutes? How can they find a substitute for a top-flight manager? The answer, of course, is that the choice of a manager is not that important any longer.

Morningstar has more than 60 different rating categories from which a retail adviser can choose, and the fund sponsors are busy filling many, if not all, of them.[21] The particular companies within a category, or within a fund, are just details; a fund manager's job is to track the benchmark . . . period.

---

*A high price-earnings ratio may also suggest that the earnings are temporarily depressed, so that at almost any price, the P/E ratio will be high; but the com-puter won't know that. See generally, the author's *Sense and Nonsense in Corporate Finance* (Reading, MA: Addison-Wesley, 1991), ch. 10.

The term "stand-alone" was an artfully crafted reference to the days, now past, when the goal of a fund was simply to make money and to outperform the market as a whole. Two or three funds were commonly thought to be the right number (perhaps a couple of stock funds, plus a bond fund); taken together, they would provide all the diversification one needed. And with the responsibility for deciding when to invest in energy or consumer durables resting with the funds, investors had no need for a costly retail adviser to manage the managers.

I suppose it was inevitable, but as with the fund sponsors, we see the same absence of serious analysis at the retail level. More than half the financial advisers who responded to a FRC study used portfolio optimization systems or other software to make their asset class decisions.[22] These easy-to-use programs are basically mathematical models that compute the best combination of asset classes in order to maximize the "risk-adjusted returns" and to compare how one portfolio might fare against another. They may or may not take a client's age, time to retirement, and so on into consideration. These models are based on rear-window studies that assume a consistency in market fundamentals, as if nothing radical will ever happen.[23] They push the broker or other adviser more toward the role of a salesperson and further away from anything resembling security analysis. Investing involves math, parsing financial statements, and other quantitative analysis that can often begin with computing power. But investing *wisely* also involves a great deal of experience and judgment that software programs are unable to provide. The broker has moved yet another step away from providing a client like Terri with the personalized advice she expected. Unfortunately, however, the fat booklet then given to Terri suggests that this portfolio has been crafted personally, just for her.★

Who needs top-notch managers when there's a benchmark to follow? It's a system that permits the fund families to create thousands of

---

★Customers are also being misled by the increasingly popular separately managed accounts (SMAs). They suggest that "you're getting something special, just for you." In fact, it's typically the brokerage firm that has designed the portfolio, relieving the broker of the burden. Suzanne McGee, "Different Toppings, Same Scoop," *Barron's*, February 19, 2007, 39.

products—over 600 new stock funds were born in the years 2005–2006★—run by at best modestly skilled, modestly paid teams. Stars might leave to form a hedge fund or, as happened at Mutual Beacon in 2005, a new mutual fund, taking investors and press notices with them. The teams, however, are virtually anonymous; so, if two or three people were to leave a management team this year, no one would notice. Indeed, it happens all the time.[24]

All this product proliferation and style consistency reflect, of course, the enhanced role of the retail advisers. Our Advisor Class shares, T. Rowe Price announced in January 2006, "have been well received by advisors . . . and other intermediaries, demonstrating the appeal of our . . . *consistent style discipline*."[25] (Italics added) That is exactly what you would want if you were buying a car, perhaps, but a mutual fund?

Asset Allocation

Let's take another look at the Mutual group's parent company, Franklin Resources, which published late in 2006 "A Guide to Asset Allocation," which it then advertised in the press. The 14-page brochure made it clear that the "secret to long-term investment success" lay in allocating money across different categories of assets, and set out a full-page table of the performance over time of the various styles and sectors. Using a mechanistic formula, an investor would become diversified across asset classes, thereby reducing "the overall volatility"—meaning reducing the expected (according to a computer) short-term fluctuations relative to a market index.

Not surprisingly, Franklin offers "every major asset class," including funds as specialized as gold, utilities, financial services, real estate, and global health care. Being fully aware that no amateur would know how to allocate money across these categories, Franklin took pains to advise the reader to meet periodically with a financial adviser. Some groups may "grow more quickly than others," Franklin noted, leading them then to recommend what today is the accepted wisdom, that the asset

---

★Even during the roaring 1990s, the annual rate of new funds was only 125. John C. Bogle, "The Mutual Fund Industry 60 Years Later: For Better or Worse?" *Financial Analysts Journal* 61 (2005): table 7.

class that has done well now be reduced as part of a periodic *rebalancing* to "reflect [one's] original allocation." Stated succinctly, the investor should play a market-timing game, betting that what has *not* gone up this year will do better in the next than the ones that had.[26] This is not investing! This isn't even really asset allocation, at least not in any meaningful sense. It is the equivalent of investing with a Ouija board. But since a major fund complex, such as Franklin, cannot pick dozens on dozens of star managers, it is the best they can offer us.

Rebalance My Portfolio . . . You Said What?

Forget what's sensible. The currently hot fashion among retail advisers—those dealing with the public—is to recommend that we, the investors, *rebalance* our portfolios of funds at least once a year, shifting dollars among the various styles and sectors with nary a glance at the fundamentals of price and value. Are good values in stocks currently scarce, as some value managers were saying early in 2007, so that it seemed sensible to keep more in bonds? It doesn't matter; *Business Week*, echoing the common wisdom, would have us rejiggle, even if the proportion of bonds has shifted by a mere 3 percent from the agreed-upon formula, whatever that happens to be.[27] Conversely, suppose that years ago, with skill and a dollop of luck, you had bought shares of an extremely well-positioned, well-managed company, say Microsoft, and for 10 years or so you were content to hold a concentrated investment in Microsoft, watching the earnings grow, relaxing on the beach . . . whatever. *Sorry, that was a mistake.* Stocks are to be selected only in groups and as parts of a designated style. They are treated like checkers on a board, some red, some black, with nothing of substance to distinguish one from another.[28] The Financial Research Corporation study, published in 2006, found retail advisers had been rebalancing along the following lines:

- Increased international allocations, including emerging markets.
- Shifted to large-cap equities and out of mid- and small-cap equities.
- Shifted to a greater emphasis on growth stocks.

The most frequently cited reason for the changes was the retail firm's expectations about where the market was headed, as if they knew.[29]

(Happily, the study also showed that funds had become more sensitive to expense ratios, reflecting the impact of low-cost index funds and of watch-dogs like Morningstar.[30])

Martin Whitman, the manager of the successful Third Avenue Value Fund, reports that time and again, his fund is told that having performed well in the preceding year, various institutional investors will now take money away from the fund, so as to rebalance the overall portfolio between one style and another; otherwise his fund would exceed its allotted share. In effect, the fund is punished for having performed well. It is, as he said, a model for mediocrity.[31]

Worse yet, this mechanical process ignores the alternative model, the one followed by Whitman, Buffett, and other distinguished investors, to sell only stocks that have gotten too pricey *relative to their business funda-mentals*, as distinct from merely having gone up a lot. (Even though Toy-ota, for example, had gone up a great deal over the years, Whitman con-tinued to hold it, because the fundamentals of price and value remained sound.) The conclusion is painfully obvious: Since a truly able manager will sell those pricey stocks for us, we don't have to "rebalance," i.e., sell his fund! That is why we hired him in the first place.

Whitman smiled, adding that the adviser "has to justify his fee"— whatever the outcome for the client. The adviser is in competition with more than 600,000 others; he cannot just sit there, from one year to the next, telling his clients not to do anything.[32] Most brokers, as well as planners, are working these days not for commissions on buy-sell trans-actions, but rather for an annual fee—perhaps a fixed dollar fee but often one calculated at, say, 1 percent of the account's value. Sometimes called wrap accounts, they place brokers under obvious pressure to do *some-thing*. Count on it—they are not going to say, "Hey, the managers of those three funds of yours are first-rate; just relax and we'll talk again next year." That may be good tax and financial advice, but Rick and Terri will eventually ask themselves, if these funds are so good, who needs the broker?

That is just one of the self-serving secrets underlying much of the retail market advice. In the late 1990s, brokers and advisers, victims of their lackadaisical approach to stock analysis, neglected to tell their cli-ents (customers) to rebalance or sell their tech stocks or tech funds—a classic bubble at least as clear as the real estate bubble of more recent vintage. These folks don't want to be caught napping the next time around. Their current advice: Underweight, as they like to say on Wall Street, whatever has gone up, whenever we have experienced what David Swensen, who has successfully run the Yale endowment for over 20 years, calls a period of "excessive volatility"[33]—as if we would surely recognize one.* Swensen practices what he preaches, checking the Yale endowment every trading day to see if the asset classes have deviated from their target allocation. Swensen devotes page after page of a recent book to explaining why rebalancing "represents supremely rational behavior," using the market crash to make his point. And then 20 pages further on, as if to repent, he praises the notable Philip Fisher for having encouraged investors to pick an adviser who searches for good companies and then lets the profits run.[34] (Perhaps Swensen, while checking his asset allocation every day, doesn't actually act on it quite so frequently.)

A majority of investors hold mutual funds with an eye to retirement,[35] meaning that their funds should be managed with a patient, long-term perspective, ignoring the inevitable fluctuations. No one knows when the market will hit periodic peaks and bottoms. Why move dollars from here to there, and a short while later back again? Wholly apart from taxes, there are significant costs incurred. No matter; as John Maynard Keynes said, "[L]ife is not long enough; human nature desires quick results, [and] there is a peculiar zest in making money quickly." None of us likes to admit that we really, *but really*, don't know the market direction. Our psyche abhors the unsettling passivity of leaving things as they are. We need a story, and given the inherent ambiguity of how to invest, we need the social validation of someone telling us what to do.

Smith Barney certainly got the message. In a brochure distributed to its brokers, it asked "Is It Time to Rebalance?" and then immediately answered its own question, saying, "It's a good time to rebalance your clients' portfolios." It declares that "regular rebalancing can help."[36] Alas, little could be more useless than the admonition that a technique "can help." Of course it can. It can also hurt. Either could be said of a slot

---

*Even if volatility has been low, as it was in 2005, that may change, so . . . rebalance! Paul J. Lim, "Ignore the Ups and Downs at Your Peril," *New York Times,* February 5, 2006, sec. 3, 8.

machine as well. Short of a certainty or at least a strong probability about the eventual outcome, such advice leads more toward speculation and less toward prudent long-term investing. Yes, it is possible to make money speculating, but it's time-consuming, daily if not hourly work. It's expensive, most assuredly beyond the ken of most people, particularly those of us who are occupied in careers. It is also highly risky, and really, how many of us can do what George Soros has done without losing it all? Those who have not just the skills but the temperament as well are few and far between. At the end of the day, it is doubtful whether Smith Barney and other brokers and advisers are contributing anything at all beyond some personal attention, mostly computer generated. A quite systematic study by several B-school people concluded that while brokerage customers pay substantially higher fees, they end up getting funds with *lower* risk-adjusted returns than funds sold directly to the public.[37]

Not even the staid *New York Times* is a voice of quiet sanity. One week the *Times*, like *BusinessWeek*, hits the "rebalance" key,[38] and another week it urges even readers who have found the haven of index fund investing to *do something*—buy a country fund or whatever to "turbocharge" the index.[39]★

Warren Buffett remarked recently to a group of B-school students that (1) people get convinced they have to be doing something in investing at all times, (2) chicken tracks in the past don't predict where chicken tracks will go next, and (3) the market is there to serve you and not to instruct you.[40] In a sense, Buffett was simply paraphrasing Mark Twain, who, in *Pudd'nhead Wilson* (1894), wrote:

> Behold, the fool saith, "Put not all thine eggs in the one basket"—
> which is a manner of saying, "Scatter your money and your attention"; but the wise man saith, "Put all your eggs in the one basket and . . . watch that basket."

Most funds do scatter their attention, watching too many eggs, and constantly flipping some eggs out, putting others in. Just as the consultants,

---

★There has been a similar proliferation of exchange-traded funds (ETFs), which began as classic index funds. Now there are some 700 varieties, and the heavy trading in them soon overwhelmed the concept of low-cost diversification. John Authers, "Winning Concept's Meteoric Rise," *Financial Times*, January 23, 2007, 8.

brokers, and the like are flipping the dozen or so funds in their portfolios. Focused on the movement of markets, measured over the shortest of increments, they are trying just to match their "risk-adjusted" benchmarks, and perhaps to outperform them by a few basis points (a basis point is 1/100th of a percentage point). The risk they have in mind, however, is the short-term fluctuation of stock prices, not the *business* risk that one of their portfolio companies will do something dumb, commit an accounting fraud, or fail to keep its products current, and thus lose value over an enduring period. The risk-adjusted yardstick is measurable and fits neatly into their computers, unlike business risk, which requires digging into annual reports, talking to people in the industry, and the like. In any event, sensible or not, it's how they (the managers and brokers) are measured, so they ignore such yardsticks at their peril.

Actually, the fund is not a basket; it's a turnstile. It's widely agreed, as Kevin Laughlin of the Vanguard group said to me, that the "trick" is to keep a fund's largest holdings within a few basis points of the index's weighting, to be sure of staying in the ballpark, then to "churn" around that core in an effort to add "value," meaning a few basis points better than the index.[41] Years ago, when there was not the same manic focus on benchmarks, the churn was far lower. In the mid-1960s, for example, the average annual turnover was 17 percent, meaning that funds kept stocks on average for six years.

The cost of living in that turnstile—the cost of trading in and out of stocks—is not broken out for the investor. Fund managers, therefore, are typically indifferent to the tax burden on investors of what is often short-term trading. "It's irrelevant" to the managers, though not to investors, as one well-placed observer said.[42]

A Witch's Brew

It is hoped this discussion of rebalancing makes the point, perhaps obvious by now, that we have the makings of a witch's brew, a compound made up of 90 million fund investors, few of whom have the skills, much less the time, for the analysis of a business, its prospects, its financial underpinnings—investors who have poured roughly $6 trillion into equity funds to be managed by intermediaries, large numbers of whom

are little more than pen pushers in financial conglomerates whose primary concern is to gather those assets, rather than to manage them well,
bureaucrats who have learned through experience that their personal
success will be measured by how well they stay abreast of the market
trends, rather than by a deep, abiding sense of trusteeship. It is a model
that works well for the retail advisers, works well for the fund companies, works well for Morningstar and the other rating services that fashioned the model, and works well for the journalists always looking for
the next new thing . . . everyone, I guess, except for the forgotten thee
and me.

Mutual funds are *not* soap. Funds are a lifeline to the golden years;
they are a reflection of the trust we have in the people who run them,
and of our hope that the managers will grasp the human aspirations that
are at stake. Selling them like soap is indecent.

About Those Benchmarks . . .

While it might not have any substance, a fund's designation as mid-cap
blend matters a great deal in the world in which we live. The fund will
be measured in the marketplace not by how much it gained in absolute
dollars over the years, nor even by whether it did better or worse than
the market as a whole, say the S&P 500. Instead, it will be compared
with a benchmark of other funds like it. The most visible of these benchmarks is the Morningstar system, which awards one to five stars, depending on the style or sector. Is the manager perhaps one whom I can trust
for some years to come? Don't ask; as Morningstar acknowledges, the
ratings are myopic, weighted toward the near-term results.

The FPA Capital Fund, for example, one of the top-notch Goldfarb
10 discussed earlier, received early in 2007 a meager two-star rating. It had
done quite poorly in 2006 relative to its small-cap value benchmark, but
nonetheless, it had outperformed the S&P 500 over five years by an average of 6 percent *per year*, and over 10 years by 5 percent a year. No doubt,
the fact that the fund's returns had been more volatile than those of the
benchmark hurt its ratings.[43] For the two years 2005–2006, it had produced average returns of 11 percent a year, but while it had outperformed
its Morningstar category by 11 percent in 2005, it had underperformed

the category by an equal amount the following year. It's that damn tracking error again. In fact, the fund manager, Bob Rodriguez, has said time and again that his investment horizon is three to five years, but those computer programs obsess about the recent numbers and tend to choke on insights like Rodriguez's.★ So what the world sees are those two stars, and as Bill Nygren of the Oakmark group said to me, the intermediaries are, in turn, measured by their benchmark deviation, not by whether they made or lost money.[44] He added that for a fund with only two stars, invitations to appear on CNN and elsewhere will dry up.

Some of the Morningstar ratings are equally absurd in the other direction. Consider the recent five stars awarded the Jacob Internet fund, which the reader may remember as having lost over 90 percent of its value when the bubble of the late 1990s collapsed. As the early years of this century rolled off the star-rating calculus, however, the fund's score no longer reflects its roller-coaster history. Credit at least a Morningstar analyst with having simultaneously reported that this is a fund "to avoid," noting the fact that the same "unimpressive [sic] manager" is still there.[45]

Whatever its true merits, this system of benchmarks and stars serves an important marketing function for the fund families. Fidelity has hundreds of funds, and even T. Rowe Price almost one hundred. Any such family will always have several funds with five-star ratings, which can then be highlighted in ads in the financial media, such as *Barron's* or *Money* magazine. These are institutional ads, designed to burnish the brand name of the fund family in the public eye. The presence of the five-star funds featured in the ads lends an air of quality to the group as a whole. Never mind that as the size of a fund complex grows, it becomes impossible for the group to achieve outstanding performance on average. As we discussed earlier, the universe of stocks in which a fund can achieve a meaningful position shrinks rapidly as the fund increases in size. This is exactly why so many of the value funds discussed in Chapter 2 capped their growth and closed their funds at some point. But for the major fund complexes, bent on asset accumulation, the

---

★In a remarkably prescient speech in June 2007, before the Chicago Society of Financial Analysts, Rodriguez outlined what he saw as a "bubble of massive proportions . . . in the housing market," and how he had increased the cash and equivalents in FPA Capital dramatically. Sorry, the computer still said "two-stars."

pressures are the same as with any mass-marketed product or service. Consistency of style, yes; benchmarking, yes; but as for performance, it need only be "just good enough so that you don't sell."[46] Or, as a director of one of the more visible fund management companies acknowledged, speaking of the industry generally, performance is a small portion of the [management] game.[47]

Once upon a time, Fidelity was a good place to look for creative talent, notably Peter Lynch at the Magellan Fund, but those days are long gone. (Although he was no longer in the kitchen, Lynch continued to appear in consumer advertising. And the fund continued to grow, but the performance fell.) Now, Fidelity simply creates products to cover every need an investor might have, and to maintain style consistency.[48] Fidelity is not alone. Lipper has come up with 50 different equity categories.[49] The fund complexes will fill them all. What kind of soap would you like?

Wrapping Up the Benchmarks

The Sequoia Fund, which was founded in 1970, reports to shareholders its results for the year and for the 10 years past, alongside the comparable results for the Dow Jones Industrials and the Standard & Poor's 500 indexes. Morningstar says that Sequoia is a large-cap blend fund, but Sequoia's reports don't mention that. Sequoia is one of the few major funds that holds an annual shareholders' meeting, and it takes a large banquet room to accommodate those who attend. In 2006, there were about 400 in attendance, including rival money managers who were eager to glean the managers' insights about the stocks in the fund's tightly constructed portfolio. I am confident that no one, but no one, has ever asked the managers how the fund's performance compared with its large-cap blend benchmark, and if someone were to do so, the answer would have been along the lines of, "Gosh, we don't know what our benchmark is." Just as they wouldn't know the *beta* of the fund, meaning the volatility of its stock price relative to the benchmark.

The Sequoia shareholders seem content to know how the fund has done, and how that compares with the stock market generally, for which the Dow Jones Industrials and the S&P 500 are reasonable proxies. (Over the years, the fund has comfortably outperformed both.) All of these indexes have their flaws, which is inevitable. The Dow Jones index is a group of very large, blue-chip stocks—such as Alcoa, Honeywell, Pfizer, and Procter & Gamble—that are not especially trendy and will at times be out of sync with the market as a whole. During the dot-com episode, for example, the blue chips neither rose as high nor fell as deeply as the market generally. The S&P 500 is a better measure of the broad market, containing as it does about 75 percent of the capitalization of all U.S. stocks. But it, too, has faults, which in a sense are the converse of the Dow Jones Industrials', because it can be overly sensitive to whatever does happen to be hot at the moment. The S&P 500 is a market-cap-weighted index, meaning that the index figure we see, say 1,480, is the product of weighting each of the 500 component stocks by its market capitalization. During the frothy years of the late 1990s, therefore, as the tech and media stock prices surged, their impact on the index was excessive. In 1999, for example, the S&P 500 rose 21 percent, even while half of all stocks were falling or failing to rise.[50] Various other benchmarks also suffer from the same tendency to overweight what has gone up recently.

But over time, given the tendency of most stocks to even out, the S&P 500 is a reasonable guide to how Mr. Market has performed. The turnover in the 500 component stocks is small, about 4 percent a year, the result of mergers, spin-offs, and the like. Also, people who buy and hold an S&P 500 index fund have no trading or management costs.

Morningstar and Lipper have tried to do something that is far more bold, even risky, namely to create indexes based not on stocks, but on funds, so as to measure the performance of a fund against the average of its peers *in the same niche*. As we saw, the ratings are based on past performance, with all the pitfalls that entails. For one thing, the past is not prologue. Indeed, Morningstar's five-star-rated funds, the ones investors gravitate toward, have subsequently tended to underperform the market as a whole, and by significant amounts.[51] By 1999, for example, when tech shares had for several years enjoyed stellar performance, 90 percent of the rated tech funds had acquired five-star ratings. Two years later, after the collapse, the average rating for tech stocks had fallen to 2.4 stars. Swensen summarized the results succinctly, saying "Morningstar's record proved perfectly perverse."[52]

Heeding the criticism, Morningstar revamped its rating system, but the inherent limitation of all these systems is the reliance on past performance and computerized measures of risk. Remember, real risk, meaning business risk—such as whether a company will lose market share or stumble when it tries to expand—these issues are a function of the inherent *uncertainty* of the future and are simply not quantifiable, though sometimes a careful investor can at least frame the odds.

Note, too, that the median actively managed mutual fund has all-in costs of about 2.3 percent per year, which includes the cost of trading, though not the sales loads or the tax burden from portfolio turnover.[53] Because of these costs, using the Lipper and Morningstar indexes as benchmarks will make all actively managed funds look far better than they would if compared against a passive index fund. Funds should, and some do, give a side-by-side comparison of their performance with, say, a Morningstar benchmark *plus* the S&P 500. It's the only fair way to go.

Managing by Rote Can Hurt . . . Badly

Managing money by fixating on style boxes and sectors, maintaining the requisite style consistency, doing a copycat rebalancing—all this has stripped away the precept of critical analysis and judgment. And it hurts investors. Charles de Vaulx, the then manager of the First Eagle Global Fund, ignored the styles that were a fetish elsewhere, buying, as he said in 2006, wherever the opportunities lay, whether in small, midsize, or large companies; by a willingness to hold cash whenever "we cannot find enough securities at prices we like"; and by "worrying a lot about what can go wrong."[54] Someone investing for the future by how the style boxes behaved in the past would have missed out on First Eagle Global's performance over the five years from 2002 to 2006, which averaged 20 percent a year.

For most fund families, therefore, the result will be mediocrity; and in times of stress, it might be much worse. Working in a straitjacket, fearful of style drift, fearful of even short-term tracking error (which would preclude the holding of cash), they have abdicated their managerial responsibility, all the while being rewarded handsomely by investors. Investors may think that they are buying topflight talent, experience, and even wisdom. Actually, they are getting a shipwreck in the making. Any mechanical process, followed with statistical rigidity, relying on stock price changes rather than the analysis of an underlying business, can produce seriously unpredictable results, whether the formula is based on riding the recent winners or rebalancing away from them.

Consider the portfolio insurance computer programs of the late 1980s. They were a popular device for minimizing losses by selling stock index futures if and when the market declined by some designated amount. The rationale was that a rapidly falling market would necessarily continue to fall, so that a portfolio manager should act immediately, without hesitation; hence the need for a computer-driven program. The players had forgotten the need for critical reflection, to see what was happening in the real world, outside the stock exchange. Thus, they failed to recognize that with so many of these computer schemes in place, they alone would be enough to overwhelm the market, driving prices down by 22 percent in a single day.

It's literally mindless, this investing for the future based on mechanical formulas, whether asset allocation or more sophisticated formulas such as those used by Long-Term Capital Management. Would a broker have advised a client, at year-end 2001, to rebalance and buy back into the T. Rowe Price Science and Technology Fund, which had fallen so sharply that the client's asset allocation was now out of whack? We hope not. It's true, in 2002 the fund would slightly outperform its category, but that would prove to be small comfort for a second successive loss of over 40 percent.

Will the current fad of asset allocation and rebalancing collapse in some catastrophic losses? Who knows, but thoughtful managers always worry about the bad stuff that can happen. The common tendencies to follow the herd can only exaggerate the losses.[55] Consider international stocks, for example. In 2006, almost $150 billion flowed into international equity funds, more than 10 times the inflows to U.S. funds. These large inflows came on top of a strong showing in 2005, when 77 percent of inflows were channeled overseas. The impact on foreign stock prices was predictable; the Morgan Stanley Capital International (MSCI) Europe, Australasia, Far East (EAFE) index, an index of over 1,000 companies in 21 foreign countries, rose 27 percent just in the year ended October 2006, so that its bargain pricing relative to stocks in the United States was drying up. Reflecting those gains, an index of world equity funds had a banner year, topping out at 25.6 percent for 2006 as a whole.

Rather than chase the trend, the First Eagle Global Fund, mentioned previously, *reduced* its overseas holdings, moving money to U.S. stocks and keeping over 20 percent of its portfolio in cash and bonds. Of its top 10 stocks, four were now U.S. stocks.[56]

The First Eagle fund follows a lonely path, however. Fidelity, in contrast, has over 20 international funds, the largest of which by far is the Diversified International Fund, with assets of $48 billion. Like the First Eagle fund, it is rated five stars by Morningstar. But consider how differently the managers perceived their roles. The Fidelity fund so faithfully tracks its benchmark that it is generally regarded as being closet-indexed.[57] (The statistical measure for benchmark tracking is the R-squared, which for Diversified International is a high 95.) It thus holds no U.S. stocks, and a relatively modest 7 percent in bonds or cash. To catch a little performance here or there, it has been spinning its 300+-stock portfolio at twice the rate of the First Eagle fund (59 percent vs. 29 percent). One of those funds is keenly aware of the risk of loss, while the other, like its peers, has its eyes tuned to a benchmark. We can't peek inside FMR, the Fidelity sponsor, being privately owned. But here is a hint of how well all this is working for the management: The largest FMR shareholders, Ed Johnson and his daughter Abigail, are worth $7 billion and $13 billion, respectively. Abigail is 16th on the *Forbes* list of the 400 richest Americans.

For those eager to learn more about closet-indexing, there's even an index, called the "sheep index," the result of a study that concluded that three-fourths of institutions display conformist behavioral patterns, or a positive sheep value.[58]

What then is the manager of an average fund doing, while spinning a huge portfolio 100 percent or more a year? He's obviously not reading financial statements with the same intense scrutiny as a Whitman or Rodriguez, if indeed he's reading them at all. Instead, he's asking, "Where are small-cap funds headed this year?" It's all about market segments, not even the overall market, and it's certainly not about the strength of the underlying businesses.

This makes me think of. . . Joe McGinnis. Looking back 20 years after writing *The Selling of the President,* McGinnis bemoaned the "surrender of something so sacred . . . to cynical, mercenary (and technologically superior) soldiers of fortune." He added, "It's not what's there that counts; it's what's projected."[59] I can't say it better.

Chapter 8

Through a
Window . . . Darkly

P aul Cabot, an architect of one of the first mutual funds, State
Street Investment Corporation, testified in 1928 before a New
York Stock Exchange committee about the abuses among the
investment trusts of the day. The speech, published in the *Atlantic Monthly,*
summarized his accusations in succinctly damning terms: "(1) dishonesty; (2) inattention and inability; (3) greed."[1] The investment company
industry today is a whole lot healthier, but neither is it squeaky clean.
The inherent conflicts of interest are still there, as are the frailties of
human nature that lead us to temptation . . . with other people's money.
While Cabot's three charges tend to bleed one into the other, we focused
in Chapter 7 on the second of them, what we today might call the industry's indifference and incompetence. Fund families, rather than trying for
superior long-term management, are playing short-term games that will
enable them to gather the assets that will make the managers' personal
profits grow.

Cabot also observed the "infinite number of ways whereby [an] unduly large slice of the spoils [are] kept by the insiders. They may . . . take out the money in the form of expenses or management fees of one sort or another," and their "slices" are "*not clearly set forth*." (Italics added) Sound familiar? As the French say, the more things change, the more they remain the same. The industrialization of manufactured fund products has facilitated explosive growth, such that the suits could amass great wealth. Not content to be merely rich, not content even with milking those economies of scale, far too many of them became, in Cabot's words, greedy and dishonest. Those two charges, greed and dishonesty, are the focus of this chapter.

In the early 1980s, as we saw back in Chapter 5, the federal courts, with the eventual blessings of Congress, opened the way for fund managers to take their management companies public, or to sell them to a bank, insurance company, or other fund families that were themselves already public. For successful entrepreneurs, that is the American way. We don't pass our businesses on to the next generation, as Germans are prone to do. Instead we seek at some point to capitalize that stream of income, cash out, and thus to build an estate and gain the liquidity that will solve estate planning and tax issues. Among the fund groups whose privately owned management companies have been sold in recent years, in whole or in major part, are Acorn, Clipper, Evergreen, Mutual, Pioneer, Royce, Third Avenue, and Tweedy Browne. That's what the game is about, and with $6 trillion just in stock funds, there is a veritable river of fees, commissions, expenses, and other cash flows that will one day, sooner or later, fuel a buyout of the fund sponsor and mark the capstone of a successful career. No wonder investors have seen increased fees and expenses, even as the funds' assets grew.

From $45 billion in 1980, stock funds grew 90 times to $4 trillion in 2004. The industry's revenues—meaning investors' expenses—soared 125 times over those same years, from $288 million to $37 billion.[2] The growth in revenues reflected not just the growth in assets, but a higher rate of fees and expenses. From $4 trillion in 2004, stock fund assets grew again, to almost $6 trillion in 2006, an increase of 50 percent in just two years. Finally, the expense *ratio* began to fall, dropping by about 6 percent in 2005. That was nothing really to write home about; as Morningstar commented, the "slight drop [was] a paltry reward for all the increased economies of scale enjoyed by the fund industry over the [preceding] 15 years."[3]

The industry's press for more fees is a contorted tale, with many twists and turns, as one source of funding dries up and another opens. The fees and so-called expenses take various, often hidden forms. We will go through some of the major avenues pursued by the funds, one by one, and you should read and digest it all slowly, even though the reading may be painful. This is an industry that has gone astray, typically making a mockery of the concept of a free market or fiduciary duty. The management companies take money in many different envelopes, mostly legal but not always so, and too often with inadequate disclosure. The funds they control truly seem simply a fiefdom of which they are the overlords. In addition, we will see the absence of the effective, independent oversight, whether from boards of directors or elsewhere, that is essential in any well-functioning free market when dealing with an industry as complex as this one has become. Take your time; it is, after all, your money.

The First Story behind Those Numbers

Our first tale begins in 1980, when the fund industry, having suffered through a decade of net redemptions in the 1970s (when the stock market was in a long funk), began to pressure the Securities and Exchange Commission (SEC) for help. What the industry wanted seems almost incredible. It wanted to use the assets in the funds themselves—that is, the money belonging to fund investors—to spend on marketing and distribution, meaning to find new investors. In short, the funds wanted to take a portion of your investment to pay for ads in *Money* magazine and the like. The SEC had always been opposed, for obvious reasons. The investors' money was for buying stocks, right? It was fair, of course, to charge them a fee for research and for the salaries of the people who managed the money, because the research presumably benefited them. But if the management companies wanted to advertise at the Super Bowl or on the pages of *Fortune* or the *Wall Street Journal,* let them spend their own dough.

But in the late 1970s, the industry was truly hurting. Indeed, the number of mutual fund accounts had declined from almost 11 million in 1971 to 8.5 million in 1978. And so the SEC, fearing that the industry would dry up, changed its mind. The Commission decided in 1980 that investors, yes investors, would benefit by paying for the companies' increased sales efforts. It adopted a new Rule 12b-1, allowing the sponsors to cover advertising and marketing costs with shareholder funds in the form of a fee. The fee would be subject to shareholder approval at the outset and then, on a continuing basis, by the independent directors, if they periodically "conclude . . . in light of their fiduciary duties . . . that the plan will [likely] benefit the company *and its shareholders.*"[4] (Italics added). The benefit to shareholders would come, it was thought, from the increased size of a fund and the resulting economies of scale. This logic was always a bit tortured. Mutual fund performance, in general, suffers as the size of the fund grows. If there are economies of scale, companies should not need a carrot from the SEC to exploit them.

The industry is no longer on the brink of extinction, and yet most funds, even the largest, continue to charge 12b-1 fees. Depending on the class of stock, these fees may run as high as 1 percent a year of the fund's assets. Industry-wide, these fees totaled $11.8 billion in 2006.[5] (The dollars have grown as the assets have grown.)

The fee has long since outlived its raison d'être. Less than 5 percent of the 12b-1 fees are currently used for direct promotion and advertising. Instead, they have become just another stream of revenue, but a particularly useful one for fund sponsors, because it permits them to compensate brokers without having to charge a fat front-end sales load.[6] A sales load is the 5 percent or so charge levied by brokers at the time they sell shares in a fund. Since investors can see that they have immediately lost $500 of their $10,000 investment, it has always stuck in the public's craw. A 12b-1 fee escapes that onus, because it is an *annual* expense that, as a practical matter, gets lost in the overall results. Indeed, so long as the fee is capped at 25 basis points, the fund can still be described as a "no-load" fund. (A fund that does not impose any 12b-1 fee can say it is a "pure no-load" fund, as if Terri and Rick are likely to catch the distinction.) Even funds that have closed to new investors continue to charge this fee for marketing,[7] and their supine boards of directors rubber-stamp it as a benefit to shareholders. One educated guess is that the 12b-1 dollars from a group's closed fund A go to support sales efforts for fund B.

Early in 2007, Andrew Donohue, the director of the SEC's Division of Investment Management, which regulates mutual funds, suggested that the 12b-1 fee had outlived its purpose and was ripe for review.[8] It should be obvious that the cost of marketing through brokerage firms should be borne only by customers who use their services, rather than by those who buy directly from the fund or are no longer buying shares at all. But the word on Wall Street is that, given the strenuous opposition of the industry, a reduction in the fee is the best we will see.[9] The sticking point is that as investors have become increasingly allergic to paying 5 percent front-end sales loads,[10] the 12b-1 gives the industry a $11 billion kitty to cover distribution costs in a way that, as a fund manager said, is "just about invisible."[11] Donohue is only the latest of a long string of Division of Investment Management heads to have questioned the ability of investors to put the expense pieces together.[12]

The industry's fondness for the 12b-1 fee is no mystery, particularly when it is compared to the alternative. A front-end sales load is a big 5 percent or so, to be sure, but it is collected only once, and only from a portion of investors—those who buy from brokers. A rough calculation shows that about $15 billion to $16 billion in these front-end commissions were paid by such investors in 2006, a banner year with about $350 billion in new sales of load funds.[13] However, a 12b-1 fee is typically paid by all the shareholders, old and new, even by those who may have already paid an up-front sales commission on their shares. Best of all, the 12b-1 dollars just keep coming, year after year, in good times and bad.

But Rule 12b-1 is only the beginning of our story, because it has bred some remarkable offspring. Garrett Hardin, the distinguished ecologist who died in 2003, authored the oft-quoted line "We can never do merely one thing," meaning there are inevitably unexpected consequences for whatever we do. Before the adoption of Rule 12b-1, funds typically issued only one class of stock. All that changed in the years after 1980, and today it is not uncommon to see a fund with five, even eight or 10 classes of stock, with incredibly complex ongoing fee structures, some payable immediately, some annually, and still others triggered by a redemption of the shares. It is fair to ask why a mutual fund, which after all was invented to make life simple (remember?) should find it necessary to offer eight different classes of stock.

Multiclass Fund Shares

One ostensible purpose of the Rule 12b-1 fees was to allow all funds, including no-load ones, more flexibility in marketing. Vanguard had won an exemption allowing its no-load funds to charge an equivalent fee, even before the rule was adopted.[14] Following adoption of Rule 12b-1, funds of all sorts, load and no-load, added 12b-1 fees. But then investors began to complain about the poor disclosure of what, in substance, had become load funds in sheep's clothing (i.e., a trailing, perpetual commission, sometimes as large as 1.25 percent a year). Since no-load funds are supposed to be those that don't charge marketing fees, why are they tacking on those 12b-1s?

Hoping to placate the public while still allowing the fund companies to rake it in, the SEC adopted in 1995 another rule, 18f-3, permitting companies to offer multiple classes of shares in the same fund. Investors in each class would be hit with a separate expense structure, like latte sippers and espresso drinkers at the bar. Be careful what you wish for. The level of complexity today defies almost any description. Morningstar tried to produce a succinct summary, entitled "The Short Answer," but it required five printed pages, more than Terri and Rick are likely to wade through.[15]

For the moment, let's stay with the basics, Classes A, B, and C. One shareholder might prefer to pay, say, a 5.75 percent commission at the time of purchase, buying what are generally labeled Class A shares. With a time value of money calculation—not easy to do—investors like Terri and Rick might conclude that the Class A makes sense because they plan to hold their shares for eight years or so. Alternatively, there is the Class B, which has no *visible* front-end load, but the broker still has to eat. So this class carries a 12b-1 fee of 1 percent a year, and the fund company pays the broker immediately the equivalent of a 5 percent front-end load. Over time, the company will recoup the payment to the broker out of the 12b-1 fees it collects. But wait, suppose Rick sells his shares before the company has fully recovered that up-front payment to the broker? If that happens, then Rick will be hit with a contingent deferred sales charge (CDSC) to make the fund company whole. Eventually, if Rick holds his Class B shares long enough, they will convert into Class A to give him the benefit of a lower, 25 basis points 12b-1 fee. "Whew," Rick said, "I think I get all that, but maybe I'd better read it again."

Class C shares are a good deal simpler. Like the Class B shares, they include an annual 12b-1 fee of 1 percent, but unlike the B shares, the Class C shares do not convert ever, so that the fee is paid forever, year after year. The split of that 12b-1 fee between the distributor and the broker is different for Class C shares, in that the broker's share will be 75 basis points a year, instead of the 25 basis points the broker would take for Class B stock.[16] (The difference makes sense if we remember that the broker would have earned an up-front 5 percent commission for selling B shares, payable by the distributor. For example, for the sale of $20,000 in Class B shares, the broker would have earned immediately a sales commission, paid by the fund sponsor, of $1,000 but would earn only $50 a year from the 12b-1 fee. For the sale of $20,000 in Class C shares, the broker would receive no sales commission, but the broker's share of the 12b-1 fee would be $150 a year.)

The entire industry is just delighted with these multiclass stock structures. They have helped the funds to reach new constituencies and thus to gather more assets.[17] Their flexibility pleases particularly the brokers and other advisers. While brokers might prefer the front-end load shares, personal financial planners—who, being unable to sell funds directly, cannot collect a front-end sales commission—can, however, sell the same fund using the Class C variety, taking their cut from the 12b-1 fee.

The complexity alone is enough to drive Terri and Rick, their eyes glazed over, into the arms of a broker or planner. Someone buying into a multiclass fund is supposed to know whether he or she is there for the long term, in which case it makes sense to buy the Class A shares because of the lower ongoing fees. If the buyer contemplates holding the fund for a relatively short period—say, three years—then the Class C shares make sense. It is difficult to see any circumstances under which the obscurely configured Class B shares would be a good idea, and some fund shops, Franklin for one, have dropped them.[18]

Strange to say, investors who think they know which class of shares to buy may be at more risk than others. They may expect to hold for years, but, as we've seen, it doesn't always play out that way. What they don't know is that from the moment they invest, they will be subject to a steady barrage of advice from their advisers to rebalance, to do something other than to hold on to what they have just bought. At Morgan Stanley, the retail advisers, who got that up-front reward for selling Class B shares, often "forgot" to remind clients of the discounts available for larger quantity purchases of Class A stock. (For that and other violations, the firm was fined $50 million.[19]) The conflicts for these advisers are almost endless. Has the broker told them about those complex deferred charges, the so-called CDSCs mentioned earlier, or is he about to retire and would, therefore, like to sell stock with front-end loads?[20] How is a broker likely to respond if Rick asks about a pure no-load fund, one like Fairholme, with no sales load charge and no 12b-1 fee?

The underlying concern, as always, is not just one of costs, but whether Terri and Rick are getting the fund that is best for them, or at least the broker's honest opinion of what is best. As we saw in Chapter 7, a broker's advice is probably not worth much, but Terri and Rick are entitled to the best the broker has.

As investors became increasingly aware of the in-your-face front-end sales loads, they were willing to buy almost anything else, whether a different class of stock in a fund or a different fund altogether. The proportion of U.S. equity funds invested in front-end load funds has dropped from 91 percent in 1962 to 23 percent in 2006. That's quite a drop. But brokers and supermarket operators still need to eat, so the money for marketing a fund has to come from somewhere. The industry adapted by clutching to the 12b-1 and other fees.[21] As a result, despite the huge increase in assets under management during those years, which should, thanks to economies of scale, have cut the operating expense ratio, the all-in expenses (including the 12b-1 fees) actually increased over this period by 60 percent.[22] The huge drain of these annual expenses is masked, not just by the considerable volatility of mutual fund returns, but by their lesser visibility.

But wait, the broker-sold alphabet soup does not stop with Classes A, B, and C. There's a Class D, available through fund supermarkets, such as Schwab and Fidelity. An investor reading his or her annual report may find that the fund has S or Z share classes, which are now closed to new investors, as well as I or Y class shares. The American Funds group offers no less than 14 share classes.[23] It's enough to make one's head hurt. At the very least, we will understand why mutual fund managers might listen with a slight smirk when the SEC's Donohue intones that the "most fundamental principle in the mutual fund business is that fund advisers are fiduciaries, which means the investor comes first."[24]

Now Here's a Stealthy Way to Influence a Broker's Advice

One could be excused for wondering why fund families, already holding a range of tools to reward brokers for promoting their funds—front-end loads, 12b-1 fees, CDSCs, and multiclass stocks—would need to siphon off still more. But they do; the competition for shelf space at the major brokerage houses, such as Merrill Lynch and Smith Barney, is that intense. One obvious way for a fund company to get Merrill's attention is to direct its stock trading to Merrill, or whichever broker seems willing to energetically market its funds.

With stock fund turnover rates averaging at or above 100 percent a year, the total trading costs for investors, including the impact of, say, a fund's purchases on the price in the market, will run about 1 percent a year.[25] Yet even the bare commission costs appear only in that obscure SEC filing known as the Statement of Additional Information (SAI). It's a puzzle why so considerable an item does not show up in the annual report, where it would attract the attention it deserves. According to *Forbes,* the SEC's attitude seems to be "Well, it's always been that way."[26]

For years funds deliberately *inflated* the commissions paid for stock trading as an essentially invisible, no-cost-to-the-sponsor marketing device. The obvious concern, as the SEC finally acknowledged, was that the practice created "an incentive for the broker to recommend funds that best compensate the broker rather than ones that meet the customer's investment needs."[27] Belatedly, in 2004, the Commission adopted a rule explicitly outlawing the practice, known as directed brokerage. Over a dozen firms settled charges.[28] The American Funds group, while it did cease the practice, vigorously denied any illegality.

American's resistance may have been a blessing, because it turned a bright spotlight on a long-running industry abuse. The National Association of Securities Dealers (NASD) sued the American Funds group, essentially charging violations of fiduciary duty.[29] The hearing officers found against the fund family, though the fine it levied—$5 million— was altogether modest. As of late 2007, the case is still on appeal. What is interesting is that it has brought to light the intricate ways in which a major fund family, one with $1 trillion under management, had used investors' assets for its own ends. A detailed business plan was entered into with each brokerage, setting forth arrangements for meetings and conferences with brokers, including branch and regional office coverage, plus broker "business development" training to be delivered by "key American Funds personnel."[30] The flow of dollars to and from the fund family was carefully tracked, and American made it clear that a broker's continued eligibility depended on the firm's remaining among the top 50 retailers of its funds.[31]

In 2001, the fund group paid more than $34 million in directed brokerage★—that is, fees to brokers who had excelled in marketing American's funds. (The opinion failed to name the major brokerage firms receiving the money, presumably because only the American Funds group was directly involved. Think of it as professional courtesy by the panel that wrote the opinion.)

Just to complicate the analysis a bit, we need to note that the broker doing the trading for the American group of funds did not always keep the entire commission. Often they simply passed on, or "stepped out," as they say, a portion of the brokerage fee—typically 70 percent or more—to a retail firm which, though it had taken no part whatever in the stock trades, had been a major producer of new business for American. American could not direct brokerage payments directly to these producers, because they did not offer trading services. American did the next best thing: It paid a broker that was trading for one of its funds enough to pay both a market rate commission, plus sufficient added dollars to pay the producing firm that American was seeking to reward. That 70 percent step-out figure gives us a good sense of the extent to which the funds had been paying excessive commissions. The remaining 30 percent, kept by the trading firm, presumably sufficed as payment for its efforts.

The step-out firms, the ones that had been vigorously marketing American's funds, had come to depend on that source of revenue, and were said to have been "shocked and dismayed" when the American Funds group decided, in 2003 under pressure from the SEC, to discontinue step-outs. Not to worry. In reality, the American Funds group changed the form of the flow of payments, *but not the substance*. Compensation to the step-out firms continued, but now the payments would be made directly by American Funds, the management company, rather than out of trading commissions paid by the funds. And the clearing firms—the ones doing stock trades for American—that were no longer benefiting from the step-out transactions were compensated with increased trading flows, but of course at a reduced rate of commissions.

Does it matter to shareholders of a fund if the firms that are gathering assets for the American group continue to receive payments, just as

---

★The Franklin Templeton group had between 2001 and 2003 allocated $52 million for directed brokerage payments. SEC Release 2004-168, December 13, 2004.

long as the money is no longer paid directly by the fund itself? Switching the source of the payments to the management company goes by the seemingly innocuous name of "revenue sharing," and we will get to that shortly, after we have discussed still another outrageous practice, one that goes by the bland name "soft dollars."

"Soft Dollars"?—Hey, That's My Hard Cash

The mutual funds' linens are soiled indeed, and you can wash your hands when we are done, but we're not yet there. Why would fund families, having already dug into their fund shareholders' pockets to reward brokers with inflated commissions, find it necessary to dig still further? Answer: to increase the fund sponsors' (read: the management company owners') profits by shifting some of their own expenses onto the funds. Soft dollars are the trading commissions a fund manager pays to a brokerage firm over and above the market-rate cost (hard dollars) to trade stocks in the fund. In exchange, the clearinghouse will furnish to the manager a variety of research and other cost-saving services.

But haven't the investors—you and I—already paid for the research in the form of a management fee? Of course we have; hey, that's what a management fee is all about, doing research and hiring people with the skills to do it well. Those inflated commissions are a diversion of investors' assets to cover research expenses for which the manager has already been paid; we are being asked—except no one asks us, they just take—to pay for the same service twice over. This arrangement obviously delights the management company, since they no longer have to use their fee income to buy research reports and the like. By one calculation, for each dollar of market-rate trading commissions, the industry has paid an additional 50 cents in soft dollars—soft to the point of rotten.[32]

There is some history to soft dollars. Until 1975, trading commissions had been fixed at arbitrarily high rates, and the brokerage firms, to win institutional investors' (including mutual funds') business, happily provided research and other services free of charge. When commissions were deregulated, there was a question whether, given the funds' fiduciary obligation to obtain best execution for trades, they could continue to receive research services that would implicitly increase the commission.[33] Congress, in its modest wisdom, added to the Investment Company Act a safe harbor, Section 28(e), to permit funds to continue the practice, limiting it, however, to "research services."

Forget the limits; there was abuse from the outset. Money managers construed the exemption to cover overhead goods and services, certified financial analyst examination review courses, membership dues, office rent, copiers and other office supplies—even backup generators.[34] The SEC has tried time and again to clarify the limits. Finally, in 2006, it issued a 40-page interpretative release, fixing narrow limits to these difficult to measure, yet legally authorized, soft dollar payments.[35]

Even the Commission's latest efforts to narrow the exemption are not easy to police. (Try this one: Mixed-use products will still be permitted, if the costs are allocated and the allocation is disclosed to clients.[36]) It's ridiculous; soft dollars should be discontinued—period.

The pressures of the marketplace, however, are such that Section 28(e) is not likely to disappear anytime soon. Brokers' commissions have been shrinking,[37] and the clearinghouses are eager for additional revenue in any form.

Revenue Sharing

Funds may change their colors but hardly their reptilian—and greedy—nature. While they are now barred from yesterday's abuses, they adopt other techniques so as to win preferential shelf space at the brokerage houses. Now it goes by the innocent-sounding name of revenue sharing. Revenue sharing is not just an afterthought; it is big. What it means is that out of the management fees and other revenues received by the fund sponsors, a substantial portion is devoted, not to managing or administering the funds, but to marketing them. Indeed, as we saw in Chapter 7, a fund family might spend almost as much, or even more, on marketing than on all of its other management expenses combined.

The brokerage firms on whom the funds shower this money know full well they are a scarce resource, and they are ready to extract ever more dollars from the funds. In truth, the managers can't do much about it,[38] at least not if they want to become big, really big. It's not enough just to get in the door, to be among the funds available to a firm's customers. There are over 500 large-cap growth funds, with 1,800 separate classes of stock.[39] To escape from the crowd, fund families must pay . . . and pay again, in many different flavors.

Revenue sharing is legal, at least if it is disclosed. But think about it: Without these "pay to play" dollars, the management and 12b-1 fees would be much, much lower. The public loses twice over for these intense marketing efforts: inflated costs and obese, inflexible funds.

The revenue-sharing deals are typically opaque; no one talks freely about how they're calculated, hoping to maintain a competitive advantage. They can be based on new sales, new sales less redemptions, or assets under management. The managers of one substantial family of funds said to me that they are currently paying 25 to 35 basis points, depending on the administrative services provided. Even at the agreed rates, the firm, which does not charge 12b-1 fees, is sharing with brokers one-third of its management fee revenues. And the firm, I was told, is getting a "bare minimum" of sales support, meaning that for opportunities to speak at training sessions and at branch offices, further payments would be required.

Remember, the brokers and other advisers, including those employed by Schwab, and the major wire houses, are recommending funds that pay *them* well, not necessarily those they expect to perform well. Disclosure? The broker is chatting up customers, giving them brochures, trying to close a sale. Why would we expect the adviser to break the flow of his pitch to dig into a densely written disclosure document? Terri and Rick will get a prospectus, but not until the sale has closed.

To get a better sense of the scale and impact of revenue sharing, it helps to see it from the brokers' perspective. The best way to get a clear view is to have a major brokerage firm fail to make even the minimal required disclosure, and then for the SEC and the NASD to bring enforcement proceedings. All the dirty laundry gets aired.

Edward Jones is one of the four largest brokerage firms in the nation, with over 10,000 financial advisers and more than seven million clients. It is well known for its network of thousands of quite small offices; in Indiana alone, there are 358 branches. The major fund families are eager to sell through Edward Jones. While Jones has selling agreements with many funds, its seven-member "preferred list" is a tightly drawn prize.★

What did it mean to be on Jones' preferred list? Like much of the Morgan Stanley proceeding mentioned earlier (where the brokers just "forgot" to tell clients how they could pay reduced fees), the Jones case turned on the firm's failure to inform clients of the critical factors influencing their advisers' recommendations. The seven preferred families at Jones turned out to be a very mixed bag.[40] They ranged from the American group and Goldman Sachs at the high end, whose funds have been reasonably managed, down to Putnam, some of whose funds had been implicated in the market-timing scandals or collapsed in the wake of the 1990s bubble. Training programs for Jones brokers provided information *solely* about the seven favored groups; brokers' bonuses were keyed to sales of those seven, and Jones actually discouraged staff from contacting rival firms. The seven fund firms also paid for cruises, ski trips, and safaris, with five-star accommodations for Jones brokers who had met their sales targets.[41]

While all this was common knowledge in the industry, no one bothered to tell the Edward Jones clients, who no doubt assumed that they were receiving objective advice. To settle late in 2004 administrative proceedings brought by the SEC and the New York Stock Exchange, Edward Jones paid $75 million in disgorgement and civil penalties and agreed to be censured.[42] In the subsequent class action proceedings, clients won an additional $127 million in cash and credit vouchers.[43]

Nevertheless, revenue sharing continues. The Edward Jones web site now provides this information, but it's hard to believe that the advantages enjoyed by those seven families have diminished by much or that investors are better served (or maybe that they even notice the disclosures or gather the import). For the year 2005, Jones received $172 million in revenue sharing from the favored seven, *equal to about a third of its pretax income!*[44] If not for favored treatment, what were the fund companies paying for? In the years before the settlement, the favored seven had captured 98 percent of the Edward Jones mutual fund sales, with the American Funds group taking home half of that.[45] We don't know how

---

★As of October 2006, the seven preferred families were American, Franklin Templeton, Goldman Sachs, Hartford, Lord Abbett, Putnam, and Van Kampen.

big the share is currently, but the funds continue to pay and clearly it's not for nothing. You don't pay for space on the grocery shelf if they aren't selling your product. At Smith Barney, the funds with preferred shelf space—a group of 40 families—accounted for 94.9 percent of total mutual fund sales in 2005.[46] Of the 10 top revenue-sharing families at Smith Barney, five are among the Edward Jones seven.

No retailers are more dependent on revenue sharing than the so-called fund supermarkets, Schwab, Fidelity, and TD Ameritrade. Schwab, for example, aggressively promotes the fact that investors can buy any of 3,000 no-load funds through its OneSource, boasting that "you won't pay a penny to purchase" a OneSource fund.[47] Schwab also provides investors with a single, simplified report for all the funds bought through Schwab. What's the hitch? How can they do all that and not get paid? The answer, of course, is revenue sharing, which at Schwab can run a healthy 40 basis points annually.[48] Buried in expenses, the cost is thus borne by *all investors*—those who buy through Schwab and those who do not buy through Schwab (or indeed any other retailer). One fund group, Bridgeway, tried to protect those of its shareholders who bought their shares elsewhere by creating separate classes of stock with different expense ratios, but Schwab shot that down. Another family, Loomis Sayles, simply increased its overall expenses by 25 basis points. Longleaf Partners group abruptly left the Schwab system, citing a fee increase as "duplicative and excessive."[49] The fund supermarkets, however, are too important for most funds to bypass.

Corruption by Committee: The Story Gets Worse

If revenue sharing and soft dollar payments are technically legal, a charitable reader may wonder if it's fair to call the fund companies on these practices. Everyone does it (well, almost everyone), it's legal, and mutual funds are still the best bet for the average investor, so we live with these costs and added expenses. (Besides, wealthy investors pay hedge funds a lot more in fees.) I would demur, not just because investors don't get the straight story, but (more importantly) because they grievously distort the advice that we receive from our trusted brokers and their colleagues. The recommendations we get are so visibly manipulated when, as we saw in the Edward Jones case, only the few fund families that are on the firm's preferred list—those few who had paid to play—could expect any business from that far-flung network of sales offices.

Just to strip away the reader's last shred of innocence, this sordid story took an even more serious turn for the worse in two recent cases involving major banks. These weren't some kids peddling dope in the 'hood, but banks, big banks. The first, which was settled in 2005, involved Citigroup and its Smith Barney fund management subsidiary.[50] Aware that there might be savings to achieve, Citi explored the possibility of taking back the transfer agency functions (back-office functions) from the company, First Data, that had been handling it for the more than 100 Smith Barney funds. After extended and intricate negotiations and the use of a consulting firm, Deloitte & Touche, Citigroup kept First Data for all but some minor services, which it assigned to a newly created subsidiary. That subsidiary then recontracted with First Data for the essential transfer agent functions, but at much reduced rates. Citigroup, however, brazenly pocketed the $89 million saved over a five-year period. These monies clearly belonged to the funds that were paying for the services in the first place. It was fraud. And they knew it; they used a side agreement with First Data's corporate successor as cover. The funds' boards were given grossly misleading information; the side letter, in particular, was not mentioned. More than once, Deloitte had warned of the dubious legality of the arrangements.

In the end, the SEC imposed penalties totaling $180 million, but no indictments followed. The boys in the 'hood wouldn't have gotten off so easily.

The other recent proceeding also involved banks, in this case 27 of them, each with mutual fund affiliates.[51] The funds had obtained various administrative services from BISYS Fund Services, a publicly owned company that services mutual funds. In return for extending its contracts, the fund advisory companies took kickbacks from BISYS, primarily to cover—guess what?—their marketing expenses. (One adviser, dubbed Adviser A in the public record, used some of the money to pay country club fees.) In all, the kickbacks totaled $230 million over five years, or almost 75 percent of the administrative fees collected by BISYS from the banks. As of late 2007, two of the banks have acknowledged receiving inquiries, and reliable rumor suggests that settlements are under discussion, with outcomes dependent on the quality of information that had been provided to the funds' boards.

BISYS paid $21 million to settle the charges. Interestingly, the case came to light only when its new CEO became aware of the practices, froze the kickbacks, and retained outside counsel to oversee a review.* This has been the largest fraud case since the market-timing abuses came to light, and yet the media have given it scant attention.

Devious and Deceptive?

Before you buy a car, you can kick the tires, take it for a test drive, and check *Consumer Reports* for reliability. Not here. We have fixed the market-timing and directed brokerage abuses, but now, as the story moves on, we see more than two dozen banks committing fraud in one form or another. Shocking? Not really. It's inherent in the structure of absentee ownership, where all the investor owns is a piece of paper, shares of stock, representing something else, and that something else is not only out of sight and difficult to analyze, but under the control of others. Does anyone seriously believe the abuses that led Congress to adopt the Investment Company Act were ephemeral? Where are the safeguards in the system?

There are basically two safeguards, transparency and energetic watchdogs. The primary watchdogs are a fund's board of directors, the regulatory authorities, the third-party services such as Lipper and Morningstar, and the press. Obviously, it all starts with disclosure. Even watchdogs can only guard what they can see. Let's take a hands-on look at a fund family, chosen randomly, to see how well it is meeting what one public-interest observer described as the test of effective disclosure: giving investors (1) the information they need to make good decisions, (2) in a form that is accessible and useful, (3) at a time when it is likely to affect their purchase decision.[52]

---

*As I would tell students, engage in fraud and you're handing out vouchers, redeemable on demand, to rat on you.

I selected the RiverSource group of funds, and in particular the Growth Fund, which happens to be one of the large-cap growth funds that we looked at in Chapter 4. This is a family of 100 funds, with about $60 billion in assets under its wing, a group formed in the 1890s and long known as Investors Diversified Services. American Express acquired it in 1984 and then spun it off to its shareholders in 2005, under the name of Ameriprise. It got caught in the market-timing scandals, but since the spin-off is reported to have set about improving operations and disclosure. On balance, the group was a happy choice; the disclosures seem reasonably representative—not notably better or worse than those of other funds. It's a good place to see what's missing in fund disclosures generally, and particularly the conflicts of interest distorting the flow of dollars in and out of funds.

At the fund family's web site (www.riversource.com) investors can readily download for each fund a two-page fact sheet plus a prospectus, the annual and semiannual reports, and the Statement of Additional Information (SAI). The fact sheet for the Growth Fund might better be called "fact lite," because except for performance data and expense ratios, there's not much there. Stock selection, we are told, "is research driven . . . and applies a 'price conscious' strategy." (Other funds in the family describe themselves in almost identical terms.) The disclosures provide nothing to help prospective buyers see why they should buy a large-cap growth fund, or the RiverSource Growth Fund in particular. Have the results been better or worse than the market as a whole? The question is neither asked nor answered.

The annual report for the year ended July 31, 2006, is the most useful and accessible document. Early on, the reader gets a full-page report on the year's results, complete with a bar chart: The fund was up 0.98 percent versus negative results for two benchmarks, the Russell 1000 Growth Index, and the Lipper Large Cap Growth Funds Index. (Because the Lipper results reflect fund expenses, they were 1.1 percent worse than the −0.76 percent performance of the Russell index.) None of the data, however, even hint at how this fund performed *relative to the market as a whole*. Were large-cap growth funds a good place to be? In fact, the S&P 500 index, a good proxy for the market generally, was up 5.4 percent for those 12 months ended July 31, 2006, far better than the Growth Fund. In fact, this fund had underperformed the market for years. For the 10 years ended December 31, 2006, the Growth Fund showed average annual returns of 3.22 percent. It's not mentioned, but those results compare badly with the 8.42 percent per year average returns for the S&P 500.★ Forget the chatter about the fund being "research driven"; the turnover of the portfolio averaged 147 percent a year over the past three fiscal years for an average holding period of seven months.

Could the failure to discuss the overall market returns have been induced by the fact that, despite the fund's poor performance in fiscal 2006, the management fee included a $500,000 performance bonus, based on a comparison of the fund's results against those of the Lipper group of like funds? At RiverSource, it's clear, it's the benchmarks that matter, not whether investors make or lose money. Digging further into the annual report, the reader will learn that while the fund has a quite representative group of independent directors, the same group serves as the board for 100 other RiverSource funds. Fortunately, they don't have far to travel; they all live in Minneapolis, where the funds are based. No one can possibly oversee the performance of 100 funds and managers. And if Terri and Rick were the rare exceptions who read SAIs, they would have learned that except for the board chair, the average director of the Growth Fund earned the trivial sum of $2,300 for the year's work, and for all 100 funds, a total of about $140,000. Perhaps $2,300 a year was all they were worth at the Growth Fund.

As is often the case, there is one SAI for all 100 funds, and being 200 pages long, it defies easy access. Labor on to page 115, and the investor will see that the manager of the Growth Fund, Nick Thakore, manages several funds, of which this one is not a major part. As of early 2007, he had managed the Growth Fund for five years, but owned no stock in it. (The SEC's Division of Market Regulation is said to be of the view that a manager's personal holdings are "too personal" for up-front disclosure.) Further back, at page 173, assuming Terri and Rick are not soundly asleep by now, we see that the directors of the fund also owned few, if any, of the shares.

★Both the Lipper and the Russell indexes outperformed the Growth Fund over a 10-year period. In short, this has not been a good fund even within its style box.

What's Missing from the Disclosures?

The adequacy of fund disclosures needs to be seen in the context of the rapid changes in the industry. It's not just that there are $6 trillion in stock funds today, or that the number of products being offered has soared. As pension plans terminated, more and more people discovered that if their future was to be even remotely secure, they would have to learn something about funds, whether within a 401(k) plan, or bought directly. Or they would have to find someone to guide them through the complex maze, because they had neither the skills nor the time.

Ameriprise Financial, the sponsor of the RiverSource funds, happens to be a good example of the changes under way. In addition to the funds, it is a powerful group of retail financial planners, accounting today for more than 10 percent of all registered planners in the country.[53] The CEO noted recently that almost half of the company's two million individual clients work from plans, as the staff has come to realize the "leverage inherent in such a model."[54] Once a plan is established, a client is likely to purchase a range of products, including funds, and also annuities and certificates of deposits. With the clients clearly relying on the planner, it won't be easy for people to break through, to induce them to do some independent reading and analysis, so as to gain truly effective disclosure. No matter how good the paper or online disclosure may be, it won't help if they don't read it.

Some Particulars

For over three years now, the SEC has been considering a Profile Plus, a two- to three-page summary of the information investors need to make a decision.* The way the system is rigged now, it's like buying a car without learning the miles per gallon until it's been paid for. The typical investor can't sort through the disclosures that do exist, doesn't have the time or experience, but is in need of investing for retirement. What's the option? Seek a supposedly objective party whose only interest is in serving

---

*As noted in Chapter 5, the SEC has recently proposed a new mandatory short-form prospectus.

the investor, right? But before investors can even get to the core mutual fund information, it's imperative that they understand the often-skewed incentives of the advisers to whom they have turned. The industry has been fighting the Profile Plus proposal on the empty pretext that, since such a skinny document would be incomplete, it would increase their legal exposure. The SEC itself is said to be divided, with the Division of Investment Management favoring the proposal and the Division of Market Regulation taking the industry's point of view, hence dragging its heels.

Using the RiverSource Growth Fund as an example, it is clear that any point-of-sale document should include a broad market index, such as the Dow Industrials or the S&P 500, as a benchmark. And, unlike the Growth Fund fact sheet, it should include the turnover ratio, with a brief explanation that it matters, not just because of the costs but because it is a good marker for whether the fund is being managed patiently or is simply chasing trends. And yes, give Terri and Rick not just the name of the manager, but how much stock in the fund he or she owns.

The reporting of management fees and other expenses also needs some major fixes. In the early days, when investors bought funds for the dividends they paid, the expenses were reported as a percentage of the income. Although today Terri and Rick are investing for total returns, they still need an equivalent metric. What part of the total returns goes to pay the managers and the various administrative and trading costs? This is the true expense ratio: How much of the profits go to the managers? How are Terri and Rick to know if a fund's expenses are high or low, without some yardstick? Measured as a percentage of *assets*, the expense ratios all look small, so that only by projecting out the impact over 20 years or so will Terri and Rick see the true impact. When they buy a refrigerator, there is stuck across the front an Energy Star rating by the Environmental Protection Agency, comparing the energy cost of owning brand X with those of a broad range of other manufacturers' products. Cars are stickered on the window with the miles per gallon denoting their fuel efficiency. For a mutual fund, call it the "Expense Star" rating, perhaps.*

---

*The current proposal to put data in an XBRL format will facilitate interactive comparisons fund by fund. As of mid-2007, about 40 funds had adopted it.

There is another major defect in the reporting of management fees, one we mentioned in the context of the T. Rowe Price funds. A mutual fund reports only the *gross* management fee, without disclosing where the money goes, who gets what. It's as if General Electric reported annually the salaries, bonuses, options, and perks of its senior officers all bundled into a single lump sum, without disclosing how much any individual, even the CEO, was taking. Mutual funds pay their management fee to a separate corporation; and as far as the funds' investors know, that management company might as well be on Mars. They have no clue what their managers are earning, or to what extent their incentives are skewed by their holdings and options in the parent complex. There are just the scraps of information that show up in the SAI, which investors don't get and wouldn't read or comprehend if they did.★

Revenue sharing is disclosed about 20 pages back in the RiverSource Growth Fund prospectus, which is typical. That's neither good enough nor soon enough. Again, it's not just the cost, but how the payments tend to distort the advice Terri and Rick get from a broker. Martha Stewart gets paid big dollars to weave a product into her TV scripts.[55] That's not the standard we should apply to investment companies.

Boards of Directors: Watchdogs or Lapdogs?

Too often, like almost all the time, boards of directors look like lapdogs. Here are a few specifics:

- The 12b-1 fees must be approved by a fund's board as being in the shareholders' interest, the purpose being to help those who have not yet achieved a viable scale. But boards have routinely approved the fee, even at American Funds' Growth Fund of America, with assets of $190 billion. The American Funds boards are said to be among the best, but has anyone confronted them with these persistent efforts to grow, and the failure to give investors adequate warnings of the conflict underlying the revenue sharing that feeds this growth?

★TIAA-CREF, which manages $400 billion on behalf of academics and doctors, recently agreed to give its holders a nonbinding vote on executive pay. Francisco Guerrero, "Fund Group Offers 'Say on Pay,'" *Financial Times,* June 15, 2007, 15.

- As we've seen over the years, fund management companies have often been sold off, but with rare exceptions, the boards of directors of the funds in those families have never rejected a buyer. It seems that whichever buyers paid top dollar were the best qualified—regardless of their skill and prudence as managers.
- We have seen how aggressively the major fund families have poured money into marketing, using money that, from one spigot or another, comes from the funds. The boards of these funds are legally obligated to protect their shareholders' interests, but the evidence of any due diligence is hard to find. Surely a much larger share of the economies of scale would have passed through to investors if boards were looking out for investor interests. How often have boards truly examined their fees and expenses, *except* by tracking what similar funds are charging? It's like lemmings. If everyone is jumping off the cliff it must be okay, so the fee dollars go up.
- We know why funds churn their portfolios. It's to stay close to the trends, to catch the next breeze. Have boards focused on the often-absurd turnover ratios, with the high trading and tax costs imposed on investors? Perhaps those costs are as irrelevant to directors as they are to most managers.
- Due diligence loses any semblance of meaning when the same people sit on dozens of boards, much less on 100 or even 300 separate boards, within the overall family. As a managing director at Black Rock, Anne Ackerley, acknowledged, it's more "efficient" that way.[56] It sure is. How much care would you get from a doctor who saw 300 patients every day? And with only a single board for all of the 24 Fidelity large-cap growth funds, with therefore 24 different sets of owners, it would be nice to know how diligently the directors handle the conflicts inherent in deciding when, say, to buy a great stock for this fund instead of for that one.
- How often do boards ask why a manager's personal stake in a fund is zero, as at the RiverSource Growth Fund? My guess: close to never.
- The soft dollar and directed brokerage abuse of fund commission costs were common knowledge in the industry. Why did the boards of so many funds fail to stop this silent bleeding of clients' money?
- It was by looking inside management companies that we were able here to see how remarkably profitable they have become. A fund's

board of directors, were it to do so, might take a fresh look at revenue sharing and the like, so that investors would benefit from lower expenses. Do they look? What do *you* think?

- In truth, the work of sitting on hundreds of boards is just too lucrative for the directors to spoil the party. The directors of the 300+ Fidelity funds were paid anywhere from $370,000 to $500,000 each for fiscal 2006. Not bad for part-time work.

- The SEC had proposed to strengthen mutual fund boards by requiring that the chairman and at least 75 percent of the directors be independent of management. It was blocked by the courts on a procedural issue, and then buried altogether as the makeup of the SEC changed. The hope was that an independent board chair would control the agenda and bring a higher degree of skepticism to the evaluation of the fund's management and performance. In essence, the SEC was trying to change the board culture.[57] The proposal was naturally opposed by the fund industry's trade association, the Investment Company Institute. But then, *they* represent fund managements, not fund investors.

If the fund boards are not diligent watchdogs, Terri and Rick are in trouble, because the other watchdogs, the SEC and the courts, have largely deferred to the funds' directors, hoping they can do the job.[58] Unfortunately, mutual funds do not attract the same level of oversight as does corporate America. Public companies hold annual meetings of stockholders and thus are required to distribute proxy statements explaining in relatively plain English what, say, the CEO is taking home and in what form he or she is taking it. The media pounce on these disclosures, so that the *Wall Street Journal* and others can do side-by-side comparisons of how much various CEOs take home versus how well their companies and shareholders are doing. Home Depot's then CEO, Robert Nardelli, went out of his way to thumb his nose at the company's owners at the 2006 annual shareholders meeting, refusing to take questions and keeping the directors away. A few months on, and he was gone, a casualty of pressure from hedge funds, activist groups, and the press. Activists now sit on the boards of major companies, including Heinz, Wendy's, and Applebee's, as well as Home Depot.[59] For years mutual funds were passive investors, not least because their management companies saw corporate America as a source for new business, running 401(k) plans and the like. But as their stock holdings grew, so did the pressure to flex their muscles as proxies for shareholder interests, as in fact T. Rowe Price did at Laureate Education, and Fidelity at Clear Channel Communications.

But the mutual fund boards never hear an angry or confrontational message—or indeed any message at all. Because mutual fund directors are not required to stand for reelection periodically, it is the rare fund that holds an annual shareholders meeting. As a result, there is no forum for shareholders to express their views and ask questions. Do we expect a sponsor to hold 100 or so separate meetings, with the managements and boards present? Perhaps not, but with no proxy materials being distributed, most of the dirty laundry remains entombed in the SAI. Embarrassment is a potent instrument, and it would have been useful for someone at a shareholders meeting to ask a director of the American Funds group's Growth Fund of America when, if ever, it is going to close to new investors. Or to ask a Mutual Beacon director why, if Franklin Resources was spending more on marketing than on managing the funds, the fund's fees could not be slashed.

The media report on mutual funds, but the coverage focuses on how funds are performing—on who is hot now and who is not. The best coverage is from the specialized services covering the industry, namely Lipper and Morningstar. Lipper's primary source of revenue, however, is the fund families, which makes it difficult to throw stones. Morningstar is paid primarily by investors, which argues for more objective reporting.

Some Unresolved Questions

Revenue sharing builds into the price of the product the cost of distribution, and if we think of mutual funds as a business, those costs must ultimately come from the consumers of the product, Terri and Rick. The same is true in almost any business. I think it's obvious by now that, with the almost singular exception of Vanguard, this is no longer simply a profession where managers would be paid for their services, even paid well, but no more than that. For better or worse, mutual funds have moved beyond that and are no different from Procter & Gamble, the difference being that if Crest toothpaste bombs for whatever reason, customers will reject it, and investors in P&G will also notice and demand that something be done.

Even when we recognize that mutual funds have become a corporate-style, profit-maximizing industry, the fact remains that they are not soap. The social and political stakes are too large. Reflect for a moment; what we've seen here is an almost lethal conspiracy against Terri and Rick. The SEC, perhaps innocently, gives funds the right to impose a 12b-1 fee, believing that investors will benefit from economies of scale. The economies are there, but it's not Terri and Rick who profit from them. Rather than rescind the 12b-1s, the Commission sanctions a regime of multiclass stocks for funds, which only compound investors' problems. Given a green light, the industry creates a bewildering array of classes and fees, forcing Terri and Rick to seek an adviser of one sort or another—thus sending investors into the arms of yet another conflicted player.

The fund families—or at least the dominant players—are delighted. By channeling dollars to the brokers, and employing fleets of wholesalers to seduce them, the big fund sponsors are able to dominate the preferred shelf space, enabling them to capture the lion's share of the business. Marketing expenses explode; but being a scalable business, the management companies can handle that. Their margins of profit grow, their returns on invested capital so high as to be beyond belief.

The brokers and planners are delighted, too, because revenue sharing and other payments from fund complexes have become an important source of income ever since commission income dropped. Because the flow is virtually hidden from investors, brokers and planners are free to pick whichever funds help them—whichever pay the most—rather than whichever might be best for the clients. With a dizzying array of stock funds now to choose from, it has become an easy matter to keep clients coming back, thus creating a steady flow of payments. Just convince Terri and Rick that only by frequent rebalancing among all those choices—tinkering in one form or another—will they stay abreast of changes in the market. They never hear about who is a good fund manager, because to focus on who are the good guys would reduce the need for so much moving about. It goes without saying that no one mentions the costs—from taxes to transaction costs to loss on return—of all that switching.

Terri and Rick did not start out being sheep. They are bright people. The industry has, however, conspired to make them such, aided and abetted by the watchdogs; so they are kept in the dark, at which point there is no incentive to wrestle with whatever information they do get. Even then, no one tells them why the costs, some here, some there, are consuming so large a portion of their total returns and retirement nest eggs. How come, if the market is doing well, they are not?

Meanwhile, some of us, watching from the sidelines, are wondering whom the SEC is working for. Would it ever have been likely that we would see a significant change in the culture of the funds' boards of directors—who almost never see a shareholder or confront an embarrassing question—simply by making the board chair nominally independent? Even while paying him or her to chair a hundred such boards?

The SEC has from time to time taken useful steps to improve transparency and integrity, but it has picked its spots, plugging holes in the dike here and there, without stepping back for a more comprehensive analysis, such as we did here. The reality is that more significant changes by the SEC are not likely to happen anytime soon. The industry is prospering as never before, and investors are doing fairly well, even after the market declines of the summer of 2007. There is no impetus for change . . . at the moment. Should masses of investors lose a tremendous amount of money, then change may be forced; but by then it will be too late for those investors and their $6 trillion in stock funds.

Chapter 9

How to Pick a Mutual Fund

An Overview

So what's an investor to do? If the mutual fund industry is such a quagmire of money-losing (or not money-growing) tricks and traps, where is the investor to turn? It's almost enough to make you want to throw up your hands and start stashing money under the mattress. Unfortunately that's not a viable option. You need to provide for your retirement, because no one else is going to. You need to get the best return on your money possible, with an eye, of course, to risk. The reality is that it's not a simple matter. You must be cautious in picking a stock fund. Too many managers have made it clear they do not put your interests first. At times they steal. More often, the industry creates and runs funds for its own self-interest with scant regard for those who entrust to them their savings and hopes. Sad, but true.

173

The good news is that we also found some truly outstanding funds, ones that exhibit a keen sense of fiduciary duty and professionalism, typically investing on the fundamentals of a relatively small number of companies, and willing to be out of step with the crowd. Their patience has been rewarded twice over: first, by avoiding the harrowing losses that befall stocks at quite unpredictable moments, and second, by achieving quite superior results over the longer term, say four to five years. In short, you can make good profits with them.

So how do you find these funds? It just takes a few tools and a requisite frame of mind to find funds that will guard your money, and look to obtain the best total return—be it from return on the investments or from reduced costs from lower turnover (remember, less trading equals lower taxes and transaction costs). We'll review the process in the course of examining two such funds and will also look at when and how to invest in index funds.

The overriding theme—strangely ignored by so many mutual fund sages and advisers—is that the managers matter. They matter in the restaurant where you eat, and on the baseball team you root for. Even in baseball, though the manager doesn't play, he matters. Joe Torre sat there in the Yankee dugout, pensive, steady, and ever vigilant. If the game was going well, then toward the ninth inning, he would give a slight nod to tell the bullpen that it was time for the relief pitcher, Mariano Rivera, to step in. Now, though, Torre will be gone, and the Yankees will be different. The uniforms will look the same, but will they win their division 10 out of 11 years, as they did under Torre? Maybe, but I wouldn't bet on it, just as I wouldn't bet on a mutual fund, even one with a respected brand (a "uniform") without knowing about the manager. Indeed, with apologies to Joe, at a mutual fund the manager is even more important than in baseball. The manager is the pitcher, shortstop, and cleanup hitter, all rolled into one. If a top-notch fund manager exercises his right of free agency and goes elsewhere, the proper response is often to migrate with him.

Back to Pogo . . . and You!

Better managers need better investors. In "The Superinvestors of Graham-and-Doddsville," written in the 1980s, Warren Buffett concluded that we can preach the precepts of thoughtful, fundamental investing, but our words are likely to fall on deaf ears. With an army of financial advisers trying to justify their existence, and the trading in the stock market now breaking the speed limit, it's gotten even harder to get the message through. It's not that the basic precepts are complicated; they're not. It's the execution that is so difficult. If you don't grasp the principles deep in your bones, you'll be defenseless the first time a friend asks how come you missed out on some hot new sector—oil, health care, real estate, whatever—and you'll turn around and sell out of what may, in fact, have been a very good fund.

More than the itch to make money, it's the fear of loss that really unsettles investors and, particularly if they are new investors, destroys their perspective. The first time the market and, yes, *your* fund have a lousy year, you may get that sinking feeling in the pit of your stomach that the losses will spiral further . . . and further. The pundits on CNBC or Bloomberg will certainly be telling you that the outlook is bleak, and that it would be better to be in some other fund or even out of equity funds altogether. As the losses accumulate, so will your anxiety. You'll forget that the very reason you picked the fund was your confidence in the manager's ability to cope with the changing seasons. Scholars like to talk about greed, but it's that touch of panic that really unhinges people. Perhaps your spouse has heard that the Smiths down the block have lost some money, and she's wondering if you have, too; and when you give her a soft "yes," she'll ask if you should sell. Like the husband in that apocryphal couple, Quincy and Caroline, back in Chapter 6, you *will* sell . . . at precisely the wrong moment!

Think of Quincy, who sold after the market break in October 1987. Alas, it was a moment of extraordinary opportunity for a manager who could think independently of a market seemingly seized by panic, a manager blessed with the courage to think bottom-up, company by company. As the Dow Jones Industrial Average was falling 22 percent on Black Monday, October 19, the Sequoia Fund was buying, not selling. It was in the wake of the crash that Buffett found the opportunity he had long sought to align his thirst for the world's most popular beverage with his wallet, and buy a big stake in Coke at a significant discount.

This is not said as criticism of the Quincys of the world. The point is that they, like most of us, will do better if they invest in a carefully— repeat, *carefully*—chosen mutual fund, rather than trying to pick stocks on their own. Very few of us have the requisite skills or the time to do the necessary research. Even beyond those factors, there is the element of temperament, which can't be quantified but which plays a critical role. I have a reasonably high IQ; but being a child of the Depression, I am still haunted by a graphic memory of grown men selling apples for a dime on a cold street corner. Regardless of their generation, most people are haunted by "apples" of their own. Your "apple" is there, deep inside, and you never lose it.

For people trying to invest on their own, directly in the stock market, this sense of lurking peril can be sheer poison. And that's just one of the behavioral problems that make it difficult for people to be the cool, carefully calculating investors who inhabit the models that traditional economists like to build. Markets are rational, at least much of the time, but taken one by one, people are anything but. There is a whole discipline devoted to behavioral finance, and it has demonstrated persuasively how our emotions and frailties get in the way of intelligent investing. We have a powerful instinct to follow the crowd, which probably has useful genetic origins. Watch a herd of African wildebeests flee in the same direction when they catch a lion's scent. For primitive man, as well as beasts, a sense of safety in numbers helped account for our survival. Modern financial markets, however, turn this Darwinian instinct on its head. Perverse as it may sound, following the herd and the common wisdom translates into buying high and selling at the lows. It leads straight across the Serengeti to the lion waiting in the brush.

Our propensity to follow the herd shows up almost everywhere. A recent book, *Mindless Eating: Why We Eat More Than We Think*, explores the social influences that have a big impact on our food intake. And it offers some useful insights into everyday decision making, not just at Wendy's, but in other situations as well.[1] Years ago, for example, food and stock trading were both much more expensive, so we indulged less. The higher cost of a meal served to keep down our weight. My mom, for example, dished out excruciatingly small portions of my favorite, leg of lamb, to make sure it would last a second night. The same was true then of stock trading; it was expensive, so we did less of it. Before the New York Stock Exchange deregulated trading commissions in 1975, the turnover of stocks was much smaller, as low as 17 percent in the 1960s, compared to over 100 percent today, meaning that we kept stocks on average for six years. No one talked much about the stocks they had just bought, because they shuffled their holdings so infrequently. Now it's on the monitor in the restaurant, and a dinner companion may well ask with some angst, "What did the market do today?" In short, the culture has evolved, and not entirely for the better. Even light eaters will eat more if they are in a group of heavy eaters. While you and I may think we are too darn smart simply to follow the Wall Street herd, we have absorbed the growing cultural belief that we should be doing something with our investments all the time.

Whether you grew up in the 1930s, 1960s, or 1980s, human frailties are the same. If you don't have the time, the temperament, or the skill to select your own stocks (and most of us don't), or enough money to obtain decent diversification, or the follow-through to babysit your stocks once you own them, then mutual funds should be the investment vehicle of choice. If the manager is good, a reasonable fee is worth it. If a strong mutual fund manager helps to insulate you from those perverse herding impulses, he or she is worth it several times over. With their diversified portfolios, funds fluctuate far less than individual stocks. That alone is comforting, as is the fact that, having done your homework, you picked Fund X because you can see that it will do better than you.

Should you enlist the help of a financial adviser or broker in the process? Perhaps, if the task seems just too daunting. But think about it: If you have trouble picking a good stock or fund manager, what reason is there to think you will be able to pick a good adviser? There are over 600,000 brokers and advisers. They can't all be brilliant. In fact, as we have seen, the quality is uneven. How do you identify a top-notch adviser? Many, if not most, will be seeking to make of you a recurring source of fee income for themselves, rather than to help you find long-term solutions. In short, they will be committing all the sins discussed in Chapter 7. A good deal of that advice consists of self-serving strategies intended to foster a sense of dependency in the client and thus a perpetual stream of business for themselves. This is why brokers and other advisers inevitably favor tactics such as portfolio rebalancing—they require constant monitoring and trading, and thus a continued role for the broker/adviser. It is also why they will never tell the client, "Stick with what we did last year," and hang up. The broker or adviser has to eat, too. And a study of the costs and benefits of brokers found that not only were customers paying higher front-end load and so-called 12b-1 fees, but the funds they chose underperformed the ones people would have bought directly, without an intermediary, and by significant amounts.[2] For the turbulent years 1996–2002, the study found that for a sample group of equity funds, on an equally weighted, net of expenses basis, the funds bought through brokers averaged about 2.9 percent a year, which was less than half the 6.6 percent earned by funds bought directly, without a broker.[3] True, it's reassuring to talk to someone who at least *seems* totally and clearly focused on your personal best interest—even if the solutions turn out to be the ones produced en masse each month by the brokerage firm. And the broker/adviser may have useful personal counseling on financing a kid's college tuition and the like, but that may be small comfort for poor advice on where to invest your money.

Buy a Mutual Fund?

Despite the inherent conflicts of interest in the industry, it remains true that mutual funds are an intrinsically attractive and flexible vehicle. When Edward Leffler was designing that first fund, Massachusetts Investors Trust, in 1924, he was trying to bring professional management, liquidity, and transparency to the investing public. It was a stroke of genius. A mutual fund's portfolio is priced to market every working day, and, unlike those investment trusts of the 1920s or the hedge funds of today, we can redeem our investment whenever we choose, at our shares' readily calculated net asset value that very day. Compare that to some of the hedge funds that have imploded, such as Long-Term Capital Management, and more recently Amaranth, and then the fixed income hedge funds undone by the subprime mortgage mess, where the holdings are often so illiquid that the funds have far too much discretion in how they do their valuations—what Buffett calls "mark to myth." Beyond that, these hedge funds' holdings are largely kept confidential, and investors' ability to withdraw their money is sorely limited.

Leffler could not have guessed how useful and adaptable his concept would become. Worldwide, there is $20 trillion in mutual funds, with $10 trillion of that in the United States. The mutual fund concept has been put to a variety of ingenious uses. In the 1970s, for example, when interest rates in the United States rose above the rates that banks were allowed to pay, money market funds were created to allow small savers to enjoy the same high rates as the rich folks and institutions that could go directly to the bond market. Before long, checking privileges were added. Today we have over $2 trillion in money market funds and, even though they are not federally insured, we regard them as being as safe as a bank account. There are other ingenious adaptations of the basic concept, such as variable annuity funds, which surely Leffler could not have imagined.

When the statutory framework for mutual funds was first adopted in 1940, it was seen as a rather imperfect compromise, enacted in the context of an unsympathetic Congress and the growing clouds of war. We need to remember, however, as Marty Whitman of Third Avenue Value Fund reminds us, that the Investment Company Act and the tax law, as they have been modified over time, offer very important investor protections:[4]

- Having been badly burned in the 1920s, mutual funds' ability to borrow is severely limited by statute, and often, too, by a fund's own prospectus.
- Funds are required to diversify their holdings.
- Expenses *tend* to be limited. Yes, they are often needlessly high, but compared to hedge funds, managed accounts, funds of funds, and other vehicles, the costs are reasonable. Disclosure requirements, having improved over the years, will bring them down further.
- Self-dealing by affiliates and related parties, such as the corrupt transactions that were commonplace in the 1920s, are rigorously proscribed.
- Custodial and administrative requirements prevent the outright stealing of fund assets.
- As a practical matter, funds are required to distribute annually virtually all their net income and realized capital gains, which investors can then automatically reinvest, if they choose.
- The accounting audits are much more straighforward, reliable, and useful for an equity mutual fund than for hedge funds, which may hold illiquid securities for which there are no current market prices, or even for publicly owned corporations, which may have complex problems valuing inventories, pension obligations, and the like.

Yes, better disclosure, particularly at the point of sale, would help, but in an always imperfect world, the structure is not bad. The challenge is to find one of the few stock funds where the managers have the sense of mission that permits them to put their investors' interests up front, where they belong, so that we don't have to fall back on the legal constraints to get our due.

The Good Funds Fairly Shout Out Their Strengths

The bad news is that the really first-rate funds are few in number, or, as we've said, perhaps 1 percent to 2 percent of all the money in stock funds. The good news is that finding them is not a search for the proverbial needle in a haystack. First, they typically enjoy writing about their investment techniques and attitudes. If you read a report from, say, Longleaf Partners, First Eagle Global, or FPA Capital, they are looking over the investment landscape, explaining their methodology and talking of what went wrong as well as what succeeded, all with refreshing candor. It's as if they were in a B-school classroom, and not surprisingly many of them show up at Columbia, Wharton, and elsewhere. Loud and clear, they are telling shareholders that they are *not* trying to track some index, and because they are long-term investors in carefully picked companies, their returns will be lumpy from one period to the next. Consistency is the goal of most funds, meaning to match a niche benchmark quarter by quarter and year by year, not to avoid losses but to avoid criticism. The serious value funds are giving investors a clear and different message.

The web site of Longleaf Partners Funds (at www.longleafpartners .com) is a model of candor for a small fund family, with descriptions of how they manage the three funds (two of which are currently closed to new investors), their personal stakes in those funds, and more. Among their 10 "Governing Principles," they announce, first off, that they "will treat your investment in Longleaf as it were our own, [and] will remain significant investors with you." Also, "we will concentrate our assets in our best ideas . . . [and] will communicate with our investment partners as candidly as possible." Having underperformed the S&P 500 the year before, the managers reported at year-end 2006 that while they had enjoyed a stellar year, up 21+ percent versus 15+ percent for the index, the prices of the stocks in their portfolio were now rather high relative to values, and the on-deck list of opportunities had shrunk. Despite a good year, no cheerleading here; instead they reminded the reader that each of the three funds' cash holdings had risen. They would, of course, continue to search for companies having "honorable, capable management," and would adhere to their principle of buying stocks "based on their discount from our appraisal of their corporate intrinsic values." They had "no view on what markets will do," investing instead in carefully chosen *companies* with a minimum five-year horizon. The results? For the 10 years ended in 2006, the Partners Fund showed average annual returns of 12.77 percent versus 8.42 percent for the index. At year-end 2006, this picky, picky Partners Fund held just 22 stocks.[5]

What to Look for in a Stock Fund

What are the criteria that will help identify such funds? Treat these as *guidelines*, not rigid rules, in your effort to find the three or four, at most, stock funds that meet your needs. (And you really don't need more than three, or else you run the risk that the portfolio as a whole begins to look like an index fund, in which case you could save yourself the time and expense and just invest in an index fund—but more on that shortly.) The list has deliberately been kept short. There are many books on how to pick a fund, but my sense is that it's better to learn by doing. To start out, buy a copy of the most recent *Morningstar Funds 500*, which, one page to a fund, is chock-full of data on turnover rates, portfolio size, and performance. (Don't pay any heed to a fund's star rating, which, being purely quantitative, has little impact on the more nuanced Morningstar Analyst Picks.[6]) The company's web-based service (www.morningstar.com) allows you to download 50 additional reports. A real bonus is that if you look up on the web site one good fund, say Third Avenue Value, the report will refer you to others like it, much the way Amazon does when you're buying a book.

Just to start, check the Analyst Picks in the manual, and at the back of the book, the list of funds with low turnover rates. Look for a couple of funds that show up, say, both with low turnover *and* on the Picks list. Check out the funds we discuss here in this chapter and in Chapter 2, some of which are still open to new investors. Don't rush. Remember, this is a

long-term proposition. Having found a few funds, then go to the funds' own
web sites or call their offices to get the past three years' annual reports and a
prospectus. Read the managers' letters to investors; check the size of the
portfolios. Like Longleaf, the better funds will tell you how they see themselves, and how you should see them. They will confirm that they are managing for the long term, and almost inevitably will touch on some of the
other factors discussed next. They take pride in what they do; you'll see it.

Here's What to Look For

- The fund should have a small portfolio. The annual report will contain a list of the fund's stocks; just count them. Good managers have
  a tightly constructed portfolio of perhaps 30 to 40 stocks in companies with good management and strong businesses. You don't need
  to analyze the companies yourself. Those fund managers' letters will
  almost inevitably highlight the essentials, as well as the fund's insistence on buying in at reasonable prices. By contrast, a typical stock
  fund, with 160 stocks, has scattered its shots, hoping that its mistakes
  won't hurt it. Such funds lack the confidence to buy a significant
  position, to "back up the truck," as Charlie Munger likes to say.
- Look for a low turnover rate. There is a five-year performance table
  toward the back of the annual report, and the annual turnover rate is
  there, usually tucked in *at the bottom of the table*. Because they invested
  in a few well-chosen stocks, value managers will show a low annual
  turnover rate, typically 25 percent or less, compared to the 100 percent
  or more for the average fund. As one highly successful manager likes
  to say, the "single greatest edge an investor can have is a long-term
  orientation."[7] A low turnover rate tells us something about a manager's temperament—which is devilishly important but impossible to
  measure directly—and how well he or she will cope with the inevitable manic-depressive swings in the market. It's all about patience.
- Check the five-year performance of the fund—it will be in that
  same performance table, and also up front, in the annual report.
  But be sure to check out the performance for the ten-year period as
  well. First, it will enable you to see how the fund did over the ups and
  downs of a full business cycle. Secondly, it will allow you to separate
  the best managers from the also-rans. Just because funds talk the talk

of Graham-and-Dodd doesn't mean that they are all equally talented. And then compare that ten-year performance with the S&P 500. Don't let the manager rely solely on a Lipper or Morningstar sector benchmark; those benchmarks make every fund look better.

- They should "eat their own cooking"—meaning the managers put significant personal dollars on the line alongside yours.[8] A willingness to invest side by side with the public is, for this author, a critical factor. If a manager won't invest in the fund, why should you? Any fund may lag for a while, but if the manager is hurting, too, I have confidence in the ultimate outcome. Good managers will often discuss their personal stake in the annual letter to investors, but they are not required to do so; you may have to request the Statement of Additional Information from the fund or the SEC. (Shame on the SEC for allowing the information to be buried.)

- They like to talk about their search for companies with good managers, ones with a shareholder orientation who won't, say, go off doing dumb acquisitions. And that, in turn, tells us that the fund managers are out in the field visiting companies, not just reading computer screens. The computers are great for initial research and screening, and they allow good managers to sift through more information; but it's where the process ends that counts.

- They should not be new at the game. Experience matters. We saw back in Chapter 6 the collapse of a technology fund run by a 20-something manager who had, of course, never seen a major break in the market. Good managers have learned by hard experience, time and again, the wisdom of Buffett's two rules: The first rule is not to lose money, and the second rule is not to forget rule number one.

- The fund should not be too large, lest it become muscle-bound. There is no hard-and-fast limit to size, but it is not for naught that most of the 10 value funds discussed in Chapter 2 have, at one time or another, closed to new investors. The American Funds group's Growth Fund of America, with $190 billion in hand, has lost the ability to invest with the range of choices and flexibility one would like to see. "The damage that size does to performance," according to one manager, Jeremy Grantham, "is the dirty little secret of the fund management business."[9] Bob Rodriguez capped the FPA Capital fund when it approached $2 billion in assets, because it is a small-cap fund, focused on companies with relatively thin markets, making it difficult to acquire a meaningful position without pushing the price up as the fund buys. For a fund that invests in large-cap stocks, for example, the ceiling would be higher.

- If a fund talks about finding companies that are currently out of favor, then stop and take a good, hard look, because it is probably one of the disciplined value funds trying to find stocks at prices that offer a margin of safety—a discount from the price a buyer would pay for the whole company—which tells us they are doing serious, patient analysis, investing bottom-up, company by company, rather than focusing on whether the economy looks strong or the market too high. Being comfortable going against the crowd, they will try to capture those bargain stocks whenever and wherever.

- All things being equal, it makes sense to invest with generalists, managers who will try to capture good values anywhere they can find them, here and abroad, in small-cap or large-cap stocks, distressed debt or spin-offs. Since no one sector will offer good value at all times, a sector fund (such as an energy fund) has dumped back on you, the investor, the responsibility for knowing when to get in and when to get out. The asset allocation strategies built around those style or sector funds imply that an investor needs a lot of funds in order to be adequately diversified. That's just plain wrong, but we will come back to that matter shortly. Of course, investors will want to allocate their money across the basics of stock funds, bond funds, and money market funds, because no one should get caught in a stock market bust without access to some ready cash. But that is very different than rebalancing mechanically between different stock fund styles and sectors as summer changes to fall.

There are exceptions to these rules, as you would expect. An international fund, for example, may have more than the recommended number of stocks in its portfolio, because, as one fund manager explained to me, there being less liquidity in foreign markets, it can be difficult to acquire more than a modest position. Also, some funds with an appealingly low turnover rate may, on closer examination, turn out to be nothing more than index funds in sheep's clothing and not truly actively managed. (A closet-indexed fund will have an R-square rating [see the

Morningstar reports], which measures how closely a fund tracks its benchmark, at or close to 95).

My checklist did not mention fund fees and other expenses, even though I spent a good deal of time criticizing the mutual fund industry for its constant dipping into investors' pockets. Clearly costs are important, and the SEC has now made the figures more visible. Fees and expenses matter, but they do not matter nearly as much as the factors I've listed, such as finding a skilled manager, one who has demonstrated patience, talent, and intellectual integrity. (A preoccupation with costs is akin to the obsession some people have about avoiding taxes. They forget that the first and most important goal is to make money, whereas minimizing the taxes you pay on what you make is obviously second.) To return to mutual funds, FPA Capital, for example, is a load fund, and the fees are not remarkably low. But judging by the fund's performance, the cost of investing in FPA Capital is a bargain. FPA Capital has shown average annual returns of 16 percent over the 20 years through 2006. In contrast, the Janus Global Tech Fund is a no-load fund, but one that, having peaked early in 2000, lost 80 percent of its value by the fall of 2002, so no one can remember now whether the fees were high or low.

Price and Value

The combination of price and value is the holy grail for the several dozen or so fund managers who think of investing as buying a part interest in a strong business instead of trading stocks, and of buying at a discount so as to provide a margin of safety. If the concept is so simple, why is the execution so difficult? Start with the concept of margin of safety, the notion of buying into a company only at a substantial discount from what a willing buyer of the whole company would pay. The common thread is a deep, abiding, almost pathological fear of that permanent loss of capital that Ben Graham, having suffered in the Great Crash, would always retain. It runs throughout the value-investing literature[10]—fear not of market quotational loss, but of an enduring and irrevocable loss of business value.

Bill Nygren of Oakmark Select bought Toys "R" Us at about $10 a share in 2000. He fully expected a turnaround at the toy stores, but he figured, just in case, that the company's real estate provided a margin of safety. The turnaround didn't happen, but by 2005, as he said, the market had recognized the value of the real estate and he sold the stock for nearly $27 a share.[11]

Speaking of investing based on business values, not market timing, after Warren Buffett's "The Superinvestors of Graham-and-Doddsville" was published, someone noted that while the nine funds in his study had indeed achieved outsized records, on average they had trailed the market one year in three.[12] Tom Russo, a value manager, took a similar look at the Goldfarb 10 we discussed in Chapter 2. He found, for example, that four of them, while they hadn't actually lost money, had, however, underperformed the S&P 500 for four consecutive years, 1996 to 1999, and in some cases by huge amounts. Over a longer period, of course, that underperformance was sharply reversed, and then some. Value investing thus requires not just managers focused on fundamentals, but patient investors, those with the temperament as well as experience to feel comfortable even when sorely out of step with the crowd. Stocks are a part interest in a business—period. If you're fretting that the Chicago Board Options Exchange (CBOE) Market Volatility Index may be signaling fear this week, value investing is not for you.

Index Funds

Before we look at two good funds, let's take a look at the role index funds might play in a portfolio. Economists and scientists have a nifty concept, known as Occam's razor, a principle attributed to a fourteenth-century English logician and Franciscan friar, William of Ockham. Paraphrased, it can be read as "All things being equal, the simplest solution tends to be the best one."[13] An index fund would seem to be a delightfully simple solution to the nagging problem of where to put one's money.

The first index fund geared toward retail investors was created by Vanguard in 1975, and is now known as the Vanguard 500 Index Fund. As the name implies, it is based on the S&P 500 stock index of the market, which, since it consists primarily of large-cap companies, contains about 75 percent of the market's total value. A no-load index fund is a good way to track the market's performance, and it offers to investors, particularly those of us with modest accounts, a convenient, very low-cost, buy-and-hold solution.*The all-in expense ratio at the Vanguard 500 fund is a delightfully low 0.18 percent a year, and since few companies come and go from the index, the trading and tax costs are trivial. As John Bogle, who created the fund, likes to remind us, it was at first described as "Bogle's Folly." From our perspective today, when there are dozens of funds tracking every index under the sun, it does seem remarkable that there was no other fund like Vanguard's until 1984.[14]

Bogle's Folly no longer, the fund has $118 billion in assets. The numerous copycat S&P 500 index funds have another $265 billion. In fact, so successful has the concept been that the market, as noted, has bred literally hundreds of variations on the basic theme. You can buy index funds built around the bond market, foreign stocks, commodities, real estate, metals, health care, and so on.[15] There are also hundreds of exchange-traded funds (ETFs), which are closed-end index funds that trade in the open market like stocks. ETFs offer a convenient way to hedge other investments, or simply to speculate by buying or selling short.

Let's stay with a broad market index fund such as the Vanguard 500. Does it make sense for investors? For Quincy, the impatient fellow we first discussed in Chapter 6, and the many others who can't resist doing something nearly all the time, the pluses of an index fund are considerable. The expenses—not just the fees but the trading and administrative costs—are rock-bottom. For the Vanguard and Fidelity versions, there is no front-end sales load, and because of the low turnover in the underlying index, only 5 percent or so a year, the capital gains taxes are minimal. Over long periods, the benefits can be enormous because the effects of compounding are so large. Bogle has calculated that, for the 25 years through 2005, an S&P 500 index fund (assuming reinvestment of distributions) returned 12.3 percent on average per year, while the average stock fund returned only 10 percent a year because of the fees. Over those 25 years, a $10,000 initial investment in the index fund grew to $170,800 versus $98,200 in the average equity fund.[16] The magic of compounding!

Bogle is an impassioned and eloquent salesman, and at first blush it might seem that Bogle and I are worlds apart, with one of us recommending indexing—a universe of stocks—and the other recommending

---

*One would expect an index fund to be no-load, but many are not—the Wells Fargo Equity Index Fund, for one. If a broker won't sell you the Vanguard fund, this may be why.

a highly selective approach. In fact, there is more common ground than meets the eye. By enforcing the longest of time horizons, indexing washes out the daily, even the yearly, ups and downs in the market, the effects of transitory euphoria, gloom, and so forth. Over the long term, which is what indexers (one hopes) are in for, stocks will track their fundamentals and an indexer will reap a return that mirrors the underlying progress of a broad swath of the American economy. Now you start to see why Bogle and I are in accord in many respects. Not only does indexing avoid the market-timing tactics that are a prescription for disaster, but it also protects investors from the people who are often their worst enemies: themselves. Indexing keeps people from frequent and mindless churning of their portfolios and enforces the rarest investing attribute: patience.

So, where do the differences lie? Bogle's argument depends too heavily on averages—the average over a long time span, and the average of 500 companies. This obscures as much as it reveals. Index investing ignores the ability of *some* fund managers, admittedly not many, to select with discipline companies that will do *better* than average. Bogle is right: On average the funds perform poorly, but we can also invest *selectively*, one by one, not just on average. While there is safety in reliance on the 500, there is also safety in a research-driven effort to prune the list for the better businesses. The 500 group includes, for example, a number of banks, among them Bank of New York, Bank of America, Citigroup, and JPMorgan Chase. They are not all alike. Moreover, those speculative market peaks and valleys provide not just the hazards of which Bogle writes, but sometimes the opportunity to buy good companies at great prices, a discount from true value—and also times to take chips off the table or to transfer them to other tables. In short, the speculative excesses can at times be used to advantage by a truly good manager.

This may sound like market timing, but it's not. At rare times, the market simply does *not* offer value, and managers such as those in Chapter 2 know it when they see it, as they did for those hot sectors of the market at the top in 2000. The reward for not robotically following the whole market at all times can be immense. It was not until 2007 that the S&P 500 returned to its 2000 peak. What if you were 70 years old when the market tanked? Would you have been able to stick it out?

The bottom line for this author is that, yes, for most investors, indexing provides a low-cost, sensible alternative to walking into the pits of

Wall Street. The only winners at that roulette table are the croupiers, who are, by Bogle's calculation, raking in some $400 billion a year.[17] Even indexing, however, requires patience (i.e., the "average" returns of which Bogle writes are available only to those who hang around long enough to realize the average). The annual redemption rate in the Vanguard 500 Index Fund has averaged 20 percent over the past few years, not much better than the 25 percent rate in stock funds generally. Anyone who trades in and out of an index fund will realize all the pitfalls of market timing and none of the benefits of careful selection. *Know who you are.* If you are able to use the principles outlined here to find an above-average fund, also to be held over a long term, you should see returns greater than you would with an index fund.

Two Stock Funds

To illustrate the value-oriented investment philosophy recommended in the book, I chose for close-ups two no-load funds, Fairholme and Wintergreen. They are funds to buy and hold in all seasons and in weather foul or fair. Each of them is relatively young. Fairholme was founded at year-end 1999, and Wintergreen in October 2005. While the funds are quite new, and happily still not large, the managers in each have been in the business a long time and have plenty of experience. Table 9.1 shows some of their respective returns as of their respective 2006 year-ends.

As you can see, Fairholme has outperformed the index over five years by an average of 10 percent a year; and if we were to put together Winters' four years at Mutual Discovery and the most recent year at Wintergreen, he beat the market index by almost as much.

So how did they do it? At Fairholme, each of the three portfolio managers has at least 20 years of investment advisory experience, as does Winters at Wintergreen. In addition to their mutual funds, both groups manage some private funds, which may seem like a distraction, though the amounts are relatively small. They do eat their own cooking. The officers and directors of Fairholme, as a group, have $20 million in the fund. Winters reports that he and his partner, Elizabeth Cohernour, have "the majority of our assets invested in Wintergreen."

Table 9.1 Fairholme and Wintergreen Returns

Data	Fairholme	Wintergreen
Average Annual Total Returns Year Ended:		
11/30/2006★	18.71%	
12/31/2006★		20.10%
Average Five Years Ended 11/30/2006	16.04%	★
S&P 500 for Five Years Ended 11/30/2006:		
6.08%		
Net Assets ($Millions)	$3,701	$596
Percentage of Net Assets		
Domestic Stocks	51%	26%
Foreign Stocks	26%	55%
Cash Equivalents	21%	18%
Total Number of Stocks	18	41
Percentage of Assets in Top 10 Holdings	70%	40%
Turnover Rate 2006	20%	13%
Increase in Number of Funds' Shares	121%	870%
Outstanding during 2006		
Annual Expense Ratio	1%	1.91%
Minimum Investment	$2,500	$10,000

★The S&P 500's performance for the years ended 11/30/06 and 12/31/06 was 14.23 percent and 15.8 percent, respectively. Before creating Wintergreen in 2005, David Winters had primary responsibility for managing the Mutual Discovery Fund, which for the four years 2001–2004 showed average annual total returns of 9.66 percent, compared with an average annual *loss* of 0.52 percent in the S&P 500.

The funds are alike in one other important respect. Each will go anywhere, and look in any market, to find significant buying opportunities. Just as we look for outstanding managers in a fund, so, too, do they for the companies whose stocks they buy.[18] Fairholme's letters wax poetic about some of the executives running the companies in the portfolio. Even if you don't like poetry, this tells you they take pains to know the people to whom your money is ultimately entrusted. Both have invested significant stakes in Buffett's Berkshire Hathaway, though Fairholme's is much the larger, at 17 percent of its assets. Wintergreen's biggest concentration is in the tobacco industry, where Winter has found several firms with large cash flows and seemingly able managers. Tobacco, of course, is not to everyone's taste, just as some will decide they don't need a mutual fund to buy shares in Berkshire. But the point is that the typical fund manager plying those computer spreadsheets has neither the facility nor indeed the interest to meet corporate executives and size up their skills.

These funds not only seek opportunities anywhere, they are actively involved even after investments are made. Wintergreen's prospectus highlights its readiness to take an activist role in corporate governance and engage in risk arbitrage in mergers, spin-offs, and the like. They both will buy distressed securities, as Fairholme did with success in MCI. If a downturn in the economy worries you, for Winters this spells an opportunity. He will remind you that at some point in time there will be a return of the bankruptcy cycle that will present opportunities for his fund to buy securities on the cheap.

Like most value funds, these two both see their large cash positions as the wherewithal to seize those moments when others panic. But do the cash positions suggest that they might close the funds? Not in the foreseeable future, although, as Winters noted, "there will be a point at which we'll probably have to say no for a while."[19] Ditto Fairholme, if "performance is [otherwise] likely to be impacted."[20]

They are different in one respect. Wintergreen is a pricey fund, with all-in expenses of 1.91 percent, versus 1 percent for Fairholme. Perhaps given its unusually broad mandate, we should think of Wintergreen simply as a low-cost hedge fund. Ultimately, as we've said, it's the results that count. (Full disclosure: The author owns relatively modest positions in both funds.)

Should you, the investor, own more than two or three (four, tops) stock funds? Stop for a moment and think about how much diversification you need. Taking these two tightly focused funds simply as illustrations (not as personal recommendations), someone investing in both would indirectly own stock in over 45 different companies; and given Fairholme's large positions in Berkshire and in Leucadia, which are themselves diversified conglomerates, the total number of different *businesses* would quickly exceed 100. Remember, you should be seeking, through a fund, indirect ownership in outstanding companies; but the reality is that, given the intensity of competition in most industries, the truly good ones are hard to find. At some point, diversification becomes what one wag called "diworsification." You've scattered your shots, losing the ability to invest a significant part of your assets in the most attractive opportunities. For example, assume you really like Stock A, which soon doubles in value; but if you've put only 1 percent of your assets there, the profit from this great investment will add only 1 percent to your net worth. You've lost your competitive edge.

True safety lies in a research-driven search for opportunities, rather in owning what Winters calls a "menagerie, not a portfolio." Money management, as a Fairholme stock picker said to me, is often a soulless business, a bunch of people making what they need to make and then getting out, as many do. They don't really enjoy the challenge of searching here and there, far and wide, for the values that have escaped the crowd and can be bought with a margin of safety. However, there are a few who not only take to the challenge but find a sense of self in doing the best they can for clients. Amen.

Notes

Foreword

1. Alson Capital analysis of published articles in the *New York Times* and *Wall Street Journal*, 2006.

Introduction

1. Investment Company Institute, *2006 Investment Company Fact Book*, Data Tables, sec. 1, Table 4.
2. Ibid., Table 5.

Chapter 1   Mutual Funds: A Painful Birth

1. *Mutual Fund Industry Handbook* (2005), 13–14.
2. K. Geert Rouwenhorst, "The Origins of Mutual Funds," Yale ICF Working Paper 04-48 (December 12, 2004), http://ssrn.com/abstract=636146.
3. Ibid., 11.
4. Paul C. Cabot, "The Investment Trust," *Atlantic Monthly*, March 1929, 401.
5. Investment Company Act of 1940 and Investment Advisers Act of 1940, H.R. Report 2639, 76th Cong., 3d Sess. (1940), 5 et seq.; Joel Seligman, *The Transformation of Wall Street* (New York: Aspen, 1982), 222–223.

6. Michael R. Yogg, "Passion for Reality: Paul Cabot and the Boston Mutual Fund," Yogg, Xlibris.com, 127 (quoting Galbraith).

7. H.R. Report 2639, supra.

8. Seligman, *Transformation*, 222–225.

9. "Fortress Set for Storming Market Debut," *Financial Times*, February 8, 2007, 1.

10. Michael J. De La Merced, "Fortress Goes Public, a First for Hedge Funds inside U.S.," *New York Times*, February 9, 2007, C2.

11. Hearings before Subcommittee of the Committee on Banking and Currency on S. 3580, 76th Cong., 3d Sess. (1940), 971.

12. "Big Money in Boston," *Fortune*, December 1949.

13. Dwight P. Robinson Jr., "Massachusetts Investors Trust," speech, Boston, Massachusetts, November 5, 1954, 13.

14. Arthur Wiesenberger, *Investment Companies: Mutual Funds and Other Types* (New York: Wiesenberger & Company, 1965), 7.

15. John C. Bogle, "Re-Mutualizing the Mutual Fund Industry," speech, Boston, Massachusetts, January 21, 2004.

16. "Big Money," *Fortune*, supra.

17. Bogle, "Re-Mutualizing," 2–3.

18. Donald Lemay, "Massachusetts Investors Trust: A Study of Performance" (submitted to fulfill Master of Arts degree in Faculty of Political Science, Columbia University, 1956), 25, 29.

19. Bogle, "Re-Mutualizing," 3.

20. Ibid., 4.

21. Yogg, "Passion," 72.

22. Ibid., 209.

23. John C. Bogle, "Mutual Funds: How a Profession with Elements of a Business Became a Business with Elements of a Profession," speech, Boston, Massachusetts, February 24, 2006.

24. Russell Baker, "Baker's 'World,'" *New York Review of Books,* January 12, 2006, 13, 14.

Chapter 2   Searching for Rational Investors in a Perfect Storm

1. Sebastian Junger, *The Perfect Storm* (New York: W. W. Norton, 1997; Harper Paperback, 1998), 130.

2. See, e.g., Paul A. Samuelson, "Proof That Properly Anticipated Prices Fluctuate Randomly," *Industrial Management Review* 6 (1965): 41, 48; Eugene Fama,

"Efficient Capital Markets: A Review of Theory and Empirical Work," *Journal of Finance* 25 (1970): 383, 392.

3. For an overview of the literature and a cogent dissent from EMT, see Lynn A. Stout, "The Mechanisms of Market Inefficiency: An Introduction to the New Finance," *Journal of Corporate Law* 28 (2003): 636.

4. Martin Wolf, "Evolution Can Provide a Missing Link to the Modern Economy," *Financial Times*, London ed., January 17, 2007, 15.

5. Robert J. Shiller, *Irrational Exuberance* (Princeton, NJ: Princeton University Press, 2000), 5–12; see generally Roger Lowenstein, *Origins of the Crash* (New York: Penguin, 2004).

6. Robert E. Rubin and Jacob Weisberg, *In an Uncertain World* (New York: Random House, 2003), 330.

7. Ibid.

8. See this author's "A Perfect Storm: Changing a Culture," Swedish Corporate Governance Forum, December 2003.

9. Ronald J. Gilson and Reinier Kraakman, "The Mechanisms of Market Efficiency Twenty Years Later: The Hindsight Bias," *Journal of Corporate Law* 28 (2003): 715, 739 (and papers cited).

10. Nicholas Barberis and Richard H. Thaler, "A Survey of Behavioral Finance," in *Handbook of the Economics of Finance*, George Constantinides, Milt Harris, and Rene Stolz, eds. (Amsterdam: Elsevier, 2003), 1051, 1055.

11. Shiller, *Irrational*, 215, 231; Justin Fox, "Is the Market Rational?" *Fortune*, December 9, 2002, 116, 126 (Shiller and Thaler advise investors to diversify completely); cf. Jesse H. Choper, John C. Coffee, and Ronald J. Gilson, *Cases and Materials on Corporations*, 6th ed. (New York: Aspen, 2004), 191.

12. See, e.g., Charles M.C. Lee, Andrei Shleifer, and Richard H. Thaler, "Investor Sentiment and the Closed-End Fund Puzzle," *Journal of Finance* 46 (1991): 75, 80–81 and materials cited.

13. Alon Brav and J. B. Heaton, "Market Indeterminacy," *Journal of Corporate Law* (2003): 517, 534 n. 66 (italics in the original).

14. See, e.g., Gilson and Kraakman, "Mechanisms," 737–739.

15. Robert Rodriguez, "Discipline," Wharton School speech, February 23, 2004, 2; see also Warren E. Buffett, "The Superinvestors of Graham-and-Doddsville," *Hermes* 11 (Columbia Business School, Fall 1984), 4.

16. Ian McDonald, "Veteran Value Manager Took a Big Risk by Playing His Investments Safe," *Wall Street Journal Quarterly Mutual Fund Review*, October 4, 2004, 3 .

17. See, e.g., First Eagle Funds Prospectus, March 1, 2004, 3; Longleaf Partners Fund Annual Report, December 31, 1999, 11. Buffett reminds investors in each annual report that while intrinsic value can be defined simply—it's the

discounted free cash flows—the calculation is anything but simple. See, e.g., Berkshire Hathaway 2003 Annual Report, 73.

18. David Rynecki, "10 Stocks to Last the Decade," *Fortune*, August 14, 2000, 114.

19. Roger Lowenstein, *Origins*, 166.

20. Clipper Fund Annual Report, December 31, 2003, 2.

21. Ibid.

22. McDonald, "Veteran," 3.

23. Shiller, *Irrational*, 245.

24. FPA Capital Annual Report (March 31, 2000), 1.

25. The Morgan Stanley Capital International index, which is a relevant yardstick for First Eagle Global and Mutual Beacon, showed negative average annual returns of 0.77 percent, almost precisely the showing of the S&P 500.

26. Louis Lowenstein, *Sense and Nonsense in Corporate Finance* (Reading, MA: Addison-Wesley, 1991), 234–238.

27. Paul J. Lim, "Investors, Do Not Try This at Home," *New York Times*, March 14, 2004, sec. 3, 1 (169 stocks in average domestic stock fund).

28. Rodriguez, "Discipline," 4.

29. See Marianne M. Jennings, "A Primer on Enron: Lessons from *A Perfect Storm* of Financial Reporting, Corporate Governance and Ethical Culture Failures," *California Western Law Review* 39 (2003): 163, 176 (company burning through cash, very low returns on equity, etc.); see also Anthony H. Catanach Jr. and Shelley Rhoades-Catanach, "Enron: A Financial Reporting Failure," *Villanova Law Review* 48: 1057.

30. Shiller, *Irrational*, 215, 231.

31. Ibid., 9–12.

32. Gilson and Kraakman, "Mechanisms," 725, 731–732; Mark Rubinstein, "Rational Market: Yes or No? The Affirmative Case," *Financial Analysts Journal* 57 (May/June 2001): 15.

33. Rubin and Weisberg, *Uncertain*, 285.

34. Ibid., 323–324.

35. Richard A. Brealey and Stewart C. Myers, *Principles of Corporate Finance*, 6th ed. Boston: Irwin/McGraw-Hill (2000), 372.

36. Stout, "Mechanisms," 664; Brav and Heaton, "Market," 518–519.

37. See, e.g., Rodriguez, "Discipline," 5.

38. James Gipson, in *Outstanding Investor Digest*, April 30, 2004, 46 (responding to an investor query about currency plays); see also Seth A. Klarman, Baupost 2003 year-end letter, January 23, 2004, 12 (Baupost is a value-oriented hedge

fund); Berkshire Hathaway 2003 Annual Report, 21 (when there's nothing exciting in which to invest, our default position is U.S. Treasuries).

39. Legg Mason Value Trust, 2003 Annual Report, May 5, 2003, 6, 14.

40. Longleaf Partners Fund, 2003 Annual Report, December 31, 2003, 1. The fund's cash and equivalents were over 15 percent of total assets.

41. First Eagle Global annual report, March 31, 2000, at 1.

42. Gipson, in *Outstanding*, 44, 64; Rodriguez, "Discipline," 6; see Gregg Wolper, "Why Legendary Investors Are Drowning in Cash," Morningstar.com, March 25, 2004.

43. James Gipson, Michael Sandler, et al., Clipper Fund letter to shareholders, April 2, 2004 (reported in *Outstanding*, 64). See also Charles de Vaulx, First Eagle Funds, comment at March 31, 2004, annual meeting, *Outstanding*, 64 ("everything out there—is quite pricey"). The funds were not shorting stocks, because as one of them said to me, the gains are limited and the losses might be severe. Cf. Gilson and Kraakman, "Mechanisms," 726–729, 738. Query, whether the recent SEC relaxation of the rules governing short sales will have much of an impact.

44. Klarman, Baupost, 14.

45. This author's *What's Wrong with Wall Street* (Reading, MA: Addison-Wesley, 1988), 35.

46. "Invisible Fund Expenses," *Consumer Reports*, May 2004, 35.

47. See, e.g., Gilson and Kraakman, "Mechanisms"; "Hedge Funds: From Alpha to Omega," *Economist*, July 17, 2004, 69 (hedge funds trade heavily to arbitrage between markets or individual securities).

48. Buffett, "Superinvestors," 8.

49. Benjamin Graham, *The Intelligent Investor*, 4th rev. ed. (New York: Harper & Row, 1973), 87–88.

50. *Outstanding*, 15.

51. Burton Malkiel, "The Efficient Market Hypothesis and Its Critics," *Journal of Economic Perspectives* 17:59, 60; Andre F. Perold, "The Capital Asset Pricing Model," *Journal of Economic Perspectives* 18 (2004): 3; Eugene F. Fama and Kenneth R. French, "The Capital Asset Pricing Model," *Journal of Economic Perspectives* 18 (2004): 25.

52. Louis Lowenstein, *Sense*, 206–207.

53. Buffett, "Superinvestors," 13–14.

54. Rodriguez, "Discipline," 3–4.

55. *Outstanding*, 16.

56. Tweedy Browne Co., *10 Ways to Beat an Index* (1998), 7.

57. Roger Lowenstein, "Unconventional Wisdom: The Wrong Diagnosis,"*Smart Money*, March 2004, 50, 51.

58. Graham, *Intelligent*, 108.

59. Benjamin Graham and David L. Dodd, *Security Analysis* (New York: McGraw-Hill, 1934), 2, 13.

60. Graham, *Intelligent*, 277, 283.

61. Philip Fisher, *Common Stocks and Uncommon Profits*, rev. ed. (New York: Harper & Row, 1960).

62. Ibid., 91.

63. David F. Swensen, *Unconventional Success: A Fundamental Approach to Personal Investment* (New York: Free Press, 2005), 297.

64. Carla Fried, "Investing: Why the Sidelines Are Looking Good to Managers," *New York Times*, August 15, 2004, sec. 3, 6; see n. 42, supra.

65. Letter to this author dated September 15, 2004.

66. Wintergreen Fund Semi-Annual Report, June 30, 2006, 1.

67. McDonald, "Veteran," n. 16.

68. Longleaf Partners Funds Quarterly Report, September 30, 2004, 1.

69. Buffett, "Superinvestors," 13.

Chapter 3   The Anatomy of the Stock Market

1. Jonathan Chevreau, "MER Column Strikes a Nerve,"*National Post* (Canada), August 18, 2006, FP9. ("It defies logic why so many who are clever . . . in other spheres are such dolts when it comes to . . . finance.")

2. Much of what appears in this section has been adapted from earlier books by the author, *What's Wrong with Wall Street* (1988) and *Sense and Nonsense in Corporate Finance* (1991).

3. Roger Lowenstein, *Origins of the Crash* (New York: Penguin Press, 2004), 71.

4. This discussion of the market history and structure draws on a book review by the author, "Is Speculation 'The Essential Native Genius of the Stock Market'?"*Columbia Law Review* 92, 232, reviewing Walter Werner and Steven T. Smith, *Wall Street* (New York: Columbia University Press, 1991), and on the Werner and Smith book.

5. Ibid. (quoting Werner and Smith, 123).

6. Brad Stone, "Spam Doubles, Finding New Ways to Deliver Itself,"*New York Times*, December 6, 2006, A1 (most active spammers operate beyond the reach of American law enforcement, the current hot spots being Russia, Eastern Europe, and Asia).

7. Benjamin Graham, *The Intelligent Investor*, 4th rev. ed. (New York: Harper & Row, 1973), 277.

8. Benjamin Graham and David L. Dodd, *Security Analysis* (N1934), 12, 23.

9. Id. at 23.

10. James Tobin, "On the Efficiency of the Financial System," *Lloyds Bank Review*, July 1984, 14–15.

11. John Maynard Keynes, *The General Theory of Employment, Interest, and Money*, 2nd ed., Collected Writings of John Maynard Keynes, vol. 7 (London: Macmillan, Cambridge University Press for the Royal Economic Society, 1973), 155.

12. Paul De Grauwe, "The Belgian Chocolate Theory of the Dollar," *Financial Times*, January 13, 2006.

Chapter 4   Investing at Warp Speed

1. Investment Company Institute, "Trends in Mutual Fund Investing," December 2006.

2. John C. Bogle, *The Battle for the Soul of Capitalism* (New Haven, CT: Yale University Press, 2005), 73.

3. Ibid., 171.

4. American Century Growth Investors, American Century Ultra Investors, American Funds Amcap, Consulting Group Large Cap Growth, Fidelity Advisor Equity Growth, Fidelity Growth Company, Harbor Capital Appreciation, Janus Growth & Income, Janus Twenty, Mainstay Capital Appreciation, Massachusetts Investors Growth Stock, RiverSource (formerly AXP) Growth, RiverSource New Dimensions A, Vanguard Growth Index, Vanguard U.S. Growth. Two funds had been merged out, two others shifted styles, and one fund being simply the twin of another was dropped.

5. All data for the periods ending August 31, 2005, were obtained from Morningstar.

6. Data are for the eight value funds that go back 10 years; Mutual Beacon and Oakmark Select were created in late 1996.

7. Weisenberger 1965 Annual Investment Company Report, 7–8.

8. Bogle, *Battle*, 157–158; David F. Swensen, *Unconventional Success: A Fundamental Approach to Personal Investment* (New York: Free Press, 2005), 204.

9. Morningstar Alert, MIGFX expense ratio change (increase from 0.92 percent to 0.96 percent).

10. Bogle, *Battle*, 143.

11. Calls to Stephen Pesek, the lead manager, were not returned.

12. Donald Lemay, "Massachusetts Investors Trust, A Study of Performance" (submitted to fulfill Master of Arts degree in Faculty of Political Science, Columbia University, 1956), 25.

13. Statement of Additional Information, April 1, 2005.

14. Morningstar Stewardship Grade, August 10, 2005.

15. Bogle, *Battle*, 167–168.

16. Benjamin Graham and David L. Dodd, *Security Analysis* (New York: McGraw-Hill, 1934), 23.

17. "Success of ETFs Sparks Demand," *Financial Times*, June 14, 2006, 25, col. 6.

18. John Maynard Keynes, *The Collected Writings of John Maynard Keynes*, vol. 12, ed. Donald Moggridge (London: Macmillan, Cambridge University Press for the Royal Economic Society, 1983), 82.

Chapter 5   Greed Is Good

1. Paul Samuelson, quoted in John C. Bogle, *The Battle for the Soul of Capitalism* (New Haven, CT: Yale University Press, 2005), 177.

2. TROW Form 10-K, year ended December 31, 2005, Item 6, Selected Financial Data, and Item 8, Financial Statements.

3. Ibid.

4. Ibid., Item 7, Management Discussion and Analysis.

5. John C. Bogle, "Mutual Funds: How a Profession with Elements of a Business Became a Business with Elements of a Profession," speech before Boston Security Analysts Society, Boston, Massachusetts, February 24, 2006, 5.

6. In 1992, T. Rowe Price acquired a group of Axe-Houghton funds.

7. TROW Form 10-K, year ended December 31, 1999, Item 6, Selected Financial Data.

8. Bogle, *Battle*, 154–155; see also David F. Swensen, *Unconventional Success: A Fundamental Approach to Personal Investment* (New York: Free Press, 2005), passim.

9. Morningstar Snapshot, T. Rowe Price Group, February 5, 2006.

10. "The Administration of the Investment Company Act, Dec. 21, 1961," quoted in Joel Seligman, *The Transformation of Wall Street* (New York: Aspen, 1982), 364–365, quoting SEC chairman Edward Gadsby.

11. See, e.g., Samuel S. Kim, "Mutual Funds: Solving the Shortcomings of the Independent Director Response to Advisory Self-Dealing through Use of the Undue Influence Standard," *Columbia Law Review* 98 (1998): 474, 475.

12. Oakmark Funds, First Quarter Report, December 31, 2006, 1.

13. Morningstar, T. Rowe Price Growth Stock Stewardship Grade, November 17, 2005, 2.

14. T. Rowe Price Family of Funds, Sched. 14A, April 2006, 8.

15. TROW Form 10-K, year ended December 31, 2005, n. 4 to consolidated financial statements.

16. Morningstar, TROW Analyst Report, March 10, 2006, 1, 2.

17. Source: Morningstar, as of February 16, 2006.

18. Source: Morningstar, "T. Rowe Price Expands Lineup of Advisor Class Funds Distributed through Financial Intermediaries," *Wealth Management*, January 5, 2006, 2.

19. See, e.g., Growth Stock Fund, Key Facts, as of 9/30/05, 5, and Addendum to Key Facts, as of 12/31/05.

20. Deborah Brown, "Mutual Funds: Capital Pays Price for Under-Par Performance," *Financial Times*, Febuary 13, 2006.

21. Lauren Young, "Funds That Play the Field," *BusinessWeek*, March 6, 2006, 94. See also Paula A. Tkac, "Mutual Funds: Temporary Problem or Permanent Morass," *Federal Reserve Bank of Atlanta Economic Review* (4th Quarter 2004): 1, 6 (investors seek asset class consistency).

22. Ibid.

23. Bogle, *Battle*, 186.

24. Robert Rodriguez e-mails to the author, dated March 16, 2006, 10:31 A.M. and 3:06 P.M.

25. Form 497 (Statement of Additional Information) filed at SEC March 2006, 10–11.

26. "Four Former SEC Directors Agree Mutual Fund Industry Overre-gulated," *Bureau of National Affairs, Securities Regulations, & Law Report*, March 6, 2006, 376 (comments of Barry Barbash, division director mid to late 1990s; another former director, Kathryn B. McGrath, called the review of advisory fees "a big fat waste of time.")

27. "Mutual Funds: ICI Chief Economist Reid Notes Team Fund Management," *Bureau of National Affairs, Securities Regulation, & Law Report*, January 30, 2006, 164.

28. "Key Facts, Blue Chip Growth and Growth Stock Funds," November 2005. There is a passing comment in the funds' literature that a manager may advise more than one fund, but nothing to hint at the full extent of the overlap.

29. Morningstar data, as of March 15, 2006.

30. Morningstar, TROW Analyst Report, March 10, 2006, n. 26, 1.

31. "Janus Takes Another Step on the Road to Recovery," *Fortune*, March 6, 2006, 167, 168.

32. Morningstar, TROW Analyst Report, January 31, 2006, 3.

33. Arthur Wiesenberger, *Investment Companies 1955*, 15th Annual Edition (New York: Wiesenberger & Company, 1955).

34. Price Growth Stock Fund, Semiannual Report, June 30, 1986, 14–15.

35. T. Rowe Price Associates, Annual Report 1987, 1.

36. SEC Release No. IC-26323; File No. S7-03-04, *Federal Register* 69, 3472, 3473.

37. SEC Release No. IC-26520; File No. S7-03-04, *Federal Register* 69, 46378, 46383 (final rule, requiring inter alia that 75 percent of mutual fund boards be independent). The rule was subsequently negated by the courts.

38. Price Growth Stock Fund, Annual Report 1988, 17.

39. Rebecca Knight and Deborah Brewster, "Investors Weigh Up the Merrill Deal," *Financial Times*, February 21, 2006, 11; see also "Black Rock and a Hard Place," *Economist*, February 18, 2006, 73 ("Scale in equity asset management may benefit the asset manager who is collecting the fees, but it does not seem to provide a corresponding benefit to clients."); see also Martin Whitman, Third Avenue Funds, letter to shareholders, October 31, 2005, 4 (money management industry only modestly competitive).

40. See, e.g., *Gartenberg v. Merrill Lynch Asset Mgmt., Inc.*, 636 F.2dd 16 (2d Cir. 1980), cert. den., 451 U.S. 910 (1981) (relying in substantial part on comparative fee scales); see generally John P. Freeman and Stewart L. Brown, "Mutual Fund Advisory Fees: The Cost of Conflicts of Interest," *Journal of Corporate Law* 26 (2001), 609, 642–650.

41. Cf. William J. Baumol et al., *The Economics of Mutual Fund Markets: Competition Versus Regulation* (New York: Springer, 1990).

42. *Securities and Exch. Commission v. Insurance Securities, Inc.*, C.A. 9 (Cal.) 254 Fed. 2d 642 (1958), cert. den., 358 U.S.823.

43. *Rosenfeld v. Black*, 445 F.2d 1337 (1971). (per Friendly, J.)

44. There appear to have been only three instances of a fund's board rejecting the buyer before the recent instance of the Clipper Fund. See Tkac, "Mutual Funds," n. 3. This is hardly surprising, since the directors of a fund are almost invariably handpicked by the management.

45. Wiesenberger, 1955, supra, 18.

46. Bogle, *Battle*, 184.

47. Benjamin Graham, *The Intelligent Investor* (New York: Harper & Brothers, 1949), 72.

48. Ibid., 4th rev. ed. (New York: Harper & Row, 1973), 115–117.

49. Tim Hatton, *The New Fiduciary Standard* (Princeton, NJ: Bloomberg Press, 2005), 5.

50. Bogle, *Battle*, 152–153.

51. TROW Form 10-K, year ended December 31, 2005, 9.

52. Price Science and Technology Fund, Annual Report for Year 2001, Form N-30D, filed with SEC on February 21, 2002.

53. Bogle, "Mutual Funds," 5–6.

54. Ibid., 14.

55. Nicholas Barberis and Andrei Shleifer, "Style Investing,"*Journal of Financial Economics* 68 (2003): 161, 162.

Chapter 6   The Investor's Dilemma

1. Floyd Norris, "If Boomers Have It All, What's Left?"*New York Times*, September 1, 2006, C1.

2. DuPont, "DuPont to Change U.S. Pension and Savings Plan in 2008; Move Modernizes Benefits Design for Current, Future Employees," press release dated August 28, 2006; conversation with Lori Captain at DuPont, December 13, 2006.

3. Norris, "If Boomers."

4. "Markets: Investor Priorities Will Be in Flux as America Faces Up to a Pensions Gap,"*Financial Times*, December 4, 2006, 11; see also "Frontline: Can You Afford to Retire?" Public Broadcasting System, airdate May 16, 2006 (correspondent and senior producer, Hedrick Smith) (www.pbs.org/wgbh/pages/frontline/retirement/etc/script.html).

5. See "Frontline," supra.

6. See "Markets: Investor Priorities," supra.

7. See "Frontline," supra.

8. See "The Case for Automatic 401(k) Enrollment,"*New York Times Digest*, August 5, 2006, 5.

9. See "Frontline," supra.

10. Ibid.

11. Kathy Chu, "Long Life Is a Blessing and a Challenge,"*USA Today*, December 1, 2006.

12. See generally, "Recent Changes in U.S. Family Finances: Evidence from the 2001 and 2004 Survey of Consumer Finances," Federal Reserve Board, March 22, 2006. www.federalreserve.gov/pubs/bulletin/2006/06index.html.

13. See "Frontline," supra; see also Vanguard, "How America Saves 2005," 4.

14. Andrew Delbanco, *The Death of Satan: How Americans Have Lost the Sense of Evil* (New York: Farrar, Straus & Giroux, 1995), 117 (quoting George Frederickson, ed., *William Lloyd Garrison: Great Lives Observed* (Upper Saddle River, NJ: Prentice-Hall, 1968), 143.

15. Roger Lowenstein, "How the Other Half Lives,"*SmartMoney*, October 2006, 53.

16. See "Recent Changes," supra, A12.

17. Peter Lynch, *One Up on Wall Street* (New York: Penguin, 1990), 96.

18. See, e.g., Nicholas Barberis and Richard Thaler, "A Survey of Behavioral Finance" (2002), forthcoming in *Handbook of Economics of Finance*; Robert J.

Shiller, "Bubbles, Human Judgment, and Expert Opinion,"*Financial Analysts Journal* (May/June 2002): 18, and sources cited therein; Cass Sunstein, ed., *Behavioral Law & Economics* (New York: Cambridge University Press, 2000).

19. Securities and Exchange Commission, "Public Policy Implications of Investment Company Growth," H.R. Rep. No. 2337, 89th Congress, 2d Sess. (1966), 203.

20. Terrance Odean, "Do Investors Trade Too Much?"*American Economic Review* 89 (1999): 1279; cf. Mark Hulbert, "Buy and Hold? Sure, but Don't Forget the 'Hold,'"*New York Times,* July 2, 2006, sec. 3, 5.

21. David Leonhardt, "The N.F.L. Draft: A Study in Cockeyed Overconfidence," *New York Times,* April 24, 2005, sec. 4, 14 (citing study by Cade Massey and Richard H. Thaler).

22. Warren Buffett, Memo to Berkshire Hathaway Managers, September 27, 2006 (cited in *Wit & Wisdom,* compiled by David Greenspan, Blue Ridge Capital, 2006).

23. *Quantitative Analysis of Investor Behavior* (Boston: Dalbar, 2006).

24. Ibid., 18.

25. Christine Benz, "How Did Investors Really Do?" November 13, 2006, http://news.morningstar.com/article/printArticle.asp?id=178504.

26. Paul De Grauwe, "The Belgian Chocolate Theory of the Dollar,"*Financial Times,* January 13, 2006.

27. John Maynard Keynes, *The General Theory of Employment, Interest, and Money,* 2nd ed., Collected Writings of John Maynard Keynes, vol. vii (London: Macmillan, Cambridge University Press for the Royal Economic Society, 1973), ch. 12, 157.

28. Ibid., 147, 158.

29. Robert E. Rubin and Jacob Weisberg, *In an Uncertain World* (New York: Random House, 2003), 323–324.

30. Nassim Nicholas Taleb, "Life Is Unpredictable—Get Used to It,"*NewScientist .com* news service, July 5, 2006; see generally Nassim Nicholas Taleb, *The Black Swan* (New York: Random House, 2007).

31. Roger Lowenstein, *Origins of the Crash: The Great Bubble and Its Undoing* (New York: Penguin, 2004), 159–164.

32. Ibid., 105.

33. Ibid., 102–103, 111.

34. Ibid., 111.

35. Ibid., 119.

36. Ibid., 71.

37. Ibid., 116.

38. Henrik Cronqvist, "Advertising and Portfolio Choice," Working Paper 44/05, Center for Research on Pensions and Welfare Policies, 2005, 3.

39. Sendhil Mullainathan and Andrei Shleifer, "Persuasion in Finance," Working Paper 11838, National Bureau of Economic Research, December 2005 (www.nber.org/papers/w11838), and the studies cited therein.

40. Prem C. Jain and Joanna Shuang Wu, "Truth in Mutual Fund Advertising: Evidence on Future Performance and Fund Flows," *Journal of Finance* 55 (2000): 937.

41. "The World Is Your Oyster: Fidelity Can Help You Find the Pearls," *Barron's*, July 10, 2006, L4.

42. FFG: David Rynecki, "10 Stocks to Last the Decade," *Fortune*, August 14, 2000, 114.

43. Ibid.

44. Ibid., 118.

45. Dan Culloton, "It's Time to Close the Door on Invesco," December 9, 2003, http://news.morningstar.com/article/printArticle.asp?id=101171.

46. Lisa Reilly Cullen, "The Triple Digit Club," *Money*, December 1999, 168–170 (online ed., 3–4).

47. Ibid., 3.

48. Joanna Glaser, "Net Fund Longs for Happier Days," *Wired.com*, February 28, 2003.

49. "The Best Investments for 2000 and Beyond," *Money*, January 2000, 7–77 (online ed., 13).

50. Peter Coy, "Riding the Bull into 2000," *BusinessWeek*, December 27, 1999 (online ed., 17).

51. Ibid., 13.

52. Ibid., 38.

53. Ibid., 39.

54. Lowenstein, *Origins*, 115–116.

55. "Investors' Mutual Fund Purchase Practices at Odds with Those Recommended by Investor Educators, Survey Finds," Consumer Federation of America, June 12, 2006.

56. Tom Lauricella, Diya Gullapalli, and Shefali Anand, "What's New? Try Another Question: Does This Innovation Make Sense?" *Wall Street Journal*, January 4, 2007, R1.

57. See "Investors' Mutual Fund Purchase Practices," supra.

58. William C. Nygren, Oakmark Select Fund, Semiannual Report, March 31, 2006, 6–7, citing Shane Frederick, "On the Ball: Cognitive Reflection and Decision Making," *Journal of Economic Perspectives* 19 (Fall 2005): 25–42.

Chapter 7 The Industrialization of Mutual Funds

1. Joe McGinnis, *The Selling of the President 1968* (New York: Simon & Schuster, 1969).

2. Investment Company Institute, *Trends in Mutual Fund Investing,* December 2006.

3. Source: Investment Company Institute.

4. Deborah Brewster and David Wighton, "Black Rock Chief Points to European Mergers," *Financial Times,* October 2, 2006, 20.

5. Morningstar Tax Analysis, Fidelity Adv. Fifty A, March 1, 2007.

6. Andrew Gogerty, Morningstar Analyst Research, Fidelity Independence, November 10, 2006.

7. Morningstar Fidelity Independence Stewardship Grade, April 11, 2007.

8. Ibid., 3.

9. Michael Santoli, "Fixing Fidelity," Barron's April 9, 2007, p. L5, L8-9; Leslie Norton, "Quietly Bangalore Connection Grows," Barron's April 9, 2007, p. L10.

10. Deborah Brewster, "Fidelity in Consumer Banking Push," *Financial Times,* September 14, 2007, 127.

11. Morningstar, Total Returns for Franklin Resources, report dated February 7, 2007; see also "Talk of Consolidation Helps Mutual Funds Beat S&P 500," *Financial Times,* January 30, 2006, 20 (global index of asset managers valued at 22 times earnings).

12. Franklin Resources Form 10-K, year ended September 30, 2006, filed at SEC December 20, 2006 (Item 6: Selected Financial Data).

13. Conversation with Michael Price, November 7, 2006.

14. Conversation with Tim Melvin, November 3, 2006.

15. John C. Bogle, *The Little Book of Common Sense Investing* (Hoboken, NJ: John Wiley & Sons, 2007), 131.

16. *Mutual Fund Industry Handbook* (2005), sec. 1, 3.

17. Conversations by author with Michael Bills (Janus) and Joanne Mason (Third Avenue).

18. Morningstar, "Fund Times: American Century Going More Load?" April 2, 2007.

19. "Effectively Servicing and Supporting the Independent Financial Advisor," Financial Research Corporation (2006), 41–50.

20. The Morningstar Rating Methodology (2003), 3.

21. Ibid., 5.

22. "Effectively Servicing," supra, 45.

23. John Authers, "The Short View," *Financial Times,* March 15, 2007, 15, quoting Henry Kaufman.

24. Morningstar, "Fund Times: Artisan to Close Another Successful Fund," March 12, 2007 (Fidelity changes managers at nine funds).

25. "T. Rowe Price Expands Lineup of Advisor Class Funds Distributed Through Financial Intermediaries," January 5, 2006.

26. James B. Stewart, "Make the Market Work for You," *SmartMoney,* December 2006, 49–50 (acknowledging that rebalancing "injects an element of market timing into investment decisions").

27. "Set a Course for Higher Returns," *BusinessWeek,* December 26, 2005, 104 (rebalance if the percentage in bonds "strays" by about three percentage points).

28. Paul J. Lim, "Hitting the Reset Button on Your 401(k)," *New York Times,* January 8, 2006, sec. 3, 5 (rebalancing small caps vs. large caps).

29. "Effectively Servicing," supra, 45–46.

30. Ibid., 48.

31. Conversation with the author, August 30, 2006.

32. Anne Kates Smith, "Finding the Right Pro," *Kiplinger's Personal Finance Adviser,* Special Edition, March 17, 2006 (Yahoo! Finance).

33. David F. Swensen, *Unconventional Success: A Fundamental Approach to Personal Investment* (New York: Free Press, 2005), 193.

34. Ibid., 184, 217.

35. *Mutual Fund Industry Handbook* (2005), sec. 1, 2.

36. Citigroup Smith Barney, "The Financial Advisor," July 21, 2006, 15.

37. Daniel Bergstresser, John M.R. Chalmers, and Peter Tufano, "Assessing the Cost and Benefits of Brokers in the Mutual Fund Industry," working paper dated January 16, 2006.

38. Lim, "Hitting," sec. 3, 5; see also "Bargain Financial Advice," *Consumer Reports,* February 2006, 29, 32 (Cambridge planner advised rebalancing annually).

39. Jack Egan, "Investing: Start with a Stock Index; Now Try to Turbocharge It," *New York Times,* December 18, 2005, sec. 3, 7 (the best funds behave "a bit like index funds on steroids").

40. "Warren Buffett's Question and Answer Session with Harvard Business School Students," December 22, 2005, notes by students Osias, Lie, and Sender, 3.

41. E-mail from Kevin Laughlin to author, dated February 14, 2007; see also author's conversation with David Winters.

42. Conversation with Martin Whitman, August 30, 2006.

43. The Morningstar Rating Methodology, October 1, 2003, 3–4.

44. Conversation with author, November 8, 2006.

45. Russel Kinnel, "Five-Star Funds to Avoid," http://news.morningstar.com/article/id=163463.

46. Conversation with Tim Melvin, November 1, 2006.

47. Conversation with Michael Bills, October 10, 2006 (telephone).

48. Deborah Brewster, "Fidelity Targets Pensions Cash," *Financial Times*, January 29, 2007, 15.

49. Morningstar Special Advertising Section, "Top Fund Analyst Picks for the New Year," *Wall Street Journal,* January 20, 2007, S6–S7.

50. Roger Lowenstein, *Origins of the Crash* (New York: Penguin, 2004), 118.

51. Larry Swedroe, "Managing Portfolios: Three Strikes, You're Out!" www.webcpa.com, June 23, 2006 (citing study by the *Hulbert Financial Digest*).

52. Swensen, *Unconventional,* 180.

53. Ibid., 266.

54. Charles de Vaulx, "Letter from the Portfolio Manager," First Eagle Funds, Annual Report, year ended October 31, 2006, 5–6.

55. Nerissa C. Brown, Kelsey D. Wei, and Russell R. Wermers, "Analyst Recommendations, Mutual Fund Herding and Overreaction in Stock Prices," working paper, March 2007.

56. De Vaulx, "Letter," 6.

57. Dan Leflovitz, Morningstar Analyst Research, Fidelity Diversified International, January 11, 2007.

58. Dresdner Kleinwort, "Global Equity Strategy," January 10, 2007, 4, citing Dasgupta, Prat, and Verardo, *The Price of Conformism* (2006), available at www.ssrn.com.

59. Joe McGinnis, *The Selling of the President*, new intro. by the author (New York: Penguin, 1988), xx–xxi.

Chapter 8   Through a Window . . . Darkly

1. Paul Cabot, "The Investment Trust," *Atlantic Monthly,* March 1929, 401, 404–405.

2. Source: John C. Bogle, Vanguard Group.

3. Russell Kinnel, "Fund Spy: Fund Expense Ratios Continue to Fall," Morningstar, May 22, 2006.

4. SEC Investment Company Act Release No. 11414, October 28, 1980 (creating Rule 12b-1).

5. "Independent Directors Council Outlines Ideas for Rule 12b-1 Reform," *Sec. Reg. L. & Reg.*, July 23, 2007, 1140; Morningstar Fund Spy: Andrew Gogarty, "Memo to SEC: 12b-1 Fees Must Go," April 19, 2007, www.morningstar.com.

6. Gogarty, "Memo."

7. See, e.g., First Eagle Global and FPA Capital.

8. Gogarty, "Memo" (comment by Andrew Donohue, director of the division); see Deborah Brewster, "SEC Considers Axing Mutual Fund Market Fee," *Financial Times,* April 10, 2007, 18.

9. Institutional Investor News, Fund Action Daily, "Good Cop, Bad Cop Routine Aims to Shrink 12b-1," April 23, 2007.

10. Brad M. Barber, Terrance Odean, and Lu Zheng, "Out of Sight, Out of Mind: The Effects of Expenses on Mutual Fund Flows," working paper, December 2003.

11. Interview with Liz Cohenrour, November 2, 2006; see also Travis Plunkett, Legislative Director, Consumer Federation of America, "Testimony Regarding Mutual Funds: Hidden Fees, Misgovernance and Other Practices That Harm Investors," before Senate Governmental Affairs Subcommittee on Financial Management, the Budget, and International Security, January 27, 2004.

12. David F. Swensen, *Unconventional Success: A Fundamental Approach to Personal Investment* (New York: Free Press, 2005), 180–181.

13. Correspondence with Kevin Laughlin, Vanguard Group, April 30, 2007.

14. *Mutual Fund Industry Handbook* (2005), 163–164.

15. Christine Benz, "The Short Answer: Which Is the Right Fund Share Class for You?" Morningstar, August 23, 2005, http://news.morningstar.com/article/.

16. See, e.g., RiverSource Growth Fund, Prospectus, September 29, 2006.

17. Vikram Nanda, Z. Jay Wang, and Lu Zheng, "The ABCs of Mutual Funds: A Natural Experiment on Fund Flows and Performance," working paper, June 1, 2004.

18. Benz, "Short Answer," 4.

19. In the Matter of Morgan Stanley DW Inc., Admin. Proceeding File No. 3-11335, November 17, 2003.

20. Edward S. O'Neal, "Mutual Fund Share Classes and Broker Incentives," *Financial Analysts Journal* (September/October 1999): 76, 83–84.

21. Andrew J. Donohue, Director, SEC Division of Investment Management, "Keynote Address at 2007 Mutual Funds and Investment Management Conference," March 26, 2007.

22. Barber et al., "Out of Sight."

23. Benz, "Short Answer," 1.

24. Donohue, "Keynote," 4.

25. John C. Bogle, *The Battle for the Soul of Capitalism* (New Haven, CT: Yale University Press, 2005), 158 (1 percent); Janet Paskin and Nicole Bullock, "Best 35 Funds 2007," *SmartMoney,* February 2007 (1 to 1.25 percent).

26. James M. Class and Michael Maiello, "Hidden Expenses," *Forbes,* January 31, 2005, 108.

27. SEC, "Prohibition on the Use of Brokerage Commission to Finance Distribution," SEC Rel. No. IC-2591, Part II, September 9, 2004; see also In the Matter of Morgan Stanley DW Inc., supra.

28. NASD News Release, "NASD Charges 15 Firms with Directed Brokerage Violations, Imposes Fines Totaling More than $34 Million," June 8, 2005; SEC Press Release, "Franklin Advisers and Franklin Templeton Distributors to Pay $20 Million to Settle Charges Related to Use of Brokerage Commissions to Pay for Shelf Space," December 13, 2004.

29. *Dept. of Enforcement v. American Funds Distributors, Inc.,* NASD Disciplinary Proceeding No. CE3050003, August 30, 2006.

30. Ibid., n. 18.

31. Ibid., 7.

32. Bear Stearns, "Brokers and Asset Managers: Hard or Soft? Determining the Fate of Soft Dollars," June 2003.

33. Jennifer S. Conrad, Kevin M. Johnson, and Sunil Wahal, "Institutional Trading and Soft Dollars," *Journal of Finance* (February 2001): 397, 399.

34. SEC, "Commission Guidance Regarding Client Commission Practices under Section 28(e) of the Securities Exchange Act of 1934," Release No. 34-52635, November 25, 2005, 21–22.

35. SEC, "Commission Guidance Regarding Client Commn. Practices under Sec. 28(e) of the Exch. Act of 1934," Release No. 34-54165, July 18, 2006.

36. Debevoise & Plimpton LLP, "SEC Updates Its Guidance on Use of Client Commissions," July 25, 2006, 5.

37. "Share Trading: The Big Squeeze," *Economist,* October 7, 2006, 83.

38. Rich Blake, "How High Can Costs Go?" *Institutional Investor,* May 2001, 56.

39. Correspondence with Don Phillips, Morningstar, May 21, 2007.

40. Laura Johannes and John Hechinger, "Conflicting Interests: Why a Brokerage Giant Pushes Some Mediocre Funds; Jones & Co. Gets Payments from 'Preferred' Vendors; Cruises and Safaris, Too; Mrs. Wessels Loses on Putnam," *Wall Street Journal,* January 9, 2004, A1.

41. Ibid.

42. NASD Press Release, "Edward Jones to Pay $75 Million to Settle Revenue Sharing Charges," December 22, 2004.

43. *Enrique v. Edw. D. Jones & Co.*, Civ. No. 042-00126 Cir. Ct., St. Louis, Mo., and others, hearing July 20, 2007.

44. Edward Jones, "Mutual Funds: Mutual Fund Families, Including Information about Our Preferred Fund Families and Revenue Sharing," www.edwardjones.com/cgi/, October 8, 2006.

45. Cerulli Associates, "Mutual Fund Revenue Sharing: Current Practices and Projected Implications, 2005," Epilogue: Edward Jones Case Study.

46. Smith Barney, "Mutual Funds: Revenue Sharing Fund Families; What Every Investor Should Know," www.smithbarney.com/products, September 18, 2006.

47. Schwab advertisement, "Choice is a good thing," *New York Times,* January 7, 2007, C28.

48. Karen Damato, "Fund Supermarkets Harbor Hidden Costs for No-Fee Investors," *Wall Street Journal,* July 5, 2005, C1.

49. Swensen, *Unconventional,* 175 (citing Karen Damato, "Longleaf Leaves Schwab," *Wall Street Journal,* May 2, 2003).

50. In the Matter of Smith Barney Fund Management LLC & Citigroup Global Markets, Inc., Inv. Co. Act Rel. 2390, May 31, 2005.

51. In the Matter of BISYS Fund Services, Inc., Investment Adv. Act of 1940, Release No. 2554, September 26, 2006; see also Tom Lauricella, "J.P. Morgan Receives SEC Inquiry Related to Bisys," *Wall Street Journal,* October 28, 2006, A3.

52. Travis Plunkett, "Testimony Regarding Mutual Funds: Hidden Fees, Misgovernance and Other Practices That Harm Investors," before Senate Governmental Affairs Subcommittee on Financial Management, the Budget, and International Security, January 27, 2004, 11.

53. Jack Willoughby, "Good Morning, Ameriprise: A Financial-Services Giant Awakens," *Barron's,* August 21, 2006, 15.

54. Ibid.

55. Burt Helm, "Queen of the Pitch," *BusinessWeek,* April 30, 2007, 40.

56. Interview with the author, July 25, 2006.

57. SEC Investment Company Governance, Proposed Rule, Rel. No. IC 26323, January 23, 2004, 3474.

58. Alan R. Palmiter, "Mutual Fund Boards: A Failed Experiment in Regulatory Outsourcing," Brooklyn Law School Symposium, March 31, 2006, working paper, 2.

59. "Hail, Shareholder!" *Economist,* June 2, 2007, 65–67.

Chapter 9   How to Pick a Mutual Fund

1. Cass R. Sunstein and Richard H. Thaler, "The Survival of the Fattest," *New Republic,* March 19, 2007, 59–63, reviewing Brian Wansink, *Mindless Eating: Why We Eat More Than We Think* (New York: Bantam, 2006).

2. Daniel Bergstresser, John M.R. Chalmers, and Peter Tufano, "Assessing the Costs and Benefits of Brokers in the Mutual Fund Industry," working paper dated January 16, 2006.

3. Ibid., Table 7.

4. Conversation with the author, August 30, 2006; see also "Dear Fellow Shareholders . . . , Excerpts from Letters to Third Avenue Funds Shareholders 1990–2005," 343 (excerpt from January 31, 2004, letter to Third Avenue Value Fund shareholders).

5. Source: Longleaf Partners Fund Trust, www.longleafpartners.com/about/principles/fund (letter to shareholders of the funds, year ended 2006).

6. *Morningstar Funds 500,* 2007 ed. (Hoboken, NJ: John Wiley & Sons, 2007), 20–21.

7. Seth A. Klarman, Baupost Limited Partnerships, 2005 Year-End Letter, 10.

8. A recent academic study bears out the relationship between a manager's stake in the fund and the fund's performance. Ajay Khorana, Henri Servaes, and Lei Wedge, "Portfolio Manager Ownership and Fund Performance," working paper, August 10, 2006 (e-mail: hservaes@london.edu).

9. Rich Blake, "The II300: Passive Aggressors," *Institutional Investor,* July 2004 (from http://proquest.umi.com/pqdweb?index) (quoting Jeremy Grantham).

10. Seth A. Klarman, *Margin of Safety* (New York: HarperCollins, 1991).

11. Oakmark Select, Semi-Annual Report, March 31, 2005, 13.

12. Cited in Tweedy Browne Co., *10 Ways to Beat an Index* (1998), 7.

13. "Occam's razor," from Wikipedia, the online encyclopedia, 1.

14. John C. Bogle, " 'Value' Strategies," *Wall Street Journal,* February 9, 2007, A11.

15. Ibid.

16. John C. Bogle, *The Little Book of Common Sense Investing* (Hoboken, NJ: John Wiley & Sons, 2007), 44–45.

17. Ibid., xviii. Most of that $400 billion flows to broker-dealers—about $250 billion—with roughly another $75 billion going for mutual fund advisory fees and other charges, and $40 billion for hedge fund fees. Correspondence with Kevin Laughlin, Vanguard Group, April 10, 2007.

18. Wintergreen Fund, Inc., Annual Report, December 31, 2006, 3; Fairholme Fund, Investment Adviser's Letter, January 22, 2007, 2.

19. "Value Investing with David Winters," *NYSSA News,* March 2006, 1.

20. Fairholme Fund, Annual Report, year ended November 30, 2006, 6.

Index